Race, Gender, and the History of Early Analytic Philosophy

Race, Gender, and the History of Early Analytic Philosophy

Matt LaVine

LEXINGTON BOOKS
Lanham • Boulder • New York • London

Published by Lexington Books
An imprint of The Rowman & Littlefield Publishing Group, Inc.
4501 Forbes Boulevard, Suite 200, Lanham, Maryland 20706
www.rowman.com

6 Tinworth Street, London SE11 5AL, United Kingdom

Copyright © 2020 The Rowman & Littlefield Publishing Group, Inc.

All rights reserved. No part of this book may be reproduced in any form or by any electronic or mechanical means, including information storage and retrieval systems, without written permission from the publisher, except by a reviewer who may quote passages in a review.

British Library Cataloguing in Publication Information Available

The hardback edition of this book was previously catalogued by the Library of Congress as follows:

Library of Congress Cataloging-in-Publication Data Is Available

ISBN 978-1-4985-9555-1 (cloth)
ISBN 978-1-4985-9557-5 (pbk.)
ISBN 978-1-4985-9556-8 (electronic)

For Krista and Marguerite

Contents

Acknowledgments	ix
Preface	xi

PART 1 — xvii

Introduction — xix

PART 2—RACE, GENDER, AND ANALYTIC PHILOSOPHY (THE METHOD) — xxxvii

1. Discursive Injustice and the History of Analytic Philosophy: The Marcus/Kripke Case — 1
2. The History (and Future) of Logic (and Ethics) — 29

PART 3—RACE, GENDER, AND ANALYTIC PHILOSOPHY (THE MOVEMENT) — 59

3. Starting Points in Philosophy and Starting Points in the Analytic Tradition — 61
4. Post-Tractarian Critique of Metaphysics and Ethics — 85
5. Logical Empiricism and the Scientific Worldview — 109
6. Black Lives Matter and the Logic of Conversation — 141
7. Quinean Naturalized, Socialized Epistemology for Critical Theory — 163

PART 4   **191**

Conclusion   193

Bibliography   207

Index   223

About the Author   231

Acknowledgments

While lots of people say things like this, this book *really* would never have happened without people being willing to talk with me, share with me, and teach me. As I said at the outset of my dissertation, and still strongly believe,

> As I see it, philosophy is in large part about understanding and bettering humans' connections between, and behaviors toward, each other. So, I think philosophy is social to its very core. For this reason, my philosophical development has occurred almost exclusively by talking with people. Thus, I have an embarrassingly long list of people to thank for their help. (LaVine 2016a, iii)

This is certainly true here again and I would like to very sincerely thank the following folks for help along the way. Beginning with the actual writing, I would like to thank Iva Apostolova, Matt Chick, Catarina Dutilh Novaes, Dwight Lewis, Jeff Maynes, Krista Medo, Tim Murphy, Mike Tissaw, and an amazingly diligent and helpful reviewer for Lexington Books. Thank you all for being willing to look at this work in various stages and for giving extremely useful feedback. A special shout out to Iva and Dwight—who gave feedback on *a lot* of the manuscript!

With respect to the ideas contained therein, I have specific memories of helpful feedback and conversation from these folks mentioned above, as well as Tewentenhawihtha Aldrich, Zaneta Bailey, Thomas Bittner, David Braun, Liam Kofi Bright, Chris Brown, Priscilla Burke, Walter Carnielli, Breanne Ciovacco, John Corcoran, Rick Creath, David Curry, Marcello D'Agostino, Randy Dipert, Christine Doran, Juliet Floyd, Claudia Ford, Marilyn Friedman, Latesha Fussell, Alicia Gayken, Joseph Goodrow, Lewis Gordon, Cole Heideman, Jill Hernandez, David Hershenov, Kate-Nicole Hoffman, John Kearns, Teresa Kouri Kissel, Rebecca Kukla, Sandra

Lapointe, Jacob MacDavid, Maria Manzano, Nikolay Milkov, Mike Moran, Jwuan Murphy-Rodriguez, Israel Payero, Michael Popovic, Lewis Powell, Machella Raymond, Stephanie Rivera Berruz, Gillian Russell, Sheryl Scales, Shaili Singh, Karlee Square, Nimo Sugulle, Maie Thomas, Abel Ulloa, Gaylynn Welch, Starr Williams, Lonel Woods, Nicole Wyatt, and John Youngblood. For those I have forgotten, my apologies.

I also need to thank a couple of scholars and activists who were extremely gracious in allowing me to reprint their words here. Thank you, Jonathan Cunningham, for allowing me to reprint your insightful words that appeared in the Macklemore, Ryan Lewis, and Jamila Woods song, "White Privilege II." Your thoughts make a very important point clear—namely, that there is a certain sense in which what the Black Lives Matter movement is calling for is obvious. For those who do not know, Jonathan Cunningham is cofounder of The Residency, a youth development through hip-hop social justice program based in Seattle, WA. Please check it out at www.theresidencyseattle.org! Lastly, thank you Liam Kofi Bright for allowing me to reprint some of your thoughts from "Empiricism is a Standpoint Epistemology" and "Carnap Did Nothing Wrong" from your awesome blog—*The Sooty Empiric*. Again, readers, please check it out at http://sootyempiric.blogspot.com/. There is more important thinking in several paragraph posts there than in entire issues of most journals.

Finally, and most importantly, I need to thank my family. K, Momma, Arles, Izit, Alyssa, and DK—what would I do without you? I know I have been basically nothing but trouble for y'all. So, your unwavering support never ceases to amaze me. Thank you for everything you do for me to keep me going each day.

Preface

The fall of 2010 was a fortunate one for me. Not only had I recently been given a fresh start after recovering from nine months of cancer treatment—during which I read Wittgenstein and Quine constantly while working on an MA in mathematics—four of the most intellectually stimulating events of my life occurred that first semester of graduate work in philosophy at Buffalo. First, I was introduced to, and began learning from, John Corcoran. Next, I stumbled upon Scott Soames' *Philosophical Analysis in the Twentieth Century* while hanging out in the *Talking Leaves* bookshop near my first apartment in Buffalo. After this, I heard Sandra Lapointe give a talk on Bolzano for the Buffalo Logic Colloquium. Finally, I heard Sally Haslanger give a talk on the semantics and politics of generics for a UB Philosophy Department Colloquium. Displaying her ever-admirable character, I asked a very silly question and Haslanger very supportively took it in a direction that was able to teach me something. Without these experiences, this book would never have been able to come into existence. They have largely set the agenda for my thinking of the last ten years that this book finally begins to articulate.

What all of these experiences had in common for me was their contributing to my thinking constantly about connections between history, analytic philosophy, and practical concerns of social and public life. To this, John Corcoran contributed an interest in the history of logic and an understanding of the "Inseparability of Logic & Ethics." Sandra Lapointe opened my eyes to the history of analytic philosophy as a distinct subdiscipline, one I have adopted as my primary academic home. Sally Haslanger introduced me to the type of philosophizing I aspire to do most—analytically rigorous, while grounded in, and inspired by, social justice concerns. And, lastly, Soames explicitly articulated the neutralist stance that I saw all around me, but only implicitly, and that I wanted to argue against.

The thinking and writing which culminated here really started that semester and has not stopped since. The earliest presentation of any of the writing, which would become one of the following chapters, was an early version of chapter 4 given at the first annual meeting of the Society for the Study of the History of Analytical Philosophy at McMaster University. Seeing this manifestation of the society she created continued the inspiration given to me by Sandra Lapointe. Since that time, I have given talks on various versions of these chapters in a number of places. So, in addition to the above acknowledgments, I would like to thank audiences in Buffalo, Potsdam, Istanbul, Calgary, Milwaukee, Boston, San Diego, Montreal, St. Louis, Miami, London (Ontario), and London (England). The most recent of these was the 2019 version of SSHAP at Boston University. Serendipitously, this brought the last decade full circle for me with a fantastic roundtable on analytic feminism, which included Sally Haslanger, along with Naomi Scheman, Carol Hay, Julie Walsh, Samia Hesni, Ann Cudd, and Nancy Bauer.

Before I get into presenting the fruits of the studies inspired by those four events, I need to address my engaging in them in the first place. This is especially the case given that I will most closely align myself with the logical empiricists and their allies when it comes to the history of analytic philosophy. One of the things I admire most about analytic philosophers in this orbit is the fact that they held self-criticism to be so important. They made lots and lots of mistakes, but were very open to being told so and learning from those mistakes. In fact, one of the few bits of the standard story on the logical empiricists which is clearly correct is that the movement was partly brought down from the inside by their own criticisms.

With self-criticism in mind, more important than addressing the history of early analytic philosophy portion of the book is addressing the race and gender aspects of the book. This is particularly necessary given that I am a privileged, white, cisgender man writing about oppressed people, as well as activism and theorizing intended to empower them and support their resilience. World history, principles of participatory and procedural justice, as well as standpoint epistemology all point toward the fact that to do this in an even *potentially* responsible way, I need to be doing what I can to center the thinking of people of color and those with gender identities other than my own.

In line with this, many of the arguments I put forward here are defenses and extensions of views gained from reading the work of, or having discussions with, people with marginalized and oppressed social identities. In a surprisingly close to literal sense, I'm really just saying something along the lines of, if there is going to be a reason for the continuance of a distinct tradition of analytic philosophy, it should be because the thoughts of Moore, Russell, Wittgenstein, Stebbing, the Vienna Circle, ordinary language philosophers, and Quine have been significantly transformed by thinkers like Liam Kofi Bright, Sally Haslanger, Meena Krishnamurthy, Charles Mills, Catarina Dutilh Novaes, Rebecca Kukla, and others like them I do and do not cite.

On top of this, Haslanger, Mills, and others have shown there has been a gross exclusion of people of color and women from analytic philosophy. And, far too many of the people within analytic philosophy do all they can to ignore the real world at all—let alone social justice. Because of this, I believe movements for opening up the field require every person available. Furthermore, as I will discuss later in relation to the Black Lives Matter movement, one is simply not paying attention to the world if they think rationality and morality are anything but sorely needed in our public discourses. If analytic philosophers understand these concepts as well as we claim to, we should hope to get to a point where we can support real-world movements for rationality and morality by engaging such matters. And, maybe most simply, as the front cover photo points out, silence is complicity in many cases—complicity with systems and processes I'm not okay being complicit with.

All of that said, this does not yet justify *my* writing a book on race, gender, and oppression even if it does open up the possibility for genuine race traitors and gender traitors. Simply because I recognize those possibilities and desire to bring them about, that does not mean I will actually achieve being either. Another related worry is that I, as a person trained within hegemonic institutions on completely different matters, will unwittingly contribute to what Tommy J. Curry has called the underspecialization problem and the derelictical crisis in American race theory (Curry 2010, 2011). The underspecialization problem arises from the fact that:

> By simply continuing to proclaim American philosophy's "potential" to deal with racism as proof of the field's ability to contribute to race theory, American philosophy permits whites, who are willing to gesture toward a capacity to speak about race, to be recognized as legitimate race theorists. In organizational meetings, peer-reviewed journal articles, and at the general level of visibility, American philosophy permits whites pursuing a budding interest in the "concept of race" to be respected and recognized as having a specialization in "race theory." Under this current practice, many scholars interested in exploring the themes of racism (marginalization, silencing, power, etc.) are taken to be authoritative, regardless of their formal education in the histories of oppressed peoples in the United States, or a functional knowledge of the development of white supremacy within America's geography. (Curry 2010, 53)

On the other hand, the derelictical crisis comes from a particular view of race theory which I have tried to avoid, but could be guilty of:

> *The problem with this view is that it fails to fulfill the basic need in the field for organic and visceral connection to the people it seeks to study and theorize about.* When Black thinkers are not seen as the primary theoreticians of their own thought, the unnamed but powerfully cogent reflections on Blackness are usurped by the established categories of philosophical legitimacy. (Curry 2011, 319)

The latter traces back to my earlier discussion about the standpoint from which I theorize about race and gender. Furthermore, as somebody not trained in critical theories of race or gender, I did have worries about the former.

That said, I was not trained in the history of analytic philosophy, either. I was trained in the philosophy of language and logic. Of course, I have been intensely studying the history of analytic philosophy and immersing myself in institutions connected to the history of analytic philosophy for a decade or so. Similarly, I have been intensely studying and immersing myself in anti-racist, feminist, and queer institutions for a decade or so. It is these experiences and the immensely helpful feedback I have received from experts in doing so which finally made me feel qualified to write this book. I do have reservations still, but I can only put it out there as a good-faith effort rather than something that actually achieves an allyship to those fighting underspecialization and the derelictical crisis. I will work to move that effort into achievement for the rest of my days.[1]

Because of the reasons given in the preceding paragraphs, I will engage, but try to take the lead of scholars and activists, with more experience, and thus, knowledge, than I have. Where not, I will try to focus on the few dimensions of identity where I am not so privileged—as an LGBTQ+ individual and somebody with lifelong mental health issues. That said, if the trainings I lead on implicit bias, stereotype threat, contractually oppressive ignorance, and so on have taught me anything, it is that I should expect that my privileged perspective has likely gotten the best of me. I hope readers will not hesitate to point those places out.[2]

Before we move forward, I need to make one last point. Much of this book will take an approach that is very cool and conciliatory. I want to make it clear that this is not meant as an implicit endorsement of moderate approaches to politics. I am a radical through and through. My goal in writing this book is to start pushing those in the discipline of a certain persuasion to move in a more radical direction. So that I am not mistaken, though, I want to end with as clear of an articulation of my goals as I can imagine—Fuck the patriarchy! Fuck white supremacy! Fuck heteronormativity! Fuck ableism! Fuck all oppression (but these former manifestations of oppression are the only that I discuss here)!

NOTES

1. I will also try to do so in a way that keeps in mind the words of Cornel West:

   When it comes to Black intellectuals, we have to, on the one hand, be very open to insights from wherever they come. On the other hand, we must filter it in such a way that we never lose sight of what some of the silences are in the work of White theorists, especially as those silences relate to issues of class, gender, race, and empire. Why? Because class, gender, race, and empire are fundamental categories which Black intellectuals must use in order to understand the predicament of Black people. So, there is, I would say, a selective significance of White intellectuals to the critical development of Black intellectuals. (hooks & West 1991, 35)

2. An example of how I would do this in my own work comes from my first journal article (Chick & LaVine 2014). There, we were trying to show that there were internal inconsistencies in a certain self-conception of analytic philosophy. In doing so, we allowed a Eurocentric framework to frame our own contribution. As a result, our own work was unwittingly Eurocentric. Similarly, "today, we may no longer teach students that the birth of spirit occurs with the Greeks, flowers in the modern period, and comes to fruition in contemporary times, but we might as well be—the structures of our departments, the programming of our curricula, and the presentation of our canon all work together to give precisely this effect" (Rivera Berruz & Kalmanson 2018, 2).

Part 1

Introduction

§0.0 OVERVIEW OF INTRODUCTION

In this introduction, I will motivate my investigation into the connection between the history of early analytic philosophy and concerns of social justice gleaned from critical theories of race and gender by introducing representative examples of wildly varied positions on the matter from prominent members of the field. From there, like many works on the history of analytic philosophy, I will discuss what I take "analytic philosophy" to mean. In doing so, I will argue that the phrase is ambiguous between a reading on which it refers to a style or method of doing philosophy and a reading on which it refers to a social-intellectual movement, which placed great emphasis on the potential for that method to contribute to human progress. That style of doing philosophy is one which places logical and linguistic analysis at center stage. The early period of that movement (~1898–1970), which I will focus on, is broken down into five stages. Finally, I will sketch the primary argument of this book, which will involve connecting both types of analysis and all five stages to discussion of social justice.

§0.1 CONTEMPORARY DISAGREEMENTS ON SOCIAL JUSTICE AND THE HISTORY OF ANALYTIC PHILOSOPHY

There is much to be gained by bringing together inquiry into race, gender, and social justice and inquiry into, as well as the use of, analytic philosophy. Furthermore, there is actually some significant historical precedent for this. While they may seem rather tame, I think these are of great importance and are the two primary theses I will spend the next couple hundred pages arguing for. I start here because, even though there are many philosophers today who are displaying and evidencing these facts (in fact, there is a very real sense in which I am arguing for the claim that, when understood aright, we will see the culmination of analytic philosophy up to today as Liam Kofi Bright, Catarina Dutilh Novaes, Sally Haslanger, and Charles Mills),[1] very few people have taken the time to say this explicitly and argue directly for it. On top of that, there are far too many voices who have been saying for far too long that there is, and/or ought to be, a significant disconnect between analytic philosophy and critical theories of race, gender, and oppression.

Going back as far as 1937, analytic champions have been characterized quite to the contrary, with Horkheimer claiming that "radical positivism . . . is connected to the existence of totalitarian states," fascistic tyranny, and the fear of social upheaval (Glock 2008, 183). Following up on the dominance of logical empiricism, the loose conglomeration of thinkers surrounding Wittgenstein and Oxford that have come to be known as "ordinary language philosophers" have been said to be necessarily conservative in their respect for the ordinary and the common. As Toril Moi sums it up nicely, "[t]heorists from Gellner and Marcuse to Butler and Žižek accuse ordinary language philosophy of being inherently conservative or even reactionary, largely because they take this philosophy to endorse common sense" (Moi 2017, ch. 7).[2] Since that time, analytic philosophy's center has shifted to the United States and has been led by Quine and Kripke—who have said things like the political activity at Harvard in the 1960s was "mischief in the service of . . . headlong ideals" in response to which he was an "ineffectual" part of the "conservative caucus" (Quine 1985, 352) and "the intention of philosophy was never to be relevant to life."[3] This should not be taken lightly either as, for example, Soames (2003a, 2003b) has argued that Kripke is the culmination of the first century of the analytic movement in philosophy.

Views on the primary topic of this book—the relationship between analytic philosophy and social justice activism—are quite difficult to discern not just among these historical figures, but those working on that history as well. Scott Soames, for instance, in his aforementioned two-volume history of early analytic philosophy—which has become the standard text used to teach advanced undergraduates—said that "philosophy done in the analytic tradition aims at truth and knowledge, as opposed to moral and spiritual improvement" (Soames 2003a, xiv). Sally Haslanger, on the other hand, has said that a "critical analytical project," which combines critical theories of race and gender, as well as analytic methods, is of the utmost importance (Haslanger 2012, 226–28). Hans-Johann Glock, recognizing the existence of such differing opinions, published a chapter, which investigates such wildly conflicting hypotheses as (a) that analytic philosophy is characterized by excluding all moral and political philosophy, (b) that analytic philosophy is apolitical and conservative, and (c) that analytic philosophy is liberal and progressive (Glock 2008, 179–203).

Furthermore, as Meena Krishnamurthy[4] and Charles Mills (1997, 2015, 2017) have pointed out, this state of affairs is not helped by the existence of a Rawlsian Myth among the analytic mainstream that there was no important political philosophy between Mill's death and Rawls' *A Theory of Justice*. Such a picture should be easily seen as extremely exclusionary as it ignores such important figures as Anna Julia Cooper, Martin Luther King Jr., Simone de Beauvoir, Mohandas Gandhi, Jawaharlal Nehru, and Malcolm X (just to name a few). It is so exclusionary that it even leaves out the political thought of analytic figures like Rudolf Carnap, Otto Neurath, Bertrand Russell, and Susan Stebbing. Again, this is why the primary aims of this book are to (a) weigh in on this question of the public, political, and practical goals of early analytic philosophy and (b) to investigate issues like what potential there may be for analytic work to contribute to critical theories of race and gender as well as social justice activism, why so little of such work has happened, and why the work that has happened on this front has often been forgotten or ignored. In short, the result of these investigations will be that the existence of positions as different as Haslanger and Soames can be explained by the fact that there is much potential for analytic social justice work, but this potential has all-too-rarely been realized.

§0.2 THE MEANING(S) OF "ANALYTIC PHILOSOPHY"

As should already be clear, then, there is a great deal of controversy over how to understand the larger history of analytic philosophy. I think that part of this controversy actually comes from some slippage in, and disagreement about, usage of the term "analytic philosophy" itself. Given that one of the pieces of consensus that exists about analytic philosophy is that clarity has been greatly important to it, we should spend some time getting clear on the meaning of the phrase "analytic philosophy." And, from my perspective, one of the most important things to recognize is that this term is ambiguous between multiple different readings. This, unfortunately, creates the potential for merely verbal disputes when people are debating the understanding of the larger history of analytic philosophy. That is to say, it creates the possibility that two people think they are disagreeing about the historical facts, when they are really just using the phrase "analytic philosophy" differently in their utterances. To see this, we will use a standard test for ambiguity of showing that there exist sentence types such that one token of the type is true and one token is false.

To get to such sentence types, we will begin with another piece of the small consensus that exists in the subfield of the history of analytic philosophy. Given that there is some general agreement that it is difficult to characterize the meaning(s) of "analytic philosophy," one of the common places that meta-philosophers and historians start such discussions is simply by listing those they take to be paradigm cases of analytic philosophers. Interestingly, despite much agreement on these lists, there are some figures that have become something of standard problem cases as well. In particular, Gottlob Frege is squarely in the extension for some and squarely out of the extension of "analytic philosopher" for others. As representative examples, Schwartz says, "I do not consider [Frege, Godel, Tarski, Turing, and Chomsky] to be analytic philosophers" (Schwartz 2012, 7), but Klement that "Frege has become so influential that it is almost unthinkable that any reasonably comprehensive history [of analytic philosophy] would omit him" (Klement 2014).

Interestingly, while Schwartz does not include Frege as an analytic philosopher, he agrees with Klement on the influence of Frege—discussing him on no fewer than forty-six pages, more than Anscombe, Austin, and Ayer, among others. So, in a certain sense, they agree on the facts of the matter with respect to Frege and analytic philosophy. They simply disagree on whether or not those facts make it the case that "analytic philosophy" applies to Frege's work. One reason for this could be that they are using the term "analytic philosophy" with different meanings and one makes the following sentence true, while the other makes it false:

(1) "Gottlob Frege was an analytic philosopher."

Of course, another explanation may be that they are after one and the same concept with "analytic philosophy," they simply have different conceptions of it, which make them disagree on whether or not Frege belongs in the extension. A third could be that, again, they are after the same meaning, they are just working with a vague meaning.

To see a related example that I think speaks against these alternative explanations, consider the sentence:

(2) "Bernard Bolzano was an analytic philosopher."

Prior to the work of Haller (1988), Dummett (1993), and Smith (1994), very few would have thought this was anything but clearly false. Since the groundbreaking work of Lapointe (2011), many more tend to think that it is true. This is because Lapointe makes clear that Bolzano "anticipated groundbreaking ideas such as the (Fregean) distinction between sense and reference, the (Tarskian) notion of logical consequence and the (Quinean) definition of logical truth" (Lapointe 2011, 6). As she argued several years later, these and "other Bolzanian theoretical innovations ... warrant his inclusion in the analytical tradition" (Lapointe 2014, 96). That said, in Michael Beaney's editor's foreword to Lapointe's book, he says that "[d]espite these similarities, however, Bolzano had no direct influence on any of the acknowledged founders of analytic philosophy." So, rather than being a part of the analytic tradition, "[Bolzano's] philosophy—like his life—can be seen as offering a bridge between Kant's seminal work and the birth of analytic philosophy" (Lapointe 2011, ix—Beaney's foreword).

Here, I think Lapointe claims that (2) is true and Beaney that it's false because they are using the term "analytic philosophy" differently. For Lapointe, that "analytic philosopher" applies to Bolzano has to do with the way he did philosophy—namely, that he anticipated the use of tools from the philosophy of language (e.g., the sense/reference distinction) and logic (e.g., logical consequence and truth). For Beaney, he does not disagree with respect to Bolzano's role in the development of these linguistic and logical innovations, but rather suggests that "analytic philosopher" fails to apply to Bolzano because of a lack of direct lines of influence to paradigmatic analytic philosophers. In the first case, "analytic philosophy" seems to be connected to a particular philosophical method—one that places the philosophy of language and logic at the center of philosophizing. This would be natural as the linguistic turn, an event that made philosophy of language first philosophy, has been connected to analytic philosophy for a long time. Furthermore, the use of, and/or response to, the "new logic" of the nineteenth century, which superseded classical logic, has long been thought to be a defining feature of analytic philosophy. In the second case, though, "analytic philosophy" is not connected to just the use of a certain philosophical method (or methods). Rather, one needs to be connected to that particular movement within the history of philosophy, which was founded by thinkers like G. E. Moore, Bertrand Russell, and Ludwig Wittgenstein to count as an analytic philosopher.

Here we have the basis for two different meanings, which make good on the claim that "analytic philosophy" is an ambiguous term. On the one hand, it is sometimes used to refer to a style or method of doing philosophy, one which focuses on philosophy of language and logic. This is what is meant when people talk of philosophical analysis, analytic methods, and the like. This is also how it can be seriously said that "Leibniz would be the first modern analytical philosopher" (Sebestik 1997, 34). On the other hand, "analytic philosophy" is sometimes used to refer to a specific movement within the larger history of philosophy, which is defined by lines of direct influence emanating out from thinkers like Moore, Russell, and Wittgenstein. This is what is meant when people talk of twentieth-century analytic philosophy, the analytic/continental divide, and the like. One subsidiary goal of the book is to explain why this ambiguity has been missed[5]—namely, one of the defining features of the early phase of that social-intellectual movement was a great hope for that method in its relation to philosophical/scientific progress and their connection to human progress.

For now, I provide just a few more examples of sentences that speak toward this claimed ambiguity. For instance, consider the following two sentences:

(3) "Analytic philosophy may have started coming to an end in the 1970's."
(4) "Analytic philosophy requires logical and/or linguistic analysis."

While many philosophers today would be very surprised to hear somebody utter (3), something like it has been put forth by a number of prominent philosophers, whose work was collected together for an edited volume by John Rajchman and Cornel West with the suggestive title, *Post-analytic Philosophy* (Rajchman & West 1985). A number of these post-analytic philosophers come very close to something like (3) with thoughts such as "I think that analytic philosophy culminates in Quine, the later Wittgenstein, Sellars, and Davidson—which is to say that it transcends and cancels itself" (Rorty 1982, xviii) and "at the very moment when analytical philosophy is recognized as the 'dominant movement' in world philosophy, analytical philosophy has come to the end of its own project—the dead end, not the completion" (Putnam 1985, 28). Again, I claim that the explanation for this disagreement is that we have a merely verbal dispute. Those focusing on a potential truth expressed by (3) are noticing the fact that something significant in analytic philosophy—the historical movement—changed in the early 1970s, while those denying (3) are focusing on the fact that not much about the use of analytic philosophy—the method—changed here.

Something similar goes on with (4), as precisely how seriously to take, or how to understand, the "analysis" that is cognate to "analytic philosophy" has also been a point of contention. As Glock has argued, "many contemporary explanations of what analytic philosophy is are curiously silent on the issue of analysis. Yet the idea of putting the idea of analysis back into the definition of analytic philosophy is hardly far-fetched" (Glock 2008, 153). Summarizing the state of this debate, he considers Russellian, decompositional, logical, connective, constructive, and Quinean analysis, among others. Ultimately, he concludes that "while weightier and more specific notions of analysis no longer cover the whole range of analytic philosophy, the less demanding and wider notions are too indiscriminating" (Glock 2008, 159–60). On the other hand, the aptly titled textbook *Philosophical Analysis: An Introduction to Its Language and Techniques*—which was popular enough to go through three editions and multiple printings—set out to "provide the materials for a program of familiarization with the language and techniques of analytic philosophy" by introducing students to logical analysis, linguistic analysis, and the analytic/synthetic distinction (Gorovitz et al. 1979, ix). Hopefully my next move has become clear—there is no real disagreement here. Rather, (4) is true when "analytic philosophy" expresses a method and false when "analytic philosophy" expresses something about a particular historical movement.

§0.3 THE PROGRESSION OF ANALYTIC PHILOSOPHY—THE FIVE-STAGE PICTURE

Given that this book is on social justice and the history of analytic philosophy, and that the main part of the book will involve a series of chapters connecting each of the stages of early analytic philosophy to concerns of justice and oppression, it will be important to give a picture of the way I see the development of early analytic philosophy, the historical movement. As my continued use of "early" when talking about the history of analytic philosophy should make clear, I take there to be multiple phases of analytic philosophy. As mentioned earlier, there is a significant prehistory that culminates in the beginning of the analytic movement by 1898. From there, I split the first ~100 years of the analytic movement into the early analytic period (1898–1970) and the middle analytic period (1970–1995). This distinction is justified by the weight given to the new directions in speculative metaphysics and grand normative theory that Kripke and Rawls are taken to have initiated around 1970 with *Naming and Necessity* and *A Theory of Justice*, respectively. In addition to (roughly) 1970 marking a rise in new trends, it also marks the culmination of various stories from the analytic tale. Around this time, (a) Paul Grice brought ordinary language philosophy down from the inside, (b) Marcus, Prior, Kripke, and others completed the modern logical revolution, and (c) Russell and Carnap died, just to name a few. This second phase, the middle analytic period, then comes to an end around 1995. By this point, Kripke and Rawls have published all of their most important works. This also marks the time at which there began to be a distinct subdiscipline of the history of analytic philosophy with publications like Coffa (1991), Dummett (1993), Hacker (1996), and Friedman (1999), followed by the formation of the Society for the Study of the History of Analytical Philosophy, the *Journal for the History of Analytical Philosophy*, and Palgrave Macmillan's History of Analytic Philosophy series.

After breaking the history of analytic philosophy into the early period (1898–1970), the middle period (1970–1995), and the contemporary period (1995–present), the early period is further broken down into five stages.

These five stages are characterized by the emergence of different torchbearers and a group of problems they focused on, which served as a background for debates. First, Moore and Russell led their critical revolt against British idealism (1898–1914), which, in the second stage, was built into positive, large-scale philosophical systems with Russell's and Wittgenstein's logical atomisms (1914–1926). The third stage then consisted of a less-than-heated debate between different evolutions of Wittgenstein's *Tractatus Logico-Philosophicus*—logical empiricism and Cambridge analysis (1926–1940). Influenced by them, but distancing themselves from both groups, was the ordinary language philosophy of 1940–1960. This early period was then brought to a close with a decade of debate and fragmentation of the analytic movement caused, in large part, by Quine's questioning of long-held principles before new paradigms were established by Kripke and Rawls.

With respect to this first stage, very little of what I have said about it so far is controversial. Stephen Schwartz, for example, starts his history of analytic philosophy with a chapter on Russell and Moore, arguing that "Bertrand Russell—aristocrat (3rd Earl Russell), anti-war activist, prolific writer, and brilliant philosopher and mathematician—is the father of Anglo-American analytic philosophy" (Schwartz 2012, 8) and "Russell's wider outlook was shaped with his contact with G. E. Moore—a philosopher only slightly less significant in creating analytic philosophy than Russell himself" (Schwartz 2012, 27). Scott Soames' history of analytic philosophy concurs, beginning with part one on Moore and part two on Russell (Soames 2003a). Ayer, too, begins his history of twentieth-century philosophy with a chapter on Russell and Moore entitled "the revolt from Hegel" (Ayer 1982, 19). Glock can be added to the chorus as well, saying "their revolt against [British idealism] marked a decisive moment in the emergence of analytic philosophy" (Glock 2008, 31).

Furthermore, an *1898* revolt against British idealism as a starting point for this process is rather standard as well. P. M. S. Hacker's history of (Wittgenstein's role in) analytic philosophy says both that "twentieth-century analytic philosophy has its twofold root in Cambridge at the turn of the century in the work of G. E. Moore and Bertrand Russell" (Hacker 1996, 5) and "Moore's revolt against idealism began with his 1898 dissertation" (Hacker 1996, 6). In fact, 1898 as a significant date for this decisive step comes from Russell himself as well. In his intellectual autobiography, Russell says "it was towards the end of 1898 that Moore and I rebelled against both Kant and Hegel" (Russell 1959, 42). Hence, all we really need to explain here is the choice of 1914 as the time of transition between the first and second stages of early analytic philosophy.

This second stage of early analytic philosophy spanned roughly 1914–1926, or the early mid-1910s to the mid–late 1920s anyway. As mentioned earlier, this time was marked by the development and dominance of Russell's and Wittgenstein's logical atomisms. Again, claiming that this development was that which followed Moore and Russell's move away from idealism is not particularly controversial, either. Part 2 of Soames (2003a) ends with a chapter on Russell's logical atomism and part 3 is on Wittgenstein's atomism developed in the *Tractatus*. Glock also follows up his section on the rebellion against idealism with a section on "the linguistic turn," which claims this came to fruition in Wittgenstein's *Tractatus* and discusses that "a similar type of *logical atomism* was developed by Russell" (Glock 2008, 34–35). So, evidence of the significance of 1914 comes from multiple fronts:

(1) Russell published his first systematic work involving an exposition of logical atomism, *Our Knowledge of the External World*, in 1914.
(2) Because of this, Volume 8 of Russell's collected papers—the one focusing on logical atomism—begins with his published works of 1914.
(3) The background for the development of Russell's and Wittgenstein's logical atomisms was Wittgenstein's time as a student of Russell's, which lasted through 1912 and 1913.
(4) Wittgenstein's notebooks that contain the beginning of his work, which would eventually become the *Tractatus Logico-Philosophicus*—his major exposition of logical atomism, begin in 1914. Cf. "The fruits of his seven years' labour were presented in his first masterpiece, the *Tractatus* (1921)" (Hacker 1996, 22).

Yet again, there is not much controversy about placing the heyday of logical empiricism as our next stage. Soames (2003a) follows up part 3 on Wittgenstein's *Tractatus* with part 4 on logical positivism. Schwartz (2012) follows up a discussion of Wittgenstein's *Tractatus* with sections dedicated to "The Vienna Circle and their Allies" and "The Elimination of Metaphysics and the Logical Positivist Program." Coffa (1991) completes part I with a chapter on the *Tractatus* and then moves to part II on "Vienna, 1925–1935." Ayer (1982), too, has a section on logical empiricists—Schlick, Neurath, and Carnap—immediately after his section on the *Tractatus*.

What is likely more controversial is adding the Cambridge analysts to this time period. That said, it is not without some prominent backing. After introducing logical empiricism, Glock's historical development discusses Frank Ramsey, Susan Stebbing, and John Wisdom, saying "[m]eanwhile in Cambridge there emerged a new generation of logical analysts" (Glock 2008, 39). Hacker, too, has a separate chapter from the one on the influence of the *Tractatus* on the logical empiricists of the Vienna Circle. This subsequent chapter is on the *Tractatus*' influence on "the younger generation of Cambridge philosophers" where "its influence was very different in Britain, merging, as it did, with the Cambridge styles of analysis, in contrast with the Machian heritage of the philosophers of the Vienna Circle" (Hacker 1996, 67). While these Cambridge analysts are certainly not discussed today as much as the logical empiricists, I agree with Glock and Hacker that we do a disservice to the history if we leave them out. While Stebbing's influence will be discussed much more in chapters 3 and 5, we can now point out that she served on the board of the *International Encyclopedia of Unified Science*, introduced logical empiricism to the English-speaking world, and gave the first clear account of the relationships between the views of the logical empiricists and Cambridge analysts.

Furthermore, evidence of the significance of 1926 as a completion point for Stage 2 of logical atomism and the beginning of Stage 3 of logical empiricism and Cambridge analysis also comes in multiple forms:

(1) Though the Schlick-led incarnation of the Vienna Circle had been meeting for several years by this point, it was in 1926 that Rudolf Carnap—the intellectual figurehead of logical empiricism and its influence on the larger history of analytic philosophy—joined.
(2) The Vienna Circle read the *Tractatus* together page by page through much of the whole calendar year of 1926.
(3) This was also the year that Schlick would convince Wittgenstein to start scheduling meetings with a subset of the Vienna Circle including Waismann, Carnap, Herbert Feigl, and Maria Kasper-Feigl, which would last in some form from 1927 until 1935.
(4) Russell's work also took a different direction by this point, as indicated by Volume 9 of Russell's collected papers applying his logical atomism to matters on language, mind, and matter ending in 1926 and the next volume being entitled *A Fresh Look at Empiricism*.
(5) After not publishing more than five papers in any particular year prior to that, Stebbing's career took a significant turn with at least a dozen publications in 1926 (Chapman 2013, 202–3).
(6) Ramsey was appointed university lecturer in mathematics at King's College, Cambridge in 1926.
(7) Braithwaite earned his highest degree, an MA, from King's College in 1926.

Hence, while it can certainly be challenged, there is at least prima facie reason to treat 1926 as a time of transition for the analytic movement.

Going back to more of a consensus picture, there is little controversial about placing ordinary language philosophy at the center of the analytic movement following logical empiricism. Soames (2003b) follows up his discussion of logical positivism and Quinean reactions to it from Soames

(2003a) with a part on Wittgenstein's *Philosophical Investigations* and three parts on ordinary language philosophy (including its demise under Grice). Schwartz (2012), too, goes to chapters on "Oxford Ordinary Language Philosophy and Later Wittgenstein" and "Responses to Ordinary Language Philosophy" after chapters on logical positivism and responses to it. Hence, we need only say a bit about the choice of 1940 and 1960 as the transition points from logical empiricism/Cambridge analysis to ordinary language philosophy and from ordinary language philosophy to the decade of debate, fragmentation, and turmoil.

(1) Many members of the Vienna Circle had been forced to leave the European continent by 1940 as a result of Nazi activities—Neurath and Reidemeister fled to England in 1940, Kurt Godel reached the United States in 1940, Rose Rand emigrated to London in 1939, Phillip Frank made it to the United States in 1938, Friedrich Waismann to England in 1937, and Rudolf Carnap to the United States in 1935, among others (Uebel 2016).
(2) As a result, the last congresses on scientific philosophy were held in Cambridge, Massachusetts, in 1939 and Chicago in 1941.
(3) Stebbing's major works, *Thinking to Some Purpose* and *Ideals and Illusions*, were published in 1939 and 1941, respectively.
(4) Wittgenstein was elected to Moore's chair in philosophy in 1939.
(5) J. L. Austin's first publication to focus on meanings and words comes out in 1939 in a symposium on "Are There A Priori Concepts?"

As for the choice of 1960 as the transition point between the fourth stage led by ordinary language philosophy and a fifth stage where there was no single story, school, or set of problems clearly leading the analytic movement, this is much more arbitrary. That said, this is partly a result of the fragmentation of this era itself. Rather than a group like the Vienna Circle setting the institutional tone, as was done in earlier stages, this fifth stage saw a number of distinct and significant threads. There was a revival in traditional ethical theorizing from G. E. M. Anscombe, Philippa Foot, and R. M. Hare, which would ultimately lead to the applied ethics of thinkers like James Rachels, Peter Singer, and Judith Jarvis Thomson. During this time, the significance of modal and intensional logics was intensely investigated by Saul Kripke, Ruth Barcan Marcus, Richard Montague, and A. N. Prior. Finally, as the center of analytic philosophy shifted to the United States the traditions of pragmatism and naturalism were explored, and used to criticize some common themes of stages 3 and 4, in the works of W. V. O. Quine, Donald Davidson, Hilary Putnam, Nicholas Rescher, Susan Haack, Cornel West, and Cheryl Misak. Thus, given this complication, I will have to leave full discussion of the choice of 1960 to chapter 7 on Stage 5.

§0.4 PRELIMINARY SKETCH OF THE BOOK

With my understandings of the meanings of "analytic philosophy" and of the outline of the history of early analytic philosophy sketched, we are now in a position to sketch the main argument of this book. As was mentioned at the beginning of this introduction, my primary thesis is that there is much to be gained by bringing together inquiry into critical theories of race and gender and inquiry into, as well as the use of, analytic philosophy. That is, because of the entrenched nature of a belief in a disconnect between analytic philosophy and matters of necessity to "moral and spiritual improvement" such as racial and gender justice and oppression, the book has the modest, but I believe important, goal of showing that there is practical value to exploring the connections between them.

Now that we have discussed the fact that I believe there to be at least two relatively distinct meanings of "analytic philosophy," we can specify that I will argue that this primary conclusion is true on both readings of the term. That is to say, I will try to give reasons to believe (a) that there is much to be gained by bringing together inquiry involving matters of race, gender, and analytic philosophy, the method of philosophizing which emphasizes the centrality of the philosophy of language and logic and (b) that there is much to be gained by bringing together inquiry involving matters of race, gender, and analytic philosophy, the historical movement in the discipline of philosophy. Furthermore, I will argue for both disambiguations of this thesis with specific examples, which directly show something gained for our understanding of social justice issues, for our understanding of analytic philosophy, or both in some cases. More specifically, I will focus on arguing for the historical claim that many early analytic philosophers intended for their work to be public and political in nature, while trying to make good on this intention by showing how analytic thought can be useful for work on social justice issues of contemporary concern.

Given that we have two different readings of the primary thesis, I will argue for them in two separate sections. The first will be dedicated to the primary thesis on the philosophical method reading of "analytic philosophy" and the second to the historical movement reading of "analytic philosophy." Since the method I associate with the words "analytic philosophy" focuses on the philosophy of language and on logic, this first section will include one chapter on each. In particular, chapter 1 will be on a specific example showing how we can be better practitioners of analytic philosophy and understand its history in a more just fashion by utilizing tools from analytic philosophy of language concerning how social identity influences the reception of certain speech acts. More specifically, we will use Rebecca Kukla (2014)'s notion of discursive injustice to weigh in on the (in)famous debate between Scott Soames and Quentin Smith over who deserves initial credit for the so-called "new theory of reference"—Ruth Barcan Marcus or Saul Kripke. Slightly oversimplifying, I will argue for something of a compromise position where, rather than Kripke being guilty of plagiarizing Marcus, the entire discipline of philosophy is guilty of gendered discursive injustice with respect to the reception of Marcus' philosophical work. In chapter 2, I turn to arguing that we do not have a proper understanding of logic if we do not recognize its ethical, political, and practical significance. Here, I build off of John Corcoran's "The Inseparability of Logic and Ethics" as well as some of Marcus' and Arthur Prior's work connecting logic and ethics that we might hopefully spend more time on if we had taken some of the historical lessons from chapter 1.

After providing specific examples of how the philosophy of language and logic can be importantly helpful for inquiry into ethical and political matters, the next section will focus on how the early phase of the historical movement of analytic philosophy can be similarly connected to matters of race, gender, and justice. Here, I will continue the pattern of structuring the argument around specific examples showing particular contributions to each of these dialectics by bringing together inquiry into critical theories of race, gender, justice, and oppression and inquiry into the history of analytic philosophy. As a reminder, I structure the history of analytic philosophy into the early phase of 1898–1970, the middle phase of 1970–1995, and the contemporary phase of 1995–present. From there, I break down the early phase into the following five stages:

[S1] 1898–1914: Moore, Russell, and the rebellion against British idealism
[S2] 1914–1926: Wittgenstein, Russell, and logical atomism
[S3] 1926–1940: Logical empiricism and Cambridge analysis
[S4] 1940–1960: Ordinary language philosophy
[S5] 1960–1970: Naturalism, modal logic, and traditional ethical theorizing.

Again, because the feeling is that such a thing cannot be done, this section will primarily consist of direct and individual case studies showing that we can shed some light on debates over, for example, the Black Lives Matter movement, the silencing of women, and ignorance of contributions of, and injustices faced by, people with marginalized social identities by bringing these debates into contact with thought and trends from each stage of the early analytic movement. So as to avoid the rebuttal that these examples are cherry-picked and do not show anything of general interest, attention will be paid to indisputably central trends from each of the five stages of early analytic philosophy. In particular, I will discuss issues of race and gender in relation to:

[S1] The focus on common sense from the first uncontroversial analytic philosophers, G. E. Moore and Bertrand Russell. In particular, I will look at one common way of understanding "common sense" and how standard problems from judgment aggregation theory show that sets of beliefs meeting this criterion are likely to be inconsistent and standard work from sociologists, political scientists, philosophers, and critical theorists show that giving a place of privilege to such beliefs is likely to perpetuate problematic biases, prejudices, and oppressive ignorance.

[S2] The critique of metaphysics and ethics from Ludwig Wittgenstein's *Tractatus*. More specifically, I argue that Wittgenstein's *Tractatus Logico-Philosophicus* started a trend of viewing metaphysics as almost like a disguised form of ethics. I illustrate this general view, and problems with it, by showing how it can be applied to Liam Kofi Bright (2017)'s account of the logical empiricists' views on the metaphysics of race (voluntarist racial eliminativism) and their ethico-political motivations (ending racist divisiveness and promoting internationalist politics).

[S3] The verification principle and scientific worldview of the logical empiricists. I argue that these pieces of the overarching framework of the logical empiricists had ethical and political motivations throughout. In doing so, I enter into a debate involving Thomas Uebel, Sarah Richardson, and Amy Wuest over whether or not the logical empiricists had a "political philosophy of science." I ultimately argue that recent work from Liam Kofi Bright and Catarina Dutilh Novaes give us good reason to think they did. This is also shown to be less of an aberration than it might have seemed as other major figures of this stage who were only associates of the logical empiricists (n.b. Susan Stebbing) and those who set themselves in direct opposition to them (n.b. Karl Popper) had similarly political philosophies of science.

[S4] The ordinary language philosophy of H. P. Grice and J. L. Austin. I argue here for the claim that trying to replace, or even respond to, someone's saying "Black lives matter" with someone's saying "all lives matter" is mistaken and misdirected. Furthermore, I will show how we can utilize Paul Grice's logic of conversation to build a strong case for this thesis and Luvell Anderson's work to show that this is not a unique case.

[S5] The naturalism of W. V. O. Quine and the development of modal logic, which made Saul Kripke's *Naming and Necessity* possible. In particular, I will discuss applications of Quinean methodology to issues of race and gender by Charles Mills and Sally Haslanger, as well as how we can see these two as more Quinean than Quine sometimes was. In particular, their use of social science and moral theory surrounding race and gender utilizes the consequences of a naturalized epistemology and ontology more consistently than Quine's own work.

Before moving on, this sketch of my argument provides another opportunity to recognize my own standpoint as a privileged white man writing about, and for the sake of, people with marginalized and oppressed social identities. Again, I recognize there are many potential pitfalls in doing so and that I must take, for example, Kristie Dotson's "caution that when addressing and identifying forms of epistemic oppression one needs to endeavor not to perpetuate epistemic oppression" (Dotson 2012, 24). This sketch begins to make clear some of what I will use to limit the hindrances that inevitably come along with a standpoint like my own. In particular, as the references to work I will engage show, I will be building off of the work of thinkers whose standpoints give them more direct access to the phenomena of racial and gender oppression throughout. Furthermore, I will consistently be looking to come up with suggestions for constraints to be put on the types of engagements I am encouraging—constraints which hopefully limit the potential of hegemonic standpoints to infect analytic philosophizing. That said, I hope that my readers will not hesitate to point out those places where I have failed on these fronts.

§0.5 PREVIEWING THE REST OF THE BOOK

As has been alluded to, the main themes of this book will be the history of early analytic philosophy, critical theories of race and gender, the philosophy of language, and logic. Put in relation to these themes, the goals are to investigate what potential there is for logical and linguistic analysis to contribute to scholarship and activism on race and gender, as well as whether or not there is precedent for such work in the history of analytic philosophy. After going through such investigations, we will find evidence for the following subsidiary theses—(a) analytic philosophy should be used to contribute to understanding and eradicating oppression and injustice—the book primarily focusing on racial and gender oppression, but occasionally discussing sexuality, disability, religion, and class, (b) at each stage of early analytic philosophy, there was a significant body of work which was motivated by and/or easily lends itself to such work and, finally, (c) this has been missed because the analytic movement went from a revolutionary to a hegemonic tradition—occupying this position of power in society along with several other trends helping it to develop privileged, dominant tendencies that we find all over power structures in modern western society.

Summing things up in terms of a structure to integrate these primary themes and theses, the nine chapters of the book can be broken down into a four-step progression. This introduction was intended to present the topics (the history of early analytic philosophy and critical theories of race and gender), the background which makes this a worthwhile choice of topics (the extremely varied positions on the relationship, the existence of injustices within the discipline, the public perception of philosophy), and the way I conceive of the methodology and history of early analytic philosophy, which will serve as a framework for the rest of the book (a commitment to the centrality of the philosophy of language and logic to the practice of philosophy, the ability to be broken down into five rough and overlapping stages). The first and second chapters investigate ways in which we can connect the main tools of analytic methodology—the philosophy of language and logic—to social, public, and ethical matters. The third through seventh chapters of the book then go stage by stage through early analytic philosophy, connecting some main trend from each to issues of practical importance involving race and gender such as inclusive discursive practices and the Black Lives Matter movement. Finally, the conclusion ends with some potential roadblocks to a more just, critical, and radical form of analytic philosophy, as well as avenues for further investigation of these matters.

NOTES

1. I mean this in the sense in which there is something true in saying "Hacker (1996)'s history has Wittgenstein as the culmination of analytic philosophy" or "Soames (2003a, 2003b)'s history has Kripke as the culmination of analytic philosophy." While this is not quite right, it has something to do with saying the best way to tell a history of analytic philosophy, which allows you to get the most combined historical accuracy and theoretical insight is with the culminating philosopher as protagonist. In this way, I think that the best way to tell a history of analytic philosophy, which rates highest with respect to a combination of historical accuracy, theoretical insight, and political expediency is with Bright, Dutilh Novaes, Haslanger, and Mills as protagonists.

2. This summary, which can be found in her abstract for chapter 7 at https://chicago.universitypressscholarship.com/view/10.7208/chicago/9780226464589.001.0001/upso-9780226464305-chapter-008, is far from an exaggeration as well. As Moi later points out, Gellner says that ordinary language philosophy and/or common sense "is conservative in the values which it in fact insinuates" (Gellner 1959, 296), Marcuse that "[i]t leaves the established reality untouched; it abhors transgression" (Marcuse 1964, 173), Butler that it supports "nefarious ideologies" (Butler 1999), and Žižek concurs that rather than supporting a "non-ideological common-sense form of life" this type of philosophy supports "the spontaneously accepted background which is ideology par excellence" (Žižek 2009, 21). Moi rightly argues that there is a significantly problematic elitism built into these responses where "[b]ecause they trust the ordinary, and believe that perfectly ordinary people are at least as capable

as philosophers of making relevant and useful distinctions, Marcuse assumes that Wittgenstein and Austin must be marching in lockstep with dominant ideology" (Moi 2017, 152).

3. This Kripke quote and ones similar to it can be found in his interview with Andreas Saugstad, "Saul Kripke, Genius Logician," accessed June 7, 2019, http://bolesblogs.com/2001/02/25/saul-kripke-genius-logician/.

4. Krishnamurthy's piece "Decolonizing Analytic Political Philosophy" can be found on her blog at https://politicalphilosopher.net/2016/06/03/meenakrishnamurthy/, accessed June 7, 2019.

5. It should be noted that, while I think this has not been generally accepted, it is certainly not absent from prominent discussions, either. Hacker, for example, seems to be implicitly recognizing this when he says both that "in a loose sense, one might say that all, or the bulk of, philosophy is analytic" (Hacker 1996, 3) and "one (Russellian) root of this new school might be denominated 'logico-analytic philosophy' . . . the other (Moorean) root might be termed 'conceptual analysis'" (Hacker 1996, 4).

Part 2

RACE, GENDER, AND ANALYTIC PHILOSOPHY (THE METHOD)

Chapter 1

Discursive Injustice and the History of Analytic Philosophy
The Marcus/Kripke Case

§1.0 OVERVIEW OF THE CHAPTER

The method that analytic philosophers emphasize involves, at the very least, a commitment to the utility of linguistic and logical analysis. In this chapter and the next, I discuss ways in which we can connect such close attention to the philosophy of language and logic, respectively, to issues of social importance where race and gender are particularly salient. These chapters are intended to give direct case studies, which illustrate the need for, and potential of, combining the history of analytic philosophy with considerations of justice. In this chapter, I try to illustrate both sides of this coin by looking at one particular case study—the Ruth Marcus / Saul Kripke dispute over who deserves most credit for initiating the new theory of reference.

While it led to years of heated discussion, which got overly personal at times, I do not believe this debate got to any reasonably settled point. As was mentioned earlier, I hope to show that, while Soames is right that Kripke cannot be accused of plagiarism, there is good reason to believe that the entire discipline should be accused of discursive injustice in its treatment of Marcus' works. That is to say, because Marcus was a woman in a field dominated by men,[1] her speech acts were not given the correct uptake—her expert assertions and arguments being treated as mere suggestions. I begin with this as a case study because it allows us to see a clear case of analytic tools being used to identify a distinctive type of injustice and shows us how analytic tools can actually help us fight such injustices.

§1.1 QUENTIN SMITH ON THE NEW THEORY OF REFERENCE, RUTH MARCUS, AND SAUL KRIPKE

I began the introduction with a number of quotations from philosophers with vastly different positions on how connected work in analytic philosophy is to goals of moral significance like that of increasing social, gender, and racial justice. I believe the existence of such different positions can be explained by the fact that there is much potential for critical analytic work, but this potential has all-too-rarely been realized. The theorists who are hopeful about this relationship focus on that *potential* and those who are despairing of this relationship focus on the *actual* absence. Here, I illustrate both sides of this coin by looking at one particular case study—the Marcus/Kripke dispute.

More than twenty-five years ago, Quentin Smith gave his paper at the APA on the relative priority of Ruth Barcan Marcus and Saul Kripke with respect to the "new theory of reference"—that cluster of views on naming, reference, and semantics, which took the field away from the descriptivist theories of Frege, Russell, and Wittgenstein. While this led to years of heated discussion, which got overly personal at times, I do not believe the debate got to any reasonably settled point. In this chapter, I show that, while Soames is right that Kripke cannot be accused of plagiarism, there is good reason to believe that the entire discipline of philosophy should be accused of—what Rebecca Kukla (2014) has called—discursive injustice in its treatment of Marcus' works. I begin with this as a case study, despite the fact that it comes closer to the end of the era, which I will focus on, because it:

(1) allows us to see a clear case of analytic tools being used to identify a distinctive type of injustice,
(2) allows us to see why analytic philosophy as an institution needs to—as a perpetrator of injustice—pay more attention to thinking about injustice, and
(3) gives us a model for thinking about how this can be done more going forward.

Given just how central Kripke's work is to the institution of analytic philosophy over the last fifty to sixty years, such a case exhibiting all of (1)–(3) should not be overlooked. Before we can get to any of that, though, we must first set the stage that we will be discussing with some basic historical facts.

The saga under consideration began in December of 1994, when Quentin Smith gave a paper at the Eastern APA in Boston, which "argued that Ruth Barcan Marcus' 1961 article on 'Modalities and Intensional Languages' originated many of the key ideas of the New Theory of Reference that have often been attributed to Saul Kripke and others" (Smith 1995a, 179). At the same session, Scott Soames gave a strong reply, which argued that "Smith does Kripke a grave injustice" since "providing [Marcus and others] with proper credit does not result in a reassessment of the seminal role of Kripke and others as primary founders of contemporary nondescriptivist theories of reference" (Soames 1995, 208). Consistent with APA practice, Smith also gave a reply to that reply in which he argues that, given the concessions Soames makes, "if Soames is to draw a conclusion that is consistent . . . he should have concluded that the evidence [Smith] presented established that Marcus was a primary founder of the New Theory of Reference, even though Soames does not agree with *all* of the points [Smith] made about her primacy" (Smith 1995b, 243).

Since this APA session predictably created a great deal of discussion and controversy, all three of these papers were published in *Synthese* in August 1995. Roughly a year later, Soames' colleague, John Burgess, joined the discussion with his October 1996 paper "Marcus, Kripke, and Names." Here, Burgess joins the side of both Kripke and Soames, arguing against Marcus' "claim, which has subsequently been stated more explicitly by others . . . that certain remarks on names in her colloquium talk "Modalities and Intensional Languages" anticipate in an important but unacknowledged way Saul Kripke's discussion of names in his lecture series "Naming and Necessity"'" (Burgess 1996, 1). In 1998, all of the papers mentioned so far were gathered together—along with new contributions from Burgess, Smith, and Soames, as well as some pieces providing historical context—in the book *The New Theory of Reference: Kripke, Marcus, and Its Origins*. This controversy was not limited to specialists, either, receiving popular coverage by Jim Holt (friendly to Smith's original) in the January/February 1996 issue of *Lingua Franca* and Stephen Neale (falling squarely in the Burgess/Soames camp) in the February 2001 *Times Literary Supplement*. As if to put in his last word on the matter, Soames then published his two-volume history of analytic philosophy in 2003 with Kripke as the culmination and primary hero (and almost no mention of Marcus) (Soames 2003a, 2003b).[2]

Not only has little agreement been made on the substantive issues, there was significant controversy over whether or not the debate should have even happened in the way it did in the first place. Within a year of the initial session, Anscombe, Davidson, Geach, and Nagel published a letter to the editor in the APA Proceedings stating their "dismay" due to the fact that "a session at a national APA meeting is not the proper forum in which to level ethical accusations against a member of our profession, even if the charges were plausibly defended." Furthermore, while it has not featured as prominently in the published literature, my personal experience evidences the fact that the matter has not left philosophers' minds. At my very first departmental gathering in graduate school in 2010, it became one of the significant topics of conversation—and this was not the only departmental event that involved such a conversation. Since then, I have also been a part of multiple conversations on the dispute at various conferences on the history of analytic philosophy. When I gave earlier versions of this chapter as talks at conferences, I also had responses ranging from laughter and scoffing to invitations to contribute my work.

For these reasons, I believe it is time to reopen the debate in the published literature. In doing so, I will defend a more middling position than was gotten from either the Smith or Soames side of the debate. In particular, I will be trying to flesh out what Jaakko Hintikka might have meant when he said,

> I've no doubt that Kripke has acted in good faith . . . he's not appropriating anyone else's ideas, at least consciously. . . . The real blame in all this lies with the philosophical community—which, owing to its uncritical, romantic view of this prodigy, is far too quick to give him credit for new ideas while neglecting the contributions of others. Kripke probably got his results independently, but why should he get all the credit? (Holt 2018, 328)

Focusing more on Marcus not getting credit than Kripke getting credit, again, I will argue that this mistake made by the philosophical community was perpetrating sexist discursive injustice against a woman in a field dominated by men, which implicitly expects genius to be masculine. Toward this end, we will discuss a section each on:

(1) Smith's claims from the original APA session, as well as Soames' and Burgess' responses to them,
(2) oddities that can be found in Soames' and Burgess' responses to Smith,
(3) the general background for Kukla's notion of discursive injustice,
(4) an argument that discursive injustice is the best explanation for what went on in the Kripke/Marcus dispute, and
(5) gesturing at how we might proceed with our investigations into the history of philosophy with this case in mind.

§1.2 SCOTT SOAMES AND JOHN BURGESS RESPOND TO QUENTIN SMITH

As has been alluded to, Smith's original APA paper has as primary thesis that there is a combination of six main theses associated with the New Theory of Reference (NTR), which originated in Ruth Barcan Marcus' work. A subsidiary claim is that this has been missed because Kripke originally misunderstood Marcus' work and, as a result, did not cite it. The works discussed by

Smith, which he thinks Kripke should have cited, include her pioneering works on quantified modal logic from 1946 to 1947 (Marcus 1946a, 1946b, 1947) and, more importantly, her "Modalities and Intensional Languages" (Marcus 1961). This last paper is most relevant to the central pieces of NTR and Kripke was present at the February 1962 Boston Colloquium for the Philosophy of Science where it was read and discussed. According to Smith, if Kripke and those following him had properly read, understood, and cited Marcus, they would have found a picture with all of the following theses of NTR:

[T1] Proper names are directly referential, rather than being strongly equatable with, or disguised, definite descriptions.
[T2] Just because a definite description has been used to fix the referent of a name, this does not mean that the name goes on to carry the meaning of that description.
[T3] The modal argument refutes descriptivist theories of proper names.
[T4] Statements of identity express necessary propositions (i.e., the necessity of identity).
[T5] Proper names are rigid designators.
[T6] There exist necessary a posteriori truths. (Smith 1995a, 182–86)

From here, we should also survey Soames' and Burgess' responses in Soames (1995) and Burgess (1998). Soames' (1995) primary issues with Smith (1995a) can be broken down into general worries and specific concerns with each of T1–T6. On the more general side, he says that "[Marcus'] entire discussion of the meaning and reference of names, as well as their relations to descriptions, covers only five or six pages [. . .] and defenses of the various doctrines of the so-called 'new theory' would not fit into such a small space" (Soames 1995, 193). With respect to T1–T6, individually, Soames says something different about each that he believes should make us question each one of Smith's attributions to Marcus. In particular, insofar as T1 and T3 are to be found in work by Marcus, they are also to be found in works by Smullyan (1947, 1948) and Fitch (1949). So, all three of them provided "significant anticipations of some of the central theses of contemporary non-Fregean theories of reference," but nothing that would single out Marcus as a founder of such theories (Soames 1995, 208).

Something similar can be said for Soames' response to Smith's claims about T4 and T5—there is a sense in which they contain a kernel of truth, but ultimately need to be qualified significantly. In particular, Marcus can be attributed with an implicit step along the way toward T4 and T5, but she does not anticipate the full-blown theses that Kripke argued for in the arena. To see this, lets first look at T4—the necessity of identity. Here, Soames rightly points out that this is an ambiguous phrase which can mean that:

(1) statements of identity involving variables express necessary propositions (i.e., $(\forall x)(\forall y)(x = y \rightarrow \Box\, x = y)$),
(2) statements of identity involving proper names express necessary propositions, or
(3) statements of identity involving singular terms express necessary propositions.

This is important because the necessity of identity with respect to variables and proper names—(1) and (2)—seem correct, while the necessity of identity with respect to singular terms (n.b. contingent definite descriptions) is false (Soames 1995, 202). Furthermore, while Marcus (1947) proved that the necessity of identity with respect to variables is true, she does not discuss the necessity of identity with respect to proper names—the view that Kripke (1980) got to. Given this, we can no more attribute to her the true view—(2)—that there is a necessity of identity with respect to proper names than we can the false view—(3)—that there is a necessity of identity with respect to singular terms, generally. Similarly, with respect to T5, Soames argues that "[Marcus] can be seen, following Smullyan and Fitch, as implicitly treating proper names as rigid" (Soames 1995, 203). That said, without a possible-worlds semantics, Marcus' early work does not have the notion of a referent at a world and, thus, cannot be said to have any explicit views concerning rigid designation—reference to just one object across all possible worlds.

Finally, Soames' responses to T2 and T6 are much less congenial. With respect to T2—the idea that just because a definite description has been used to fix the referent of a name, this does not mean that the name goes on to carry the meaning of that description—Soames argues that Smith misunderstands Marcus' (& Kripke's) work and cites it problematically. To make his case for this, he begins by pointing out that understanding exactly what is behind T2 is somewhat difficult. Because of this, he spends some time trying to spell out exactly what T2 asserts, ultimately claiming that T2 requires holding that:

(1) "sometimes the referent of a name is semantically fixed by an associated definite description."
(2) "even though the description is not synonymous with the name."
(3) "if the referent of a name is semantically fixed by a certain description, then being a competent speaker who understands the name will involve knowing that if the name has a referent at all, it must be one that satisfies the description."
(4) "if a name N has its referent semantically fixed by a description D, then one who understands the sentence 'If N exists, then N is D' will know, without empirical investigation, that it expresses a truth." (Soames 1995, 199–200)

Unfortunately, Soames claims nothing quite to the level of any of (1)–(4) can be found in Marcus (1961) because "What she was really saying was that despite the fact that recognizing something as a thing presupposes a readiness to apply descriptions to it, nevertheless we have a linguistic device, the proper name, which allows us to refer to a thing without describing it" (Soames 1995, 200).

As for T6, Soames again argues that Smith has failed to understand Marcus' and Kripke's views on the matters at hand. In particular, Soames points out that Marcus could not have introduced the existence of the necessary a posteriori because Marcus fails to use "a posteriori" anywhere in her paper and identifies the necessary with the tautologous, with the analytic. Furthermore, Marcus holds that co-referential proper names are intersubstitutable in all contexts. So, if the following is true—"Krista knows a priori that Hesperus = Hesperus"—so too should the next sentence be true—"Krista knows a priori that Hesperus = Phosphorus." Given this, Soames says that "it is as clear as anything can be that Marcus did not in her 1961 article embrace the notion of necessary a posteriori identities" (Soames 1995, 205).

With Soames' (1995) detailed responses to the particular theses in Smith's original paper aside, it will also be instructive to look at Burgess' (1998) responses. This is because Burgess takes a step back to argue that the paper does not just suffer from problems of detail, but also has major problems in its underlying methodology. More specifically, Burgess "begin[s] by listing ten reasons why Smith's original paper should never have been taken seriously as a contribution to historical scholarship, ten ways in which the paper conspicuously violates elementary rules of historiographical methodology" (Burgess 1998, 125). Here, I will focus on just the first four of these reasons. This is because Burgess is just straightforwardly correct about the last six. That said, admitting this does not undermine the primary goal of Smith (1995a). Rather, it shows that it needs significant work to clean it up. Furthermore, Burgess himself admits that there is an important difference between the first four and the last six when he says "[a]s a result of the four methodological errors just enumerated, Smith approaches the texts asking the wrong question," whereas the last six simply cause problems of interpretation in answering those questions (Burgess 1998, 127).

With these preliminaries aside, we move to the list of reasons that Burgess provides for saying that Smith (1995a), the beginning of this saga, never should have happened in the first place. In the order he considers them, the original paper should never have been allowed to be presented because:

[R1] Smith reduces a complex philosophical theory to a list of a half-dozen points.
[R2] Smith does not seriously examine Kripke's work.

[R3] Smith conflates introducing theses with endorsing those theses.
[R4] Smith uses highly ambiguous labels for the theses under discussion.

While these are relatively self-explanatory, a few words about each is in order. As far as R1 is concerned, Smith's reduction of NTR to T1–T6 is problematic because "the importance of a complex theory consists at least as much in the interconnections it establishes among its novel elements" and "it is very far from being [a reasonably accurate enumeration of the novelties of the 'new' theory]" (Burgess 1998, 125–26). Furthermore, this list is so problematic because of what Burgess points out in R2—that the list comes from insufficient engagement with Kripke's original texts. Evidence of the fact that Smith has not significantly examined Kripke's work is given in the form of the fact that "he omits from his list important novelties of the 'new' theory", including the "notable example [of] the historical chain account of the reference of a name to its bearer" (Burgess 1998, 126).

Similarly, R3 is supposed to result from the fact that Smith has not only failed to carefully comb the literature after Marcus (1961), but also failed to carefully comb through prior literature. As Soames (1995) pointed out, some of T1–T6 are in fact endorsed by Marcus (1961), but she could not have originated them as she acknowledged following up on work from Smullyan (1947, 1948) and Fitch (1949, 1950). Finally, R4 is meant to draw our attention to phrases from T1–T6 such as "direct reference" and "necessity of identity." Burgess takes these to be problematic because they are ambiguous and Smith has not checked to be sure that they refer to the same thing when accurately describing a view of Marcus' and when accurately describing a view of Kripke's. Again, putting R1–R4 together, Burgess concludes,

> As a result of the four methodological errors just enumerated, Smith approaches the texts asking the wrong question. He simply asks whether there are passages in Marcus (1963) that could be read as endorsements of doctrines to which the labels "direct reference" and "necessity of identity" and so on could be applied. (Burgess 1998, 127)

Hence, according to Soames (1995) and Burgess (1998),

(1) Smith (1995a, 1995b) should not have been published in the first place,
(2) even if their main theses could have been argued for responsibly, these actual attempts would still have methodological problems in arguing through T1–T6 as a stand-in for NTR, and
(3) even if they did not, the individual attributions of T1–T6 would all be problematic.

§1.3 ODDITIES IN SOAMES' AND BURGESS' RESPONSES

Now that we have sketched the basic contours of this debate, we are in a position to move toward saying something about it. Remember, my ultimate goal is to say that Smith has gotten some things right and some things wrong, with similar claims about Soames and Burgess. I will also argue that part of the explanation for this situation is that all three have had their focus in the wrong place. We should not primarily be concerned with Kripke and we should not be concerned with charges of plagiarism or misunderstanding. Rather, we should be primarily concerned with Marcus (even if occasionally in relation to how much credit she has gotten relative to Kripke). Furthermore, I suspect that, and will argue for the conclusion that, a significant cause of the insufficient amount of credit Marcus has received has been her gender—a social phenomenon. Because of that, we ought to be looking at trends within social groups and institutions, rather than isolated, individual actors. In particular, we will look at the institution of academic philosophy as a whole as culprit and gendered discursive injustice as the charge, which will explain this situation.

Before we get to that explanation, though, we need to show that there is something in need of explanation. For this, we will turn to a critique of *some* of Soames' and Burgess' work, since their work is clearer and more precise than Smith's. In doing so, we could choose to either give *external* or *internal* critiques. External critiques of a view are criticisms that come from an ideology or standpoint different from the view being critiqued. Internal critiques, by contrast, criticize a view on its defender's own terms. They show that the position taken does not live up the principles that it initially grew out of. Internal critiques like these can sometimes be more powerful due to the fact that they grant many assumptions to the opponent. It is one thing to be able to criticize your view using my own beliefs and ideology. It is quite another to be able to criticize your view using your own beliefs, ideology, and worldview.

Given this rhetorical advantage internal critiques have, I will place my focus there. In particular, I will argue that there are some internal oddities to several of Soames' and Burgess' responses such that, even if we accept some of what they have to say, we can still support the claim that Marcus has been underappreciated and underrecognized. These oddities will be part of the case that there is something in need of explanation for which discursive injustice will serve as explanans.

Soames

Turning to that internal critique, it is important to note that Soames admits that a *combination* of three to four of these six theses (namely, a combination of T1, T3, T4, and T5) originated in Marcus' work. That is to say, the individual theses—T1, T3, and an implicit acceptance of T5—do not originate with Marcus. Soames holds that Smullyan and Fitch also argued for T1 and T3, while also implicitly endorsing T5. Even on Soames' picture, the combination of these with T4—the necessity of identity (on the variables, not proper names, reading)—is original with Marcus' views, though. This is significant on its own. If Marcus can be uniquely credited with more than half of the six theses connected to NTR in the debate, shouldn't she receive more credit than she has? This is especially the case given that there is the additional oddity that Soames' hesitation to give complete credit to Marcus on T4 is at odds with Kripke, who says "Marcus says that identities between names are necessary" (Kripke 1980, 100).

Of course, one may obviously respond to this that Soames admits that Marcus, Smullyan, and Fitch, "deserve a degree of recognition that they are often not given" (Soames 1995, 200) and "should be praised for their prescient insights" (Soames 1995, 208). This is not a completely satisfactory response, though. Part of Soames' point in connecting Smullyan and Fitch to T1, T3, and T5 seems to be that there is something odd about Smith's *singling out* of Marcus. Given that Marcus clearly did much more with respect to T4 than Smullyan or Fitch, this is at odds with Soames' own points. Furthermore, Soames himself gives further reason to single out Marcus as having been particularly wronged in the lack of credit and recognition she has received. As mentioned earlier, part of his justification for saying Marcus is not deserving of "founder" status is that her discussion was not long and detailed enough. That said, Soames also admits that "although Marcus' discussion of these points is brief, it is more detailed and explicit than those of Smullyan and Fitch" (Soames 1995, 197). Again, putting Soames' own views together, this would mean Marcus is significantly more deserving of recognition than Smullyan or Fitch.[3]

While I think the preceding gives reason to believe that Marcus' contributions to NTR clearly deserve more recognition *if* T1–T6 is a good way to carry out the debate, more needs to be said about this antecedent. Remember, this is the main thrust of Burgess (1998)—that Smith's (1995a, 1995b) methodological errors set us out on the wrong trajectory to begin with. So, in order for my responses to Soames (1995) to have as much weight as I would like them to, we will need to have something to say in response to Burgess' (1998) R1–R4 as well. Again, given its rhetorical advantages, I will focus on internal critiques of Burgess' thoughts on these four reasons. In particular, I will argue that R1 and R4 are inconsistent with his praise of Soames' historical work, whereas R2 and R3 are problems that Burgess' own work falls prey to. Given this, Burgess cannot consistently say we ought to dismiss Smith's work while promoting his own and Soames'.

Burgess

Starting with those reasons that I claim Burgess' own work falls prey to, remember that Burgess argues for R2 on the grounds that Smith did not include some of Kripke's most important contributions to NTR. In particular, Burgess criticizes Smith for not having recognized the importance of Kripke's causal historical theory of reference—the idea that names and their referents are passed on from user to user after an initial baptism by being causally connected to the initial bearer. Given that Burgess is criticizing Smith for not having sufficiently looked into his interlocutor's views, this is a strange claim to make. This is because Smith brings up the causal historical theory of reference multiple times in his work, even explicitly saying "[o]f course some of the ideas in "Naming and Necessity" are genuinely new, such as the causal chain picture of the reference of names, the idea that natural kind terms are rigid designators and the theory of the necessity of origins" (Smith 1995a, 186).

One might still complain that, while Smith recognizes this, he does not sufficiently connect it to NTR since he leaves it out of T1–T6. This seems to be part of what Burgess is saying when he says "[t]he result is that he omits from his list important novelties of the 'new' theory" (Burgess 1998, 126). That said, while it is a controversial decision, the causal historical theory of reference does not have nearly the support that T1–T6 do. For starters, theorists have offered compelling arguments that being causally connected to the object of an initial baptism is neither necessary nor sufficient for being the referent of a name. For instance, despite the fact that our current uses of "Madagascar" are causally connected to an initial baptism of part of Somalia, the referent of "Madagascar" is Madagascar—the island off of East Africa (Evans 1973). Furthermore, despite none of us being causally connected to abstract objects, we refer to them quite regularly.

Perhaps even more important for our discussion is that subscribing to the causal historical theory of reference is neither necessary nor sufficient for subscribing to NTR. For instance, causal descriptivists who hold that the description that gives the meaning of a name contains reference to such a causal historical chain subscribe to a causal theory without being New Theorists and Gillian Russell subscribes to NTR without holding on to the causal theory. Russell adopts all of T1–T6, much more of Kripke's and Kaplan's work, and was a student of Soames as well as Burgess. That said, she does not accept Kripke's causal historical theory of reference because she is "uncomfortable with the idea that the reference determiner for an expression might be different for different speakers." Rather, Russell offers a plausible alternative that "it is the condition specified by the baptiser (using a description, or by pointing) and used to pick out a referent for the name when it was introduced" (Russell 2008, 47).[4]

Of course, one might still, as Burgess does, worry that without contributions above and beyond T1–T6 "the views of Kripke do not emerge clearly" (Burgess 1998, 126). This is no doubt true, but I do not think it bears on what should be our proper concerns. As mentioned earlier, I do think that Smith, and subsequently Soames and Burgess, made this debate far too much about Kripke. Our concern should be Marcus and her relationship to NTR. Kripke has many views which go beyond NTR shared by "Kripke, Kaplan, Donnellan, Putnam, Perry, Salmon, Soames, Almog, Wettstein and a number of other contemporary philosophers" (Smith 1995a, 179). With our proper concerns in mind, it is no longer such a sin to have left out some of Kripke's views—even those that are wildly important and novel.

Turning to R3, Burgess holds that it is problematic for one to claim that somebody has introduced something just by endorsing that something because it very obviously could have shown up earlier in the literature. And, as has been mentioned multiple times now, several of the theses in T1–T6 were earlier endorsed by Smullyan and Fitch, among others. Here, though, we find a potential clash with R1 because, again, "the importance of a complex theory consists at least as much in the interconnections it establishes among its novel elements" (Burgess 1998, 125–26). And, while T1, T3, and T5 may have shown up in Smullyan's and Fitch's works earlier, these in connection with a formal proof of T4 were new to Marcus' work. Furthermore, Smith argues that "[t]his modal argument [T3] goes back to Marcus' formal proof of the necessity of identity [T4] in her extension of S4" (Smith 1995a, 183). Granted, Soames and Burgess both take issue with this way of understanding the relationship between the theses. That said, this is a substantive disagreement (one that I happen to agree with Soames and Burgess on), rather than the methodological one which Burgess thinks helped make the paper inappropriate for presentation.[5] Hence, Burgess' claiming that Smith's work falls prey to R3 falls prey to his own R1—in thinking that Smith has confused endorsing and introducing part of NTR, he has failed to consider the important interconnections therein.

With R1 coming into the discussion, we should turn to it. Again, my goal with respect to R1 is to show that there is something odd about Burgess saying it should rule out Smith's work, because it would also rule out much of Soames' historical work (and much good history). Remember, Burgess claims that the way R1 contributed to Smith's work being such that it "should never have been taken seriously as a contribution to historical scholarship" was because "[Smith] attempts to reduce a complex philosophical theory to a list of a half-dozen discrete points" (Burgess 1998, 125). Unfortunately, Soames' most well-known and recognized contribution to the history on these matters—*Philosophical Analysis in the Twentieth Century: The Age of Meaning*—does this as well.

On the first page of chapter 1, Soames reduces the philosophical work of Wittgenstein's *Philosophical Investigations* to several discrete views on three discrete topics.[6] The discrete topics are:

> (i) a critique of what Wittgenstein regards as the dominant referential conception of meaning, and a proposal to replace it with a conception in which to use language meaningfully is to master a certain kind of social practice; (ii) a critique of the previously dominant conception of philosophical analysis, and the substitution of a new conception of analysis to play the central role in philosophy; and (iii) the development of a new philosophical psychology. (Soames 2003b, 3)

Now, I would argue that *Philosophical Investigations* is a more complex work than *Naming and Necessity* (and that is meant as a criticism of Wittgenstein, not Kripke). That said, I do not think this means that there is anything wrong with Soames' work.[7] This is what analytic philosophy does at its best—it breaks complex views into the simplest pieces possible and their interrelations. So, again, holding that R1 should rule out Smith's historical work would also rule out Soames' own historical work and much good work on the history of philosophy. We find a similar issue in relation to R4—Burgess' worry that Smith conducts his investigation using "especially ambiguous" terms such as "direct reference" and "necessity of identity."

Burgess' R4 would rule out much of Soames' historical work (and much good history). In fact, every class I took on the history of twentieth century analytic philosophy, which covered matters related to this debate, involved similar use of the terms "direct reference" and "necessity of identity."

The Discipline Broadly

Now, remember that my goal is not to make charges against Kripke, Soames, Burgess, or any isolated individuals. My goal is to show that analytic philosophy has institutional problems with gender and to use the lack of recognition that Ruth Barcan Marcus has received as an example of that. The point of focusing on Soames and Burgess has been to start a pattern of showing lack of recognition, which is connected to under-citation and under-engagement with Marcus' work. To continue that pattern, let us turn to the broader literature.[8]

As I mentioned in the introduction, one of the things that I think warrants marking off a new phase of the analytic movement in the mid-1990s was the development of a self-conscious subfield of the history of analytic philosophy. Consistent with this increased self-reflection, there has also been a notable increase in work dedicated to metametaphysics and meta-philosophy.

Because of their connection to NTR, both of these literatures provide a valuable resource for our discussion. Table 1.1 shows some of what we learn by looking at representative examples from these literatures (please note that the numerals in the Kripke and Marcus columns for histories of analytic philosophy and books on meta-philosophy represent numbers of pages on which they are discussed, while the numerals for the anthologies of analytic philosophy and the philosophy of language represent the number of works anthologized).[9]

So, across these eighteen works, we find 361 pages dedicated to discussion of Kripke's work and just forty-four pages of discussion of Marcus' work, with eight anthology entries of Kripke's work and none of Marcus' work. With just what has been admitted about Marcus' contributions so far, this should seem problematic. That said, I will return in the next chapter to some more of Marcus' contributions that I hope will bolster this case.

For now, I think it will be helpful to look at one further reference point to see something of the pattern of oddities in the discipline's reception of Marcus' work. One way to bring the whole discipline under the microscope is to look at the number of citations Marcus' work has received—as done in table 1.2. To give us a baseline, I will include the five most-cited works of Kripke's next to the five most-cited works of Marcus'. Also, so as to not be seen as begging the question, I include some philosophers who were ranked around Ruth Barcan Marcus in the poll that Brian Leiter ran on his blog in January 2015 asking philosophers to rank the most important Anglophone philosophers between 1945 and 2000.[10]

Table 1.1 Insufficient Recognition and Engagement

		Kripke	Marcus
Histories of Analytic	Soames (2003a, 2003b)	154	4
	Beaney (2013)	44	14
	Biletzki/Matar (1998)	19	1
	Floyd/Shieh (2001)	32	1
	Glock (2008)	8	0
	Hacker (1996)	4	0
	Hallett (2008)	15	0
	Schwartz (2012)	35	5
	Stroll (2000)	21	18
Meta-philosophy	Berto/Plebani (2015)	7	0
	Chalmers et al. (2009)	5	0
	Williamson (2007)	17	1
Anthologies of Analytic	Baillie (2003)	1	0
	Martinich/Sosa (2011)	1	0
Philosophy of Language	Martinich/Sosa (2013)	4	0
	Nye (1998)	1	0
	Stainton (2000)	1	0

Author Created

Table 1.2 Insufficient Engagement and Citation

		As of	June	2019			SUM
Most Cited Papers	Kripke	14,032	4,523	2,373	1,734	1,689	24,351
	Marcus	**_464_**	**_322_**	**_110_**	**_93_**	**_81_**	**_1,070_**
	MacIntyre	26,597	4,728	2,507	2,147	1,861	37,840
	Thomson	1,910	1,330	1,262	754	516	5,772
	Hare	4,169	2,894	2,383	351	301	10,098
	Kaplan	4,304	844	721	637	315	6,821

Author Created using data from Google Scholar citation counts.
The significance of boldfaced and underlined contents is that Marcus is being compared to each of the others.

Note that, despite finishing one spot below Alasdair MacIntyre and one spot above Judith Jarvis Thomson, Ruth Marcus has been cited thousands of times less than either of them. Since one might worry that this has to do with the areas of philosophy that the relevant thinkers worked in, I also included David Kaplan, who worked in very similar areas to Marcus. Despite finishing nine spots below Marcus in the Leiter poll, Kaplan too has been cited thousands of times more than Marcus.

Furthermore, notice that Thomson, the only other woman on this list, has the second fewest citations. Again, to try to compare apples to apples, I included R. M. Hare in the list, a fellow ethicist working at relatively similar times. Despite her finishing five spots above Hare, Thomson has thousands fewer citations. I claim that we are hard pressed to plausibly explain this insufficient recognition, insufficient engagement, and insufficient citation in any other way than gendered injustice. It is toward making good on that claim that we now turn.

§1.4 KUKLA ON DISCURSIVE INJUSTICE

With the case for the existence of these oddities behind us, we can finally turn to an explication of the notion of discursive injustice. Kukla defines it as follows:

DEF'N: One is a victim of *discursive injustice* when they "face a systematic inability to produce a specific kind of speech act that they are entitled to perform" simply because they are a member of a disadvantaged group. (Kukla 2014, 440)[11]

That is, Kukla's work is an application of Austin's (1962) theory of speech acts. Like speech act theory, generally, we begin with the distinction between saying something—the locutionary act—and the actions we engage in by saying something—the illocutionary acts. Once we recognize that there is a difference between locutionary and illocutionary acts, we should also realize that there is a difference between perlocutionary failures. Sometimes the audience does not grasp the locutionary content, other times they do not grasp the illocutionary force. Furthermore, there are times when this incorrect uptake can alter the illocutionary structure of the original speech act. Finally, within this class, there are times when that inability to produce the rightfully intended illocutionary force/act happens because of incorrect uptake due to a marginalized social identity of the speaker. These are the discursive injustices.

To make discursive injustice as clear as possible, Kukla begins with examples of the genus of which discursive injustice is a species—cases where one intends to perform one illocutionary act, but something goes awry because the audience gives it the wrong uptake. For instance, imagine I am out with my partner, say to them "will you marry me?" intending for this to be a proposal, but my partner does not think I have any intention to be serious and laughs at what I have said. If this happens, there is a very real sense in which I have made a joke, rather than a proposal (Kukla 2014, 443).[12] Furthermore, Davidson's example of an actor on stage trying to warn the audience of a fire in the back of the theater, but failing to do so because the audience thinks this is part of the performance provides us another example (Kukla 2014, 447). Again, though the speakers have intended to produce one illocutionary act, the whole speech activity was altered by the conversation partners giving the incorrect perlocutionary uptake.

Building up to our crescendo, Kukla then provides a striking example of a case where this happens as a result of gender—a case of discursive injustice.

> Celia is a floor manager at a heavy machinery factory where 95% of the workers are male. It is part of her job description that she has the authority to give orders to the workers on her floor, and that she should use this authority. She uses straightforward, polite locutions to tell her workers what to do: "Please put that pile over here," "Your break will be at 1:00 today," and so on. Her workers, however, think she is a "bitch," and compliance is low. Why? One possible explanation is that the workers are just being blatantly sexist and insubordinate. They are refusing to follow her orders, which is still a way of taking them as orders. This sort of direct transgression is relatively straightforward. However, a subtler and more interesting explanation is that even though Celia is entitled to issue orders in this context, and however much she follows the conventions that typically would mark her speech acts as orders, because of her gender her workers take her as issuing requests instead. (Kukla 2014, 445–46)

This difference between requests and orders is quite important, since following an order is obligatory and granting a request is not. Since one can always permissibly decline to grant a request, we often expect there to be thanks from the requestor when the request has been granted. Such gratitude is unnecessary for following an order, though. This means either that Celia can thank her employees and undermine her authority or not thank her employees and be called a "bitch".[13]

In addition, Kukla gives other classes of discursive injustice based on grammatical structures other than those in the imperative mood. One particular type of discursive injustice that will become important to our discussion later is in relation to what Kukla calls "entreaties to speak":

> One way the performative force of a speech act can be derailed is if one speaks as an insider—a player of a game that comes with certain discursive privileges—but is not given uptake as one. (Kukla 2014, 448)

Unfortunately,

> In many scenarios, I suggest, women have good reasons to believe that they are already participants in a discursive game, until it becomes clear from how their speech receives uptake that their attempted moves within the game are actually functioning as entreaties to join it. (Kukla 2014, 449)

This is particularly relevant given that philosophy is a field that thinks that outsiders just do not understand quite how we do things in philosophy and is a field dominated by men. As Kukla continues,

> I think we see this kind of discursive injustice frequently when women try to speak as experts in a male-dominated field. Expert speech has a specific kind of default weight. This takes many forms. An expert's claims about his subject matter, though never appropriately treated as infallible, become more than just truth claims to be subjected to scrutiny and challenge at the whim of any interlocutor. When someone makes a claim about his area of expertise, this claim, though challengeable, has prima facie standing; his recognized expert status itself gives listeners some reason to trust what he says. Conversely, other experts do not get to just overrule his claims in virtue of their own expertise, as they could with a lay speaker. (Kukla 2014, 449)

So, this will be the type of discursive injustice we will be discussing in relation to our debate—injustice on the basis of gender and unwillingness to recognize expertise.

Before we do that, though, it is important to note that there is nothing unique about gender here and nothing that requires that the relevant mistaken attitude disrupting the uptake be *about* hierarchy, even if it *creates* or *perpetuates* hierarchy. That is to say, sometimes discursive injustice occurs as a result of a stereotype that does not involve hierarchical concepts like "manager" or "expert," but which is easily connected to hierarchies. For instance, there are many stereotypes of people with mental illnesses as generally deranged or irrational. As a result, if somebody knows I have a mental illness and hears me assert something about a problem I have observed, they may dismiss my speech acts as not inherently contentful or rational, but rather simply an acoustic blast produced by chemical misfirings in my brain.[14] This may significantly impact my ability to have my problems addressed. Similar examples for many different dimensions of identity can clearly be generated based on stereotypes peculiar to that identity type and how they relate to a listener's ability to recognize the speaker as meeting the preconditions for their intended speech act.

§1.5 DISCURSIVE INJUSTICE IN THIS CASE

Now that we have been through a section on the explanandum (§1.3) and a section on the essential concept we will use in the explanans (§1.4), it is time to look at my particular application of discursive injustice as a way to explain this case. For this, we will use a simple model for abduction where a plausible inference to the best explanation must first meet Peirce's general form for abductions:

"[P1:] The surprising fact, C, is observed.
[P2:] But if A were true, C would be a matter of course.
[CONCLUSION:] Hence, there is reason to suspect that A is true." (Peirce *Collected Papers*, 5.189)

Of course, a good abduction is an inference to the *best* explanation, so we must follow some further rules above and beyond meeting Peirce's general form:

(1) A plausible abduction is compared to other explanations.
(2) A plausible explanation will be as simple as possible (i.e., abides Ockham's razor).
(3) A plausible explanation will be as consistent and coherent with background knowledge as possible (and so will admit of generalization).

With this model of abduction in mind, we can turn to the principle argument of the chapter to which we have been building. First, the basic structure meeting Peirce's general form for abductions:

P1: There is this surprising fact that Marcus has been under-cited, under-taught, under-anthologized, and underappreciated.

P2: If Marcus has been the victim of discursive injustice, then it would be unsurprising that Marcus has been under-cited, under-taught, under-anthologized, and underappreciated.

CONCLUSION: There is reason to suspect that Marcus has been the victim of rampant discursive injustice.

Filling this out a bit more, my suggestion is that part of the reason Marcus has not been sufficiently recognized for her contributions to the development of NTR and analytic philosophy, more generally, is because some of her speech acts were given the wrong uptake. In particular, her expert assertions and arguments were treated as mere suggestions because she was working in a field with sexist expectations about gender and expertise. This matters greatly because a suggestion and an argument from an expert put very different expectations on us. It is never expected that one need to respond to a mere suggestion—one can always decide to take or leave it. An argument from an expert carries with it much more weight and much more expectation—one should be prepared to engage with and have something to say about an expert's argument in their area.

To give a concrete picture of what I have in mind, I am suggesting that what happened over Marcus' career was something of an extended version of what I have seen in conference and colloquium presentations all too many times in my career. Somebody gets finished giving a talk and the Q&A session starts. After a while, a woman raises her hand and gives a comment to the presenter who responds politely enough with something like "thank you for the suggestion—I'll consider that." Several minutes pass and a man raises his hand, making very similar points, but this time the presenter responds "oh, wow—what a great argument. I will write that down and have to come up with a response for it in the published piece." So, what was treated as a mere suggestion from a woman, carrying with it no obligation to respond, is something that would be treated as an expert argument coming from a man.[15] And, to be clear that my claim about which particular speech acts were involved in this discursive injustice is not coming out of nowhere, consider the following passages from Soames:

> I mentioned that in her early work Marcus *suggested* that ordinary proper names might be Russellian logically proper names. (Soames 1995, 192, my emphasis) and

> In her later work, especially the 1961 paper cited by Smith, Marcus adopted these theses of Smullyan and Fitch, essentially *suggesting* that ordinary proper names might be Russellian logically proper names. (Soames 1995, 193, my emphasis)

Yet again, my aim here is not to single out Soames and Burgess. My point is to give another representative example, which is close to the heart of this debate and continues the kind of pattern I have been illustrating for several sections now. And with general patterns in mind, it is important to remember that an explanation in terms of sexist discursive injustice coheres well with what we know about the discipline as a whole. It should be no shock that the rampant sexism we find throughout the history of philosophy (and almost all institutions that have ever existed) would make its way into the twists and turns of the literature like this.[16] In fact, quite sadly, it coheres quite well with what we know about Marcus' career in academia.

From the time she arrived at Yale for graduate school, she was subjected to regular patriarchal structures and misogynistic actors—through "separate but not equal" housing for women, exclusion from parts of the library, and being asked by the department chair to not take her duly elected position of president of the philosophy club (Marcus 2010, 80–81). Furthermore, as Diana Raffman pointed out in her obituary of Marcus[17]:

> She would tell of having to fend off the unwelcome advances of a male professor (thankfully not a philosopher!) with a coat hanger, of being barred from all undergraduate classrooms at Yale while studying there for her Ph.D., and of being forced to publish her landmark papers under her married name. (Raffman 2012)

This is appallingly and criminally sexist behavior going far beyond the type of gendered stereotyping and conversing suggested in the preceding argument. So, again, it seems that the simplest explanation that fits in with our background knowledge best is that Marcus' reception has been a result of discursive injustice.

Given that my primary thesis was gotten at via abductive reasoning, we should consider some alternative explanations and see how they fare in comparison to mine. Again, abduction is inference to the *best* explanation, rather than inference to any old explanation. To plausibly make such a claim, we have to show a comparison to some competing explanations. Beginning with those that have been suggested in the dialectic under discussion and branching out to explanations that have been offered in the conversations I have had with other philosophers about this matter, I will briefly consider five alternative explanations and point out where I think an argument showing they go wrong would begin.

[E1] Marcus' work on NTR occurs over too few pages.

Reply: This alternative explanation suggests that it would be far outside of the norm for a significant philosophical contribution to be recognized from just a few pages. As Smith points out, though, "F. P. Ramsey is generally credited with priority for the Dutch book argument for justifying the axioms of probability on the personalist or subjectivist interpretations of the axioms. But this accreditation is based on exactly two sentences" (Smith 1995b). Furthermore, in the exact same year that Marcus (1961) actually came out in print, Edmund Gettier published his famous paper that has been cited roughly 4,000 times and that comes in under three pages (Gettier 1963). This either involves an implicit assumption that women cannot achieve such significant contributions or requires an argument that Marcus' work is not of that caliber. The first would also be sexist and the second would be implausible.

[E2] Marcus' work is overly technical and not as accessible as Kripke's.

Reply: This misses the fact that, throughout its history, analytic philosophers have been extremely interested in, and influenced by, symbol-crunching. Nobody leaves *Principia Mathematica* out of the history of analytic philosophy because it is not accessible. This response also misses the fact that Marcus' work ranges from highly technical work on quantified modal logic (Marcus 1946a, 1946b, 1947) to philosophical discussions on abstract issues, which engages with formal results (Marcus 1961) to practical discussions informed by work in logic, but fully accessible to those without a formal background (Marcus 1980).

[E3] Marcus' proofs are not as elegant as Kripke's.

Reply: If this were the case, then the recognition that Marcus has received should be similar to the credit Kurt Gödel receives for proving the completeness of first-order logic, despite the fact that Leon Henkin gave the proof of the result that has become standard. Nobody would fail to mention Gödel in relation to this work, though, quite like they have with respect to Marcus, modal logic, and NTR.

[E4] Marcus' work does not exhibit the "genius" of Kripke's work.

Reply: While one could obviously argue against the basic premise here, I think it is more important to recognize that there is misogyny built into distribution of these honorifics.[18] That said, for those wishing to see an argument for the genius of Marcus' work, please see chapter 2 of this book.

[E5] Smith's list does not encompass the import of Kripke's work.

Reply: This is absolutely right. That said, this does not separate Kripke from Marcus, because the list (T1–T6) does not encompass the import of

Marcus' work either! As we will see in the next chapter, we have a great deal that can be learned from Marcus' work on the relationship between logic and ethics, especially in Marcus (1980).

§1.6 CONCLUDING THOUGHTS ON DISCURSIVE INJUSTICE IN THE HISTORY OF PHILOSOPHY

I have not tried to provide anything more than the beginning of a reply to each of these alternative explanations, because I only want to make it clear that my claim that Marcus has been insufficiently recognized and this has been because of discursive injustice coming from systematic sexism serves as a *plausible* explanation. Simply establishing this plausibility is worthwhile because both Soames and Burgess have tried to say that this whole discussion should have never happened. In addition to Burgess' quotations already discussed, Soames began his reply, "My task today is an unusual and not very pleasant one. I am not here to debate the adequacy of any philosophical thesis. Rather, my job is to assess claims involving credit and blame" (Soames 1995, 191). It is true that Smith made this debate much more about blame directed at Kripke than it needed to be. That said, the focus was always primarily on credit for Marcus and only secondarily on Kripke. And, while Smith certainly got quite sloppy in the details, Soames and Burgess miss the importance of this primary focus of Smith's work. Importantly, this phenomenon of insufficient credit is something that is to be expected given that the discipline has been a part of sexist (and otherwise oppressive) social structures throughout its history. Because of this, if we look throughout the history of philosophy, we should expect to find such stories and, in fact, we do.[19]

For example, many recent works have recognized that traditional histories of early modern philosophy are wildly exclusionary. For the last three decades, much work has been done in response to create a sophisticated, specialized subfield of work on women in early modern philosophy. Perhaps the most distinguished thinker in this field, Eileen O'Neill, has herself pointed out that this has not been as quickly followed by corresponding changes in the larger history of modern philosophy and history of philosophy, generally, though (O'Neill 2005). Because of this, we need to develop more tactics for changing people's minds on the need for them to include previously excluded women in their teaching and work. Given that many of the best pieces on the mechanisms and mistakes of exclusion focus on *external criticisms*, in this chapter I tried to focus on an almost-entirely *internal* critique of standard scholarship on early analytic philosophy.

That is, despite a consensus on the existence of a great loss from this exclusion, there is less consensus on the mechanisms by which this ignorance has been created—with problems variously attributed to early modern gatekeepers, to our own contemporaries, and to intermediaries. Despite this variety of explanations, few have centrally utilized tools from contemporary philosophers to explain this exclusion—instead relying fundamentally on concepts like implicit bias (Gordon-Roth & Kendrick 2015), poor scholarly and pedagogical practices (Berges 2015),[20] and political/socioeconomic realities (O'Neill 1998). While these are all undoubtedly parts of the story, this chapter was built off of the premise that there can be a practical advantage with some philosophers to discussing this exclusion of women philosophers via the tools of philosophy itself. That is to say, we can perhaps get more philosophers putting time into righting these wrongs by making it clear just how central to the philosophical project it is to avoid such exclusions. Not only do we lose impressive philosophical content from the thinkers excluded and do something morally wrong, we are also being bad philosophers when we exclude people via phenomena like *epistemic*[21] and *discursive injustice*.

To further push back against Burgess' and Soames' claims that we ought not to have conversations like the one Smith started, I believe we find a similar example if we turn to Mary Wollstonecraft's *A Vindication of the Rights of Woman* (1792). That such an influential work on such fundamental issues could be discussed almost exclusively in the history of feminist thought can also be explained in terms of Kukla's (2014) notion of discursive injustice. That is to say, Wollstonecraft's speech acts were not given appropriate uptake as philosophical assertions and arguments. Rather, they have been taken to be "merely" political with an intended audience of only women or, perhaps, only feminists. Given that Wollstonecraft was working on issues central to modern philosophy and was, more consistently than Kant, extending Kantian principles in moral, social, and political philosophy, this is unfortunate. Building off of O'Neill (1998), in future work I hope to argue that this resulted from an explicitly sexist "purification of philosophy" between 1780 and 1830, just as Park (2013) has shown this period of historiographical work to have been explicitly racist.

Furthermore, Wollstonecraft (1792) should be of particular use to analytic philosophers because of her enlightenment thinking and her strong focus on logic and reason. Some of her principle arguments look something like the following:

P1: All humans have reasoning capabilities.
P2: If all humans have reasoning capabilities, then all persons can possibly attain virtue.
P3: If all persons can possibly attain virtue, then we should give each person what's needed to attain virtue.
SC1: If all humans have reasoning capabilities, then we should give each person what's necessary to attain virtue. (P2, P3, Hypothetical Syllogism)
P4: If we should give each person what's necessary to attain virtue, then we must educate women as well as men.

SC2: If all humans have reasoning capabilities, then we must educate women as well as men. (SC1, P4, Hypothetical Syllogism)
C: We must educate women as well as men. (P1, SC2, Modus Ponens)

and

P1: The most wisely formed society is the one whose constitution is based on the nature of humanity.
P2: The nature of humans is to be reasoning beings.
C: The most wisely formed society is the one whose constitution is based on reason.

These are powerful arguments for the utility of, and frameworks for thinking about, a liberal arts education involving analytic philosophy. It would be helpful to a better discipline of philosophy to bring these into the canon.

Pushing back further yet, something like what I've argued has happened with women like Marcus and Wollstonecraft with respect to discursive injustice has happened to people of color and those outside of the Western world quite frequently as well. John Mohawk, in talking about academic work on the Haudenosaunee, has said "[m]any professionals in this field operate on an expectation that rational thought is found only in the West" (Mohawk 1986, xv). Peter K. J. Park has established that many historians have done this with respect to philosophers from Africa and Asia as well.

For instance, Dietrich Tiedemann (1748–1803) wrote a history of philosophy that contains only Western philosophers by denying that any non-Western thinker's assertions counted as philosophical. Wilhelm Tennemann (1761–1819) did similarly but, instead of faulting non-Western reasons, concepts, and experiences, Tennemann held that non-Western thought cannot be counted as philosophical because of its attachment to political interests. Kant, himself, gave lectures that supported a wholly Eurocentric history of philosophy based on the claim that demonstration and pure reason are not found outside of Europe. Again, this is problematic for a great number of reasons. Of particular concern to analytic philosophers, though, is that one of the topics I believe we get a much better picture of from all of Marcus, Wollstoncecraft, the Peacemaker of the Haudenosaunee, and others excluded by these histories is the relationship between logic and ethics. It is to this topic that we turn in chapter 2.

NOTES

1. While these matters will be discussed in greater detail in chapter 2, this appearance of "man" and "woman" provide an important opportunity to make clear

how I will use a number of related, but importantly distinct terms. In particular, "male," "female," and "intersex" will be used as terms for sexes. "Man," "woman," and "transgender" will be used as terms for genders. "Masculine," "feminine," and "androgynous" will be used for gender roles, norms, and expressions.

2. It should be noted that there are only four pages in the books which mention Marcus—two times in which her name appears in a list along with others, once in which this very debate is mentioned as a "nasty controversy" (Soames 2003b, 353), and once in which it is admitted that a lack of discussion of formal logic and Marcus' role in it is part of "an undeniable gap in the story I have told" (Soames 2003b, 462). In fairness to Soames, it should also be mentioned that he says here that he hopes to return to this story in future work. This was echoed in Volume 1 of his new series on the history of analytic philosophy, where he says "[l]ooking one step beyond to Volume 3, I plan to discuss the struggle for modal logic involving, among others, C. I. Lewis, Ruth Barcan Marcus, Rudolf Carnap, and the young Saul Kripke" (Soames 2014, 632).

3. It should also be noted that Soames' reasoning for not giving Marcus any credit with respect to the necessary a posteriori might be inconsistent with his giving Kripke some of the credit he receives. Part of his reasoning here is that Marcus should not be seen as contributing to this doctrine because she sees the relevant modal concepts (e.g., tautology, analyticity, necessity, a priority, etc.) as more connected than they ought to be. This is certainly true. Of course, Kripke also sees these as more connected than they ought to be when he stipulates that "something which is analytically true will be both necessary and a priori (That's sort of stipulative.)" (Kripke 1980, 39). As Gillian Russell (2008) has shown, one can be a full-fledged New Theorist of Reference and recognize that there are contingent analytic (e.g., "I am here now") and analytic a posteriori (e.g., "Muhammad Ali is Cassius X") truths. Since a full development of how this can be is outside of the scope of this chapter and Smith's discussion of the necessary a posteriori is clearly mistaken, this point is relegated to an endnote. That said, for those who are interested in some of the relevant background, please see the discussion on analyticity in chapter 5 or any of Russell (2010, 2011, 2014).

4. For what it is worth, I also consider myself to be somebody who subscribes to NTR—I accept all of T1–T6, I was a student of David Braun (also referenced by Smith as one of the important proponents of the view), I adopted the framework of gappy propositions in LaVine (2016a) (needed to deal with empty names on NTR)—but also do not accept the causal historical theory of reference.

5. Furthermore, whether or not Marcus made this move, there are straightforward ways in which T4 can be helpful to T6—the view that there exist necessary a posteriori truths. Once we have Frege's Puzzle and the necessity of identity with respect to proper names, the existence of necessary a posteriori truths falls right out:

> P1: There exist identity statements between proper names which are known a posteriori (Frege's Puzzle).
> P2: All identity statements between proper names are necessary (necessity of identity).
> C: There exist identity statements between proper names, which are necessary and known a posteriori.

6. It is also worth noting that Soames too breaks down the significance of Kripke (1980) into six "most important aspects" (Soames 2003b, 336).

7. In fact, this fits very nicely with my own explication of Wittgenstein's philosophy from LaVine and Tissaw (2015). I hope to address the differences between my views and Soames' on Wittgenstein's *Philosophical Investigations* in future work. These differences focus primarily on the understanding of Wittgenstein as having a *deflationary* conception of philosophy.

8. Importantly, I am here just spelling out some of the details behind Marcus' own point that "There remain lengthy bibliographies and historical accounts of intensional and modal logic as well as interpretations of modalities where reference to my work is absent, but that is gradually being corrected" (Marcus 2010, 83).

9. It should be noted that there is a very unfortunate unrepresentativeness of these examples in that all of these works were published in English. As a monoglot English speaker, this is one of the areas where my book will simply unqualifiedly suffer. That said, this can also be seen as part of a further internal critique of the discipline which has a similarly problematic reliance on English.

10. The results of this poll can be found at https://civs.cs.cornell.edu/cgi-bin/results.pl?id=E_70df4a00cd504826, accessed June 12, 2019.

11. As Kukla notes, there are nontrivial issues about the metaphysics of speech acts built into this definition. That said, we can leave these aside here, since these could be avoided and the same points about discursive injustice made with the following definition:

> DEF'N: One is a victim of *discursive injustice* iff a speech act fails to occur simply because they have a social identity which has been traditionally marginalized/oppressed. For further discussion, see LaVine (2016b).

12. After all, a failed proposal would seem to change the nature of our relationship. It would also make it a sore subject if others brought up marriage around us, etc. In this case, though, it seems that none of this would be true. This suggests that no proposal ever actually happened.

13. For further discussion of the ways in which women are given norms which cannot be possibly satisfied at the same time, see chapter 1 of Haslanger (2012). We will discuss this more in chapter 2 of this book. So, while Kukla does not take a stance on how common this phenomenon is, it seems to me that part of the value in her work is giving a name to, and framework for discussing, something which is all too common. It is not just philosophers who notice this, either. Novelist and public intellectual, Chimamanda Ngozi Adichie, has a very interesting discussion, with similar examples, of similar matters on pp. 21–24 of Adichie (2014).

14. Many thanks to Cole Heideman for this example.

15. Again, this type of occurrence is clearly not limited to gender—I have seen this phenomenon occur with people of color, younger academics, etc. It is also not limited to the profession of philosophy. Adichie discusses a very similar example, saying "I have another friend, also an American woman, who has a high-paying job in advertising. She is one of two women in her team. Once, at a meeting, she felt slighted by

her boss, who had ignored her comments and then praised something similar when it came from a man" (Adichie 2014, 23).

16. For anyone who does find it to be a shock, I suggest reading through https://beingawomaninphilosophy.wordpress.com/.

17. Also relevant here is the fact that this obituary even being published in the first place required serious campaigning on the part of some feminist philosophers and friends of Marcus'.

18. For further discussion of this, see https://www.insidehighered.com/news/2016/01/11/new-analysis-offers-more-evidence-against-student-evaluations-teaching and http://benschmidt.org/profGender/#%7B%22database%22%3A%22RMP%22%2C%22plotType%22%3A%22pointchart%22%2C%22method%22%3A%22return_json%22%2C%22search_limits%22%3A%7B%22word%22%3A%5B%22genius%22%5D%2C%22department__id%22%3A%7B%22$lte%22%3A25%7D%7D%2C%22aesthetic%22%3A%7B%22x%22%3A%22WordsPerMillion%22%2C%22y%22%3A%22department%22%2C%22color%22%3A%22gender%22%7D%2C%22counttype%22%3A%5B%22WordsPerMillion%22%5D%2C%22groups%22%3A%5B%22department%22%2C%22gender%22%5D%2C%22testGroup%22%3A%22D%22%7D as well as Fan et al. (2019) "Gender and cultural bias in student evaluations: Why representation matters."

19. In fact, we can find other examples of this just from the history of analytic philosophy and just sticking to gender. For instance, Rachael Wiseman and Clare MacCumhaill argued in their 2017 Women in the History of Philosophy Lecture that failure to treat Anscombe, Foot, Midgley, and Murdoch as a philosophical school has been connected to something like discursive injustice. See https://www.sheffield.ac.uk/philosophy/research/womenhistoryphilosophy. Also, in chapters 3 and 5 I will discuss how Susan Stebbing's importance to the history of analytic philosophy has been under-recognized. I also think this has something to do with discursive injustice.

20. It is important to note that Berges does also use Miranda Fricker's notion of epistemic injustice as part of her explanation (Berges 2015, 385–87).

21. One type of epistemic injustice is testimonial injustice, defined by Miranda Fricker in the following manner:

> DEF'N: *"Testimonial injustice* happens when a speaker receives a deficit of credibility owing to the operation of prejudice in the hearer's judgement." (Fricker 2013, 1319)

I believe we can explain the fact that, for example, Princess Elisabeth is not usually taught or anthologized along with Descartes in early modern philosophy research and teaching via testimonial injustice. I hope to be able to address this in future work.

Chapter 2

The History (and Future) of Logic (and Ethics)

§2.0 OVERVIEW OF THE CHAPTER

This chapter will focus on the second subdiscipline, which gets placed at center stage in what I call "analytic philosophy the method"—namely, logic. While I am adopting a general policy of discussing formalisms and technicalities as little as possible, this chapter will be the one that discusses minutiae in more detail than any other. That said, the point of this chapter is to show that there can be significant emancipatory potential in sometimes doing so. In order to motivate sticking with this discussion of the minutiae, I begin with a number of thoughts that most clearly express the motivations of my own study of logic. First, John Mohawk on the founding principles of the Haudenosaunee Confederacy—the rightful stewards of every bit of land I have ever lived on, be it John Mohawk's own Seneca people in Buffalo, the Oneida people in Vernon, the Onondaga people in Syracuse, or the Mohawk people in Potsdam:

> If you do not believe in the rational nature of the human being, you cannot believe that you can negotiate with him. If you do not believe that rational people ultimately desire peace, you cannot negotiate confidently with him toward goals you and he share. If you can't negotiate with him, you are powerless to create peace. If you can't organize around those beliefs, the principles cannot move from the minds of men into the actions of society. (Mohawk 1989, 221)

Building on this very same idea of logic as tool for peace in the very same year, yet discussing very different temporal and cultural contexts, John Corcoran says, many exemplary moralists, including Socrates, Plato, Kant, Mill, Gandhi, and Martin Luther King, showed by their teachings and actions a deep commitment to objectivity, the ethical value that motivates logic and is served by logic. (Corcoran 1989b, 37)

Finally, to be clear that these should not be read as implicating the gendered reading of "men," but the species reading of "men," my earliest introduction to feminist philosophy:

"When men fight for their freedom, fight to be allowed to judge for themselves concerning their own happiness, isn't it inconsistent and unjust to hold women down? I know that you firmly believe you are acting in the manner most likely to promote women's happiness; but who made man the exclusive judge of that if woman shares with him the gift of reason? (Wollstonecraft 1792, 2)

§2.1 LOGIC, ETHICS, AND THE DISCIPLINE OF PHILOSOPHY

Alongside the centrality of chapter 1's focus—philosophy of language—to the development of early analytic philosophy was chapter 2's focus—logic. Logic holds a unique position as the most worked out analytic subdiscipline with the most uncontroversial progress. For somebody interested in the practical, everyday value of analytic philosophy, logic should not be overlooked. It is hard to imagine some individual manifestation of theory from any academic discipline, which more people would be willing to grant had everyday value than the computer—a piece of technology that develops through a story belonging to the history of logic. Given many communities' growing distrust and skepticism of the value of philosophy, this is something that should make us think that pitching logic is an important piece of giving a pitch for philosophy.

That said, there is a group of common misconceptions about logic[1]—that it is cold, unemotional, contrary to feelings, and separate from matters of ethics and value—which keep people from fully recognizing the importance of logic, analytic philosophy, and philosophy generally. Just as we tried to connect analytic philosophy of language to moral improvement and recipes for living one's life, by looking at its history in the previous chapter, we will connect logic to such practical matters by looking at the history of logic and how it has been connected to ethical matters.

Returning to public skepticism of philosophy, questions about where the intellectual, institutional, and social structure of philosophy will be in 25, 50, 100, and 500 years have all been asked a number of times for a number of reasons. From my perspective, the most pressing of these have to do with how we will be able to undermine the racist, sexist, homophobic, classist, and otherwise oppressive biases that the discipline has inherited from being a part of an extremely oppressive society. Other important inquiries brought up in this regard include how we will deal with shrinking budgets, increasing temporary employment, anti-intellectualism in the broader culture, etc. Among the most important questions asked for a variety of these reasons are:

[Q1] What justifies our spending public money on philosophy?
[Q2] What does philosophy give back to the world?
[Q3] What will philosophy give back to the world in the future?
[Q4] How can philosophy better itself as a community and institution?

The main goal of this chapter is to discuss why I think partial answers to these questions and the future of analytic philosophy lies (or should lay) in logic and ethics coming together to a much greater extent than they do now. In order to achieve this goal, I will enlist help from the following sources:

(1) a certain picture of the development of the modern formal logical revolution, which has come to make Kant's words infamous[2] and which gives good reason to think that there has been a natural, historical progression toward logic and ethics coming together more
(2) which will be discussed through specific works from several prominent actors in this story (n.b. Ruth Barcan Marcus, A. N. Prior, and John Corcoran) that show a great deal of potential for important work to come out of connecting logic and ethics and
(3) several examples that show the untapped potential of dedicated attention to nondeductive logics in understanding prejudice and bigotry.

These will be the topics taken up in the subsequent sections of the chapter, before a final section considering a particularly relevant objection from feminists to whom I hope to be an ally.

§2.2 THE HISTORY OF LOGIC FROM 1847 TO THE PRESENT

When trying to determine the trajectory that any discipline is going to take in the future, it is almost always prudent to investigate the path taken during the period just traversed.[3] Given that we are coming out of nothing short of a complete logical revolution, this is certainly true of the discipline of logic. For this reason, I will present a broad-strokes picture of the history of this logical revolution. Given how incomplete I will be in this context, it should be clear that this picture will be largely programmatic and will partly be based on what I see to be important for determining where logic will and should go from here. With this in mind, I take the history of the modern logical revolution to be a five-phased story, which looks something like the following:

[P1] Boole and De Morgan bring mathematical methods to the study of logical problems. This gives 1847 a particularly important place in the history of logic.
[P2] Formal systems of sentential logic are formulated, refined, and mastered. Beginning a trend that will be followed in the next two phases, its syntax is first mastered, then its semantics.
[P3] Formal systems of quantificational logic are formulated, refined, and mastered. Its syntax is relatively well understood by the time of Frege (1879). Its semantics is worked out in impressive detail in the 1930s, with the most important work coming from Tarski and Gödel.
[P4] Formal systems of modal logic are formulated, refined, and mastered. Its syntax is developed by Lewis and Marcus and the semantics is understood well enough to have completeness proofs and applications to natural language by Kripke (1963) and Kripke (1980).
[P5] From the time of Kripke's 1970 lectures, which would become *Naming and Necessity* up to today, the story of the development of logic becomes a much more disjointed and partitioned one.

With this outline in place, a bit more about each of these phases is in order.

P1: The Mathematization of Logic

Hans-Johann Glock begins his history of analytic philosophy with a section entitled "First Glimmerings: Mathematics and Logic" (Glock 2008, 26). In this section, Glock looks at the ways in which logico-philosophical problems in the foundations of mathematics surrounding algebra, geometry, analysis, and set theory set the stage for increased connections between mathematics and logic. I too believe this is a suitable place to start and, like Glock, that, with the exception of anticipations by Bolzano that have been unfortunately ignored for some time, the new logic begins in Boole's mathematization of logic (Glock 2008, 27–28). Boole's logical contributions begin in 1847 with his *Mathematical Analysis of Logic*, the same year as Augustus De Morgan's *Formal Logic: Or, The Calculus of Inference*. Both of them followed up on these works with further significant contributions in Boole's *The Laws of Thought* (1854) and De Morgan's *Syllabus of a Proposed System of Logic* (1860). Their individual contributions have been noted many times over by historians and logicians much more competent than myself (Kneale & Kneale 1962, Patton 2018, Terzian 2017). So, I will not rehearse these moves here. We should simply note that what is most important about their work from my general perspective is the bringing of mathematical methods to bear on questions in logic. This is what would ultimately allow logicism to play the role it did at the outset of the explicit movement of analytic philosophy. Though, for example, Aristotle had wanted to explain the knowledge gained in doing mathematics with his system of logic, the two had developed somewhat independently up until the nineteenth century. Boole and De Morgan changed this drastically and forever.[4]

This mathematization of the study of logic has been most significant for the methods and tools of clarity, precision, and objectivity that have been brought along with it. Most notable here are the uses of algebraic methods and notation, algorithmic procedures, axiomatic structures, recursive definitions, and set-theoretic frameworks.[5] Obviously, nothing even slightly resembling modern formal logic could exist without just the members of this short list. Foreshadowing the rest of our sketch of the history of the modern logical revolution, the use of algebra brought with it the modern logician's lexicon of variable letters, operator symbols, and function-notation. Concern with, and understanding of, algorithms culminates in the famous theorems of decidability and computability of Turing, Church, and others. The use of the axiomatic method in logic has led to the development of modern proof theories, with their bifurcation of axioms and rules of inference. Recursion theory has allowed us to give finitely expressible specifications of the infinity of grammatical constructions in our logical systems (and a means by which to wrangle the theories of their semantics in a finitely expressible way). And, finally, the set-theoretic universe has provided a domain in which to do respectably rigorous semantic work, something whose possibility was doubted even into the twentieth century (e.g., Wittgenstein 1922, Carnap 1934). Thus, the importance of the bringing together of mathematics and logic can simply not be overstated. Likewise, I hope the next revolution in logic will be brought about by the bringing together of logic and ethics.

P2: Sentential Logic

The next three phases in the history of logic form something of a cohesive unit with a similar pattern repeated at each step. That is to say, each phase is defined by the systematic development of a distinct branch of formal deductive logic, each branch being more complex than the last. In particular,

(1) we start with the mastery of sentential logic—the study of the inferential behavior of sentential connectives

(2) then move to a mastery of quantificational logic—the study of the inferential behavior of quantifier phrases, predicates, and singular terms
(3) and finish with a mastery of modal logic—the study of the inferential behavior of modal sentential operators.

This constitutes a natural progression, since we can think of

(1) sentential logic as arising from the logical relations between simple and complex sentences
(2) quantificational logic as arising from the logical structure within the simple sentences, and
(3) modal logic as arising from saying things about the different kinds of completed sentences from the previous two levels.

Thus, it is unsurprising that we find the chronological order to match this progression of complexity—sentential to quantificational to modal.

It is also interesting to note that, *within* each of these phases, a similar progression is followed. First, the syntactic side of the deductive system is developed and mastered. That is, we start with explicit, systematic treatments of the lexicon, grammar, axioms, and proof theory of the logic under consideration. From there, the semantics of the system is developed second. We then define truth, consequence, denotation, and the like, which allows us to state and prove the main meta-logical results for each of the systems—soundness and completeness. Some have only partially noticed this pattern and have been perplexed. For instance, Burgess says of this situation that

> Given how greatly model theory illuminates the significance of formulas in temporal logic, one would expect a modal model theory parallel to temporal model theory to have been developed early, and to have guided the choice of candidate modal axioms to be considered. But the historical development of a science is seldom rational. (Burgess 2009, 47)

Recognizing that the case of mastery of syntax prior to that of semantics in modal logic is part and parcel of a larger trend can make it seem perfectly rational, though. Just as we developed sentential prior to quantificational (and that prior to modal) logic as a result of the fact that one is successively more difficult than the next, semantics (model theory) developed after syntax (proof theory) at each phase because semantics is just *harder* than syntax.

In the case of sentential logic, this story played out with the mastery of syntax being achieved by Frege (1879) with respect to axioms and proof theory and Sheffer (1913) in terms of lexicographical and grammatical simplicity. Furthermore, the tools needed to understand the semantics of the sentential calculus were developed primarily by Wittgenstein (1922) and Post (1921). Here we find the introduction of models in terms of truth-table assignments and calculations—procedures that make tautology and consequence decidable questions. Despite having the rudiments necessary for a more-or-less complete understanding of the basic meta-logical questions of sentential logic from these works, significant additions and extensions are made by subsequent investigations into the soundness and completeness of extensions of sentential logic. It is to these extensions that we now turn.

P3: Quantificational Logic

The story of quantificational logic is a bit more complicated, but it follows the same basic pattern. Fundamentals of syntax are mastered, followed by semantic ideas, which then allow for the establishment of basic meta-logical results. On the syntactic side, the proof theory for quantificational logic is given in impressive detail with Frege's (1879) nine axioms and three inference rules. As is well known, though, Frege's two-dimensional notation was extremely cumbersome and not particularly reader-friendly. As a result, the notation provided by Peano (1889) was a welcome change to the lexicon of quantificational logic. This notation was made most popular by Russell, who made significant strides in our understanding of the logical grammar of descriptions, scopes, and names. That said, there was an independent tracing of this story through Americans like Charles Peirce, Christine Ladd-Franklin, and Oscar Howard Mitchell as well as Lvov-Warsaw School members like Twardowski, Kokoszyńska-Lutmanowa, Łukasiewicz, and Leśniewski.[6] Of course, the merging of these traditions was cemented by the significance and influence of the semantic work of Tarski.

Despite being the source of the canonical semantics for the subsequent three-quarters of a century of work on quantificational logic, Tarski's semantic definition of "truth," his model-theoretic definition of logical consequence, and his work defining models was predated by several years by the standard meta-logical results. In fact, Gödel had proved the completeness of first-order quantificational logic a year prior to his (1930). This may, at first glance, seem to constitute a counter-example to my picture of the development of logic during the modern logical revolution. That said, it is important to note that Gödel's work has come to be only remembered for establishing *that* the completeness theorem is true. Once Tarski developed a far superior semantics for quantificational logic than anyone else had prior in his (1933, 1936, 1944, and so on) it is not surprising that a far superior proof of completeness would have been developed. And this is exactly what we find—the canonical proof of completeness coming in Henkin (1949).[7] Thus, we still have the same pattern within the history of quantificational logic. The development is marked by *mastery* of syntax followed by *mastery* of semantics, allowing for the *mastery* of the basic meta-logical results.

P4: Modal Logic

Before we get into the modern history of modal logic, it is important to correct a mistaken view of how this modern modal story contrasts with the larger history of logic. Aside from Burgess' earlier mistake, it is often erroneously suggested that the modern modal story is the whole of the modal story. For instance, in a book which is quite good, Sider says that when looking into the history of modal logic, we find that it "arose from dissatisfaction with the material conditional of standard propositional logic" (Sider 2010, 137). Given the twentieth-century origin of this dissatisfaction, this leads to the view that C. I. Lewis was not just the first significant *modern* modal logician, but the first modal logician. While it was not as systematically developed as Aristotelian quantificational logic, a sophisticated understanding of the logic of various modal operators was achieved by the time of the Islamic Golden Age. Most notably, Ibn Sina's logic and the Avicennian tradition of logic, which came to rival Aristotelian logic, at this time included a rigorous system for reasoning with temporal modalities. That said, those working in the Aristotelian tradition did interesting related work as well—including al-Farabi, Abu Bishr Matta, and Yahya ibn Adi, among others (Rescher 1963).[8]

As I alluded to, Sider and others are correct in that the *modern mathematical* study of modal logic begins with Lewis (1918) and Lewis and Langford (1932). Given what we have seen in the previous two sections, it is not surprising that Lewis' works are syntactic tour de forces. Here, the standard lexicon ('$\Diamond$', '$\prec$'), grammar, and proof theory for modal propositional logics are all established with great precision. On top of that, several axiomatic systems still studied today are developed. That said, modern modal syntax is not mastered until Ruth Barcan Marcus' pioneering work in Marcus (1946a, 1946b, 1947). Here, we get the first systems of quantified modal logic, which contain all of the innovation in syntax from the entire period under discussion. In addition, Marcus provides the key axiom, which explains the relative logical behavior of the quantifiers and the modal operators—the Barcan Formula. And, not satisfied with purely formal contributions to the understanding of modal logic, Marcus also went on to give important reasons to believe these formal systems could weigh in on long-held metaphysical debates. Given various criticisms from Quine, which were taken to show that anything like this was impossible, Marcus' work was enormously important.

Around the same time, extensions of our understanding beyond the syntax of alethic modal logic helped beat back the Quinean offensive as well. Here, Arthur Prior did much to create and bring our attention to formalisms of temporal, epistemic, and deontic operators, which closely tracked the alethic operators. Furthermore, Prior went on to publish upwards of four dozen journal articles, monographs, textbooks, reviews, and encyclopedia entries on the larger philosophical significance of various modal systems. Included among this work and his *Nachlass* was early fragmentary work on the semantics of modal systems as well. Carnap too had contributed early thoughts to the semantics of modal terms in Carnap (1947). That said, modal semantics was not mastered until Kripke gave us a definition of a modal model as a triple of a set of possible worlds, W, a two-place accessibility relation from WxW, and an assignment of truth-values not just to each sentence letter, but to each sentence letter at each world. Along with this came the defining truth-condition for "$\Box \varphi$"—namely, "$\Box \varphi$" is true at a world, w, iff for all possible worlds, v, if wRv, then "φ" is true at v. With these in hand, Kripke proved the standard meta-logical results of soundness and completeness for various frames (i.e., worlds, accessibility relation pairs) differing only in the algebraic properties of their accessibility relations. Finally, the broader philosophical importance of this work was cemented by the paradigm-shifting lectures at Princeton in January 1970, which would go on to become *Naming and Necessity*.

P5: Logic since 1970

After the culmination of this introduction of mathematical methods into the study of logic, there has been far less unity in the story of the development of the discipline. The types of logic attaining a significant literature has exploded to include illocutionary logic, the logic of indexicals, nonclassical logics, many-valued logics, free logics, the logic of counterfactuals, tense logics, the logic of imperatives, multidimensional logics, paraconsistent logics, and relevance logics, among others yet! Of course, this is not to make it more difficult to connect the future of logic with the future of philosophy. This disunity does not disassociate the most recent history of logic from the most recent history of any part of its larger context, in fact. As Soames has noted in the epilogue to his two volumes of *Philosophical Analysis in the Twentieth Century*:

> In my opinion, philosophy has changed substantially [since 1970]. Gone are the days of large, central figures, whose work is accessible and relevant to, as well as read by, nearly all analytic philosophers. Philosophy has become a highly organized discipline, done by specialists primarily for other specialists. The number of philosophers has exploded, the volume of publication has swelled, and the subfields of serious philosophical investigation have multiplied. (Soames 2003b, 463)

Hence, the analytic tradition itself has changed in much the same way that logic has since 1970. Even Rorty, a convert away from analytic philosophy, claimed that the larger history of philosophy in America, homegrown pragmatism included, developed this way at this time (Rorty 1982). Furthermore, Hans-Johann Glock has argued that the rehabilitation of metaphysics that Kripke's work formed a part of, along with the Strawsonian tradition, involved the reintersecting of analytic and traditionalist philosophy, which allowed for the ascendancy of the analytic/continental divide in terms of which we view the current field (Glock 2008). Thus, the fragmentation of logic as a single discipline followed the rest of Western philosophy in this respect.

Given the watershed year of 1970 in terms of a unified and predictable story for the development of logic, we can think of the mastery of modal logic as the completion of the modern logical revolution. Given this, there should be a certain importance attached to the pioneering works of Ruth Barcan Marcus, Arthur Prior, Saul Kripke, and, to a lesser extent, Rudolf Carnap. It may simply be because the monumental works in the history of logic—Kneale and Kneale (1962), van Heijenoort (1967), Benacerraf and Putnam (1964)—all came while this final phase was being completed, but I do not think that their importance has been properly appreciated. Furthermore, I think that their works on the connections between logic and ethics form perhaps the best evidence for this claim. For this reason, we will now turn to a further discussion of these issues and thinkers.

§2.3 WHERE (AND WHY) WE GO FROM THIS HISTORY

Insufficiency of the Current Paradigm

Before we continue, I must deal with a potential criticism. I have claimed that the giants of modal logic have not received enough credit. With respect to Kripke, I would imagine there are some who think this is a difficult claim to back up. There are very few philosophers anywhere near as influential as Kripke is today. He has established largely followed paradigms in logic, proper, as well as logically informed meta-philosophy, metaphysics, and semantics. In my own graduate training in these areas, Kripke was read and discussed more than any other philosopher by a large margin. This being the case, my complaint is ultimately not about any of the attention that Kripke has or hasn't got, but the attention that Marcus and Prior have *not gotten*. That said, I do believe Marcus and Prior have given far more interesting views on the connection between logic and ethics than Kripke has.

Given this and the fact that Kripke has been far more influential in terms of philosophical approach, methodology, and attitude, we may want to expose the problems of the Kripkean logico-ethical perspective. While I have made more detailed criticisms of the Kripkean paradigm in relation to moral and spiritual issues in Chick and LaVine (2014), I will make a few brief remarks here.

To begin with, I take the Kripkean approach to the connection between logic, ethics, and the possibility of them working together to guide our actions to be best summed up by his claims that "a lot of philosophy does not have relevance to life" and "the intention of philosophy was never to be relevant to life" (Saugstad 2001). Scott Soames has very clearly summed up how this sentiment comes out in the meta-philosophical and methodological approach of his followers:

> In general, philosophy done in the analytic tradition aims at truth and knowledge, as opposed to moral and spiritual improvement. There is very little in the way of practical or inspirational guides in the art of living to be found, and very much in the way of philosophical theories that purport to reveal the truth about a given domain of inquiry. In general, the goal in analytic philosophy is to discover what is true, not to provide a useful recipe for living one's life. (Soames 2003a, xiv)

Many who have engaged with ideas like these have challenged the suggestion that philosophy can even possibly be done well without being useful for living one's life. I don't find this to be the interesting issue, though. Soames and Kripke are probably right that this is *possible*. What strikes me as mistaken about their view is that they would encourage detached work just because there is a potential for it. In other words, given that there is also a potential for ordinary life and philosophical work to mutually benefit each other, as many we have already discussed and more we will discuss in this book have shown, why should we not (almost) *always* be encouraging this kind of work? Put really bluntly, the world is a very scary place right now and a not insignificant portion of that scariness can be attributed to moral and rational failings. Thus, it seems to me that, so long as there *can* be work, which would develop logic and help the world, that is the work we *should* be encouraging.

Furthermore, this does seem to be the type of meta-philosophical attitude that Marcus and Prior encouraged. Perhaps most obviously, within the same decade that Kripke and Soames were encouraging a disconnect between philosophy and living our lives, Marcus gave the 2009 Dewey Lecture in the form of a lecture entitled "A Philosopher's Calling." These remarks from Kripke and Soames hardly fit with viewing philosophy as a *calling*. Thinking of the way we live our lives as essential to philosophy and logic (and vice versa) was clearly present in Prior's work as well. Again, this came out in very obvious academic ways—his first article was on using logical constructions to understand the relationship between individuals and nations, his first book was entitled *Logic and the Basis of Ethics*, and his best anthology is entitled *Papers in Logic and Ethics*. It also came out in personal ways—Prior finding logic to be important enough to have written a picture book for his children, Ann and Martin, which taught them logic as grade school children. Again, this blending of the personal and the academic—the logical, the philosophical, and the living of one's life—was omnipresent for Marcus as well. In her Dewey lecture, she sets the stage for her philosophical career and approach in terms of society and politics (Marcus 2010, 75–77). In particular, she discusses issues of class, gender, and her economic views as the context for her philosophical beginnings in Marxism, Deweyan pragmatism, and logical positivism (Marcus 2010, 78).

It is also interesting to note that there is very good reason to believe that Marcus and Prior would be on board with a political picture like mine, which is left of any mainstream views in the United States. As she says in the acknowledgments section of *Modalities*, as far back as her college days Marcus "had located [her]self in a student fringe of the *Partisan Review* milieu" (Marcus 1993, ix). While it would move to the right after, in the 1940's this was a democratic socialist publication. Marcus also got involved in activism even earlier, her obituary pointing out that

> At the tender age of 17, Marcus told her mother one afternoon that she was going out to meet friends. In fact she was headed to an anti-Nazi demonstration at Madison Square Garden. She was found out when a neighbor saw in The New York World-Telegram a photo of "Ruthie" kicking a policeman in the shins because he wouldn't let her join the protesters. In 1939, of course, many Americans were ignoring or even denying the existence of Nazi atrocities. (Raffman 2012)

Furthermore, one of the most pleasant parts of being at the Arthur Norman Prior Centenary Conference at Balliol College in 2014 was hearing stories about Prior's progressive political activity at Oxford and in New Zealand, as well as the encouragement and support of activist analytic philosophers like Adriane Rini and Martin Pleitz.[9]

If Kripke, Then Marcus, Prior, and Carnap

Despite the fact that I think Marcus, Prior, and Carnap may actually have a superior understanding of the broader importance of logic than Kripke, I do not think anything like this needs to be established in order to say that we should pay much more attention to their work. Simply building off of

Kripke's importance, we can show that this ought to be the case. This is because the majority of Kripke's most famous contributions to philosophy were anticipated in significant ways by earlier works of these three thinkers. If this is the case, then it would seem terribly unjust that the readers of the Leiter Reports Philosophy Blog recently voted Kripke the second most important Anglophone philosopher of the second half of the twentieth century, while placing Marcus and Prior thirty-eighth and fifty-first, respectively. For this reason, we turn to providing evidence of Kripke's views being fruits of seeds planted by Marcus, Prior, and Carnap. Again, this is not to belittle the importance of Kripke. Rather, it is to say, precisely because of how important Kripke is, we should see these other three thinkers are much more important than we appreciate currently.

While it would be foolish to try to come up with a definitive list of Kripke's most important contributions to logic and philosophy, I do not think anybody would argue that potential candidates include (1) his notion of rigid designation, (2) his account of the necessity of identity, (3) his examples of the necessary a posteriori and contingent a priori, (4) his framework of possible worlds semantics, and (5) his modal and epistemic arguments against descriptivism.[10] Every one of these has been significantly anticipated in earlier figures or has been significantly challenged by subsequent thinkers, though. In particular, a historical investigation into each of these candidates yields the following:

[C1] That a name (constant) rigidly designates an object (i.e., refers to it in all possible worlds) is to be expected once we have got Marcus' (1961) view that names are "mere tags" with no meaning except their referents, as Smith (1995a) argues.
[C2] The necessity of identity, and with it the impossibility of contingent identity, were proved by Marcus in her (1947).
[C3] Once the necessity of identity is proved, it is natural to explain the supposed contingency of informative identity claims as really their a posteriority. Furthermore, Kripke's standard examples of the contingent a priori come from Wittgenstein (1953).
[C4] Kripke's idea of possible worlds has a predecessor in Carnap's (1947) state- descriptions and recent work on Prior's *Nachlass* has shown that Prior had understood something like Kripke's accessibility relation three or so years earlier than Kripke (1959) (Copeland 1996).
[C5] The modal and epistemic arguments against descriptivism require the assumptions that all analytic truths are necessary and that all analytic truths are a priori. Explicitly working in the Kripkean tradition, Russell (2008) has seriously challenged the former and Salmon (1993) has seriously challenged the latter.

The Untapped Potential of Prior's Work

To understand why so many have been willing to go along with the Kripkean separation of logic and ethics, we can look to an anthology whose second and final edition came out in the same year as Kripke's *Naming and Necessity* originally did. *The Is/Ought Question* (Hudson 1972) is a collection of works by the largest analytic moral thinkers of this time, with papers starting in 1958 and including contributions from Anscombe, Black, Flew, Foot, Hare, MacIntyre, Searle, and Thomson. What held all of these writings by the dominant minds in analytic meta- and normative ethics together was a view called *Hume's Guillotine* by Max Black in his contribution to the collection. This is the belief that "only factual statements can [validly] follow from exclusively factual statements" (Hudson 1972, 100).

It seems that the popularity of this view, as well as that of some forms of intuitionism and noncognitivism, suggested that no logic would be used in coming to believe ethical statements in the first place. We must simply assume them as premises if they are going to be used in arguments at all. Even then, though, it won't be a terribly interesting use of logic in ethics, since many thought it was a simple matter to reason with ethical premises—just apply universal instantiation to a general moral principle and a particular situation in order to determine the correct course of action for that situation. Finally getting to the untapped potential of Prior and Marcus, we will now show how (1) Prior established the falsity of Hume's Guillotine and (2) how Marcus demonstrated the difficulty in, and logical acumen required to, navigate reasoning from general principles to a particular decision.

While Prior originally accepted Hume's Guillotine and expanded upon it in Prior (1949), an abrupt about-face was accomplished by Prior's (1960) "The Autonomy of Ethics." Here, Prior announces that "it now seems to me a mistake" to believe "that it is impossible to deduce ethical conclusions from non-ethical premises" (Prior 1960, 88). And, very nicely, Prior proceeds directly and constructively, producing complete counterexamples to Hume's Guillotine. These explicitly show that "one simply can derive conclusions which are ethical in a quite serious sense from premises none of which have this character" (Prior 1960, 96). I will proceed to discuss this work via updated examples, which match Prior's in all of the essentials. For this, it will be convenient to let P be any non-ethical sentence like "Every time one of my students of color tells me about a horrific act of discrimination they've faced, they are lying" and to let Q be any ethical sentence like "SUNY Potsdam is obligated to do more to stop discrimination of its students." (Please excuse the very odd nature of these sentences—P is obviously false. Things will become clearer shortly.) Furthermore, let A1 and A2 be the following arguments, respectively:

[A1] Premise 1: P.   [A2] Premise 1: P or Q.
Conclusion: P or Q.   Premise 2: Not P.
                           Conclusion: Q.

From these, Prior shows that Hume's Guillotine is straightforwardly false. This can be seen with the following argument:

P1: Either "P or Q" is ethical or it is factual.
P2: If "P or Q" is ethical, then A1 is a counterexample to Hume's Guillotine.
P3: If "P or Q" is factual, then A2 is a counterexample to Hume's Guillotine.
SC: Either A1 or A2 is a counterexample to Hume's Guillotine. (P1, P2, P3, Dilemma)
P4: If A1 or A2 is a counterexample to Hume's Guillotine, then Hume's Guillotine is false.
Conclusion: Hume's Guillotine is false. (SC, P4, Modus Ponens)

While some I have shown this to have felt that it was nothing more than a logician's trick, which does not block what is *really* going on in Hume's Guillotine, I think the more appropriate response is to recognize how this shows a lack of logical sophistication as one of the roots for belief in Hume's Guillotine. As Max Black has explained in (Hudson 1972), failure to appreciate that it is a metaphor to say that in a valid argument, the conclusion is *contained* in the premises has led to the mistaken view that no valid argument has nonlogical words in its conclusion, which did not already occur in the premises. If this were true, then Hume's Guillotine would be a simple corollary. That said, as Prior surely recognized, almost all Or-Introductions are counterexamples to this view. And this last claim is nothing controversial. Without this recognition, we never would have had relevance logic.

Furthermore, Prior includes as one of the essentials of his examples that "P or Q" be such that, had it been deduced via an argument other than the Or-Introduction in A1, nobody would have doubted its ethical status. Again, following Prior's lead, I provide such an alternative derivation.

P1: Suppose it is not the case that every time one of my students of color tells me about a horrific act of discrimination they have faced at SUNY Potsdam, they are lying. (i.e., Suppose not P.)
SC1: Some of my students of color are facing horrific acts of discrimination from the Potsdam community. (P1, $\neg\forall\neg\Phi \equiv \exists\Phi$)
P2: If some of my students of color are facing horrific acts of discrimination from the Potsdam community, then SUNY Potsdam is obligated to do more to stop discrimination of its students.

SC2: SUNY Potsdam is obligated to do more to stop discrimination of its students. (i.e., Q, from SC1, P2, and Modus Ponens)

Conclusion: If not all of my students of color are lying to me about their experiences, then SUNY Potsdam is obligated to do more to stop discrimination of its students. (i.e., If not P, then Q, via P1, SC2, and Conditional Derivation)

I assume that nobody would argue that this argument is anything but ethical through and through—deriving ethical conclusions from ethical premises. Furthermore, since "If not P, then Q" is logically equivalent to "P or Q," it is an ethical derivation of "P or Q." Again, though, even if this be denied and "P or Q" held to be factual, then A2 would constitute a derivation of an ethical conclusion from factual premises. Since A2 is the actual context in which "P or Q" occurred in my life, I am perfectly happy with this being the counterexample to Hume's Guillotine.

Given this work, we can see that traditional formulations of Hume's Guillotine are definitively false (and especially those interpretations that separate ethical thinking from logical acumen). This is significant because it would provide a way to connect Priorean logical views to the so-called revival of normative, social, and political theory led by Hardin, Foot, Singer, Thomson, Rachels, Rawls, and others in the late 1960s and early 1970s. And *that* is significant because Soames admits that leaving this revival out of his volumes may be the "omission from our discussion [which] might reasonably be regarded as the most glaring gap in our story"—a story that is inspired by Kripke throughout.[11] On top of that, Prior's insistence on the importance of logical expertise in moral thinking connects to this revival insofar as Singer (1972)—an important paper in this revival—argues that "the morally good man must try to think out for himself the question of what he ought to do," that "this thinking out is a difficult task," and that, as a result, it is mistaken to believe that "reason has no part to play in [the] formation" of ethical views (Singer 1972, 116–17).

The Untapped Potential of Marcus' Work

As mentioned already, Hume's Guillotine, the naturalistic fallacy, the open question argument, and others like them helped create a sense that logic and ethics are at odds with one another—or, at least that there is no interesting involvement of logic in ethics. The thought here was that Hume's Guillotine showed that no logic could be used to get to ethical beliefs in the first place and, thus, the only use of logic in ethics would be the trivial one of applying general principles which we have simply assumed or intuited to particular situations we find ourselves in. The last section used Prior's work to show that the first conjunct was mistaken. This section will use Marcus' work to show that the second conjunct is equally mistaken. In particular, we will focus on her famous 1980 paper, "Moral Dilemmas and Consistency" to show that applying general principles to come up with a decision in a particular context can be a difficult affair.

As the title of the paper suggests, Marcus' (1980) main thesis involves stating a relationship between moral dilemmas and consistency of moral principles leading to those dilemmas. In particular, she convincingly argues for the view that moral dilemmas following from a set of moral principles need not be a sign of any inconsistency among those principles. In order to see this, we need only give a clear definition of "moral dilemma" and of "consistency." Here, Marcus provides us with the following very helpful definitions:

DEF'N: We have a *moral dilemma* whenever "there are principles in accordance with which one ought to do x and one ought to do y, where doing y requires that one refrain from doing x" (Marcus 1980, 122).

DEF'N: A set of moral principles is *consistent* iff "there is some possible world in which they are all obeyable in all circumstances in that world" (Marcus 1980, 128).

What is particularly interesting about these definitions is that failing to appreciate the importance of certain *modalities* leads to conflating moral dilemmas with moral inconsistency. In particular, a moral dilemma is a case where we cannot *actually* obey all moral principles under consideration. On the other hand, a moral inconsistency requires much more than this—namely, that we be dealing with a set of principles for which we could not *possibly* obey all moral principles under consideration. That said, it is perfectly possible for the former to occur without the latter occurring. It just needs to be the case that there is some possible world in which all are obeyable, but that possible world is not actualized.

As an example of such a case, Marcus offers Plato's famous story of our borrowing an axe from a friend who becomes homicidal. Principles governing borrowing dictate that we ought to return the axe. Principles governing the general functioning of society dictate that we ought to not give axes to homicidal people. Obeying such rules is perfectly possible in a world better than the one we have imagined. So, no contradictions need to arise when a moral dilemma does. In fact, this can be seen quite easily when we recognize that the worst situation a moral dilemma puts us in is one where "OA&O~A" is true, rather than the contradictory "OA&~OA."

I can see somebody responding here with "interesting distinction, but who really cares?" Well, I believe we should care because I think that the failure to recognize this difference is one of the states of affairs responsible for this mistaken view that moral reasoning from ethical premises to ethical conclusions requires nothing but logical trivialities. I believe this because thinking that moral dilemmas show a type of inconsistency has made it so little thought has been put into reasoning through moral dilemmas. When moral dilemmas are not thought of as necessarily illustrating a logical problem with the principles themselves, though, how we ought to deal with and respond to moral dilemmas becomes a much more pressing issue.

As Marcus put this in her paper, once we recognize the logical possibility and reality of moral dilemmas, we will see that at the very least "it is the underpinning for a second-order regulative principle" (Marcus 1980, 121). In other words, recognizing that moral dilemmas *can* come from perfectly consistent moral principles shows how there is no sense in which moral reasoning from general principles to a particular action is trivial. The easy logic will only get us from the general principles to the dilemma of "OA&O~A" being true. From there, we will need to invoke further reasoning to see if a second-order principle can dictate which principle we go with and which action we in fact do—A or not A. And, in certain cases, this will not even be enough. For it is perfectly possible that a second-order principle deals with (the principles which led to) A and not A in perfectly symmetrical ways.

In such a case, we must still *decide* what to do, though. This will involve even further reasoning about, for example, what type of person we want to be, which actions we want to encourage, etc. On top of that, the residue and difficulty of such dilemmas should lead us to "strive to arrange [our own lives] and encourage social arrangements that would prevent, to the extent that it is possible, future conflicts from arising" (Marcus 1980, 133). We will especially want to do this since, in a discussion relevant to the objection we will consider in §2.5. Sally Haslanger provides examples, which show that oppressive social roles are often constructed in such a way that we are not actually able to obey all of the norms associated with them at once—"making it impossible to live up to them or to structure a coherent life around them" (Haslanger 2012, 44). And, as Marcus continues, "as rational agents with some control of our lives and institutions, we ought to conduct our lives and arrange our institutions so as to minimize predicaments of moral conflict" (Marcus 1980, 121). Such minimizing processes add counterfactual and inductive reasoning to the situation. Hence, I believe Marcus shows that there is simply no way in which reasoning from settled general principles to a particular action is at all logically trivial.[12]

The importance of this latest connection for my overall arguments cannot be overstated. This is the meeting of very important ideas from two of the philosophers most important to my overall framework—Marcus and Haslanger. Again, Marcus argues that there exist moral dilemmas with consistent principles behind them. She also gives reason to believe these are serious and require significant attention (especially with respect to their logical properties). Haslanger, on the other hand, points out that "norms can become internally contradictory" for women (Haslanger 2012, 44). This seems to suggest a case of moral dilemmas arising from gender norms, rather than inconsistent norms. Propositions, prescriptions, and principles do not *become* inconsistent. They are that way necessarily if they are inconsistent at all.

This is not to say that gender norms are not also inconsistent at times. In fact, Haslanger herself discusses one such example here. In particular, at many times and places, there have unfortunately been norms of womanhood and femininity such that a good woman must necessarily be asexual and that a good woman is responsive and pleasing to men's sexual desire. These are flatly inconsistent, though. Thus, Marcus' distinction can be used for categorizing different kinds of problems with gender norms as well.

Importantly, there is not anything unique about gender here, either. These phenomena are quite related to what W. E. B. Du Bois was discussing with the phenomenon of double consciousness. The strange experiences of being a problem, of being a stranger in one's own house, of looking at one's self through the eyes of others interact with the norms imposed on black Americans to lead to two unreconciled strivings (Du Bois 1897). Rap group, The Sorority, recognizes this in intersectional fashion with their lines from their song *SRTY*, "You tell us eat because we skinny and stop eatin when we're too fat. We're never good enough, hood enough, light enough." That this connection between moral dilemmas, inconsistencies, and oppressive social structures can be generalized seems to make Haslanger's discussion good reason to support Marcus' claims and subsequent prescriptions.

§2.4 DEDUCTIVE PREJUDICE

So far, I have argued that a proper understanding of the history of the modern logical revolution should lead us to place more emphasis on Marcus, Prior, and Carnap. I have also argued that doing so will lead us to connect logic and ethics to a much greater extent than we do now. It would be nice, though, if I could argue for this latter claim in a way which isn't so dependent upon historical contingency. That is, it would be good for me to point to something in the nature of logic, which connects it to ethics essentially. For this, I will turn to the work of John Corcoran.

In his 1989 "The Inseparabiltiy of Logic and Ethics," from which the second quote we started with came, Corcoran gives beautiful arguments that show both that "the ethics of the future must accord logic a more central and explicit role" and that "the logic of the future must accord ethics a more central and explicit role." The primary pieces of evidence for these statements are that "The three facts that begin logic—that humans are neither omniscient nor infallible, that humans seek knowledge, and that improvement is possible—are three facts that serve to bring humans together" (Corcoran 1989b, 37). That is, if one recognizes that the reasons to use logic in the first place are that we do not know all of the consequences of our beliefs, we desire to know those things, and that coming to this knowledge is easiest in a group, it is not a far jump to the view that the reasons to use logic are reasons to cooperate with those around us. This also seems to be part of the idea behind John Mohawk's quote that we started this chapter with. Whenever we have beings with interests and limited resources to satisfy them, those interests are going to, at times, come into conflict with one another. If we wish to avoid further conflict and violence, negotiation and reasoning (i.e., the use of logic and argumentation) are central to that process.

Not only does this motivation for using logic in the first place connect logic and ethics, though. Once we engage in the use of logic, we are being guided by ethical principles and virtues. In particular, the use of logic

> can be seen as an ongoing, imperfect, incomplete, and essentially incompletable attempt to cultivate objectivity, to discover principles and methods that contribute to the understanding and practice of objectivity, which is an ethical virtue alongside kindness, justice, honesty, compassion. (Corcoran 1989b, 40)

In other words, one great reason to be concerned with logic is the recognition that our beliefs impact others in deep ways. If we wish for our beliefs to have a positive and just impact on others, then we should be concerned with attaining those beliefs in ways that can be made sensible to others. The use of logic's objectivity is a wonderful way to attempt this.

Aside from the general sentiment involved, I am also concerned with one small detail of this most recent quote from Corcoran. In particular, I want to further discuss the claim that logic is part of an *essentially incompletable* attempt to cultivate objectivity. When a logician sees "complete" or one of its cognates, they are inclined to think of the meta-logical property that applies to a system when all of its validities are provable. As discussed earlier, all of the logical systems that formed the core of the logical revolution are complete in this sense. That said, there are further systems of deduction which are not complete and, more importantly, all systems of induction and abduction are incomplete. Thus, since I agree with Corcoran, I see the coming together of logic and ethics as wrapped up in the coming together of the study of deductive *and* nondeductive logics. I have already argued in (LaVine 2016b) that the bringing together of deduction and abduction can show us ways in which logic and ethics can be brought together. Therefore, I want to end this section with a brief remark about how bringing induction into the mix can help bridge the gap between logic and ethics.

In induction, we argue from premises about a sample that we have experience with to a target with which we have only limited experience. In doing so, we rely upon an assumption that the sample tells us something interesting about the target. Given this assumption, clear problems can arise. The most obvious one is the fallacy of *hasty generalization*—where we reason from a sample that is insufficient to tell us something interesting about the target. In hasty generalizations, the sample can be insufficient either for being too small in relation to the size of the target or for being unrepresentative of the whole target. All too often, these fallacies are discussed via silly, far from life examples—examples along the lines of "1 and 3 are prime. Therefore, all odd numbers are prime," or "My philosophy teacher is a leftist. Thus, all philosophy teachers are leftists." This is terribly unfortunate, as it seems to me to be a missed opportunity for drawing further connections between logic and ethics.

Hasty generalizations are not just a logician's construct to make a point about inductive reasoning. Hasty generalizations happen all over the place in our daily lives and in scary, abhorrent ways. For instance, to use an example that will be discussed in greater detail in the next chapter, if one watches Fox News long enough, they will eventually see somebody enthymematically invoking something like the following:

P1: 19 Muslims perpetrated the September 11, 2001 terror attacks.
Conclusion: Muslims are terrorists.

Clearly this is fallacious, as it is a terribly hasty generalization.[13] There are something along the lines of 1.8 billion Muslims alive today, so a sample of nineteen is horribly insufficient for drawing conclusions about Muslims generally. And while it involves most of the same logical considerations as the examples earlier, this example much more clearly connects logic and ethics. As I said, this is a morally abhorrent argument. Unfortunately, it is also not a unique case of hasty generalization being connected to oppressive stereotypes. People all too often generalize from media portrayals of individual black men in television shows like *Cops* and the local news to something about black men and criminality. We all too often generalize from the fact that our mother's *may* have enjoyed cooking for us sometimes to the wild and constraining idea that women like to cook for people generally. Obviously, these are not hard to multiply within and across different social identities. Thus, using them as examples illustrates that attending to logic requires us to discourage hasty generalizations *and* bigotry at the same time.

That is to say, since hasty generalizations are one of the bases for stereotypes, stereotypes are one of the bigot's favorite tools, and practicing good inductive logic involves discouraging hasty generalizations, it follows that practicing good inductive logic is to discourage bigotry.[14] This is how we can have it be the case that "[The Peacemaker] raised the idea of rational thinking to the status of a political principle" (Mohawk 1986, xvii) and why thinking in line with this chapter's epigraphs is so important. Furthermore, that encouraging logic involves discouraging bigotry and prejudice should seem natural when we think of the definition of "prejudice" as "*unreasonable* feelings, opinions, or attitudes, especially of a hostile nature, regarding an ethnic, racial, social, or religious group" (emphasis added).[15] I hope for a future of logic where logicians see discouraging of such prejudicial irrationalities as part and parcel of their charge and calling. While this first section of the book has tried to discuss some ways to do this by looking at analytic philosophy in terms of its most prominent subdisciplines, the next section will try to do so by looking at analytic philosophy through the various stages of its early history.

§2.5 A POTENTIAL CONCERN AND A PATH FORWARD

As we near the end of this section on analytic philosophy the method—which places some combination of philosophy of language and logic at center stage—we should take stock of where we have been. This section started with some feminist concerns about the reception of Ruth Barcan Marcus' work, which would lead us into investigating logic in relation to ethics, and ultimately a suggestion that we should all be very greatly concerned about bringing logic into all parts of our lives and our philosophizing. This development from feminist concerns to a broad, sweeping promotion of logic needs to be addressed as, for much of Western philosophy, "ideals of rationality . . . have typically been defined in contrast to what are assumed to be characteristic features and capacities of women: [w]omen are guided by emotion or feeling rather than reason" (Haslanger 2012, 47).

Furthermore, this association of logic, reason, and rationality with men and women with emotion has not been incidental or isolated. Rather it forms an essential part of patriarchy, white supremacy, domination of nature, and so on. This is because of a common structure to what Karren Warren calls "oppressive conceptual frameworks." Such frameworks

(i) build off of value dualisms—where some group of distinctions is assumed to be analogously mutually exclusive and exhaustive,
(ii) value hierarchies—where one side of all of these distinctions is assumed to be superior,

(iii) and a logic of domination—where arguments are made built off of the premise that superiority always justifies subordination. (Warren 1990, 127)

Thus, a whole group of oppressions are built into a conceptual framework where the following distinctions are assumed to be exclusive, exhaustive, and line up perfectly:

Man/Woman
Logic/Emotion
Mental/Physical
Civilization/Nature
Western civilization/Non-Western civilization[16]

Adding in value hierarchy, the left sides are assumed to be equally superior and, bringing in the logic of domination, the left sides are argued to be justified in subordinating the right side.

Again, because of all of this, it is important to check whether my promotion of logic is promoting a logic of domination and, thus, undermining my promotion of a feminist perspective. As a starting point toward saying that they are consistent, one natural move is to say that we simply need to dislodge the gender stereotypes and gender norms, which associate men with logic and women with emotion. While there is something right to this basic idea, it also obscures the possibility that there is something deeper and more insidious at work here. In particular, it seems to miss the potential that something about our conception of logic (or closely related notions) is, itself, gendered. This is precisely what, for example, Catherine MacKinnon has argued, though, when she says "[o]bjectivity is the epistemological stance of which objectification is the social process, of which male dominance is the politics" (MacKinnon 1987, 50). Given that this criticism is put in terms of objectivity and objectivity is one of the features Corcoran (1989b) argued is central to the account of logic I built off of here, we must engage MacKinnon's line of argument.

For that, we turn to Sally Haslanger's work on MacKinnon's arguments via the question, "is objectivity gendered?" This is particularly useful for us to focus on given that it constitutes a wonderful example of what analytic methods can bring to these debates, which are begging for merely verbal disputes. Haslanger uses fine linguistic and logical distinctions to bring intense clarity to the discussion—a necessary move since accounts of both reason and gender have come from vastly different disciplines at vastly different times with vastly different goals in mind (Haslanger 2012, 37). Moving toward what is needed to avoid such talking past one another, energy is put into answering:

(i) what do we mean by "objectivity"?
(ii) what do we mean by "gendered"?
(iii) what does a yes or no answer to the initial question (is objectivity gendered) mean for our promotion of that notion of objectivity?

Beginning with "gendered," Haslanger discusses an account of gender on which it is quite distinct from sex. While sex involves distinctions based on anatomical features—things like primary and secondary sex characteristics—gender classification is essentially social (Haslanger 2012, 40). In particular, gender is a hierarchical system of dominance and subordination partially determined by gender norms encouraging objectification of women by men. Women are those judged by feminine gender norms. Men are those judged by masculine gender norms. For something to be gendered then, it must be *appropriate* to those gender norms or *grounded* in that gender role. More explicitly,

DEF'N: "a norm is *appropriate* to a social role just in case satisfying that norm would make for or significantly contribute to successful functioning in that role."

DEF'N: "a norm is *grounded in* a social role just in case (allowing restricted background conditions) satisfying the norm is sufficient for functioning in the role" (Haslanger 2012, 55)

In the former case, it is weakly gendered. In the latter case, it is strongly gendered. Therefore, the question becomes, is there a norm of objectivity that is either appropriate to men's gender roles or grounded in men's gender roles?

Of course, the answer to this will depend on how we understand "objectivity." Here, again, Haslanger provides an impressively clear account of the notion of objectivity that MacKinnon seems to be working with. In particular, she lays out a position that she calls "assumed objectivity" and which is defined by adopting each of the following norms:

DEF'N: The norm of *epistemic neutrality* requires that if one observes a "genuine" regularity involving an entity, then they must believe that regularity is a consequence of the entity's nature.

DEF'N: The norm of *practical neutrality* requires that our decisions and actions involving an entity accommodate that entity's nature.

DEF'N: The norm of *assumed aperspectivity* requires that if one observes a regularity involving an entity, then we must assume that (1) the circumstances of observation were normal, (2) the observer's social position did not condition the observations made, and (3) the observer has not had an influence on the behavior of the entities being observed. (Haslanger 2012, 71–72)

Putting all of this together, we can further specify that our question will be, is assumed objectivity weakly or strongly masculine?

In response, Haslanger gives convincing arguments that assumed objectivity is weakly masculine, that it is not strongly masculine, and that it is strongly collaborative to masculinity. These follow from the definitions since men's dominant role is essentially connected to sexual (and other) objectification and assumed objectivity is appropriate to objectification, not grounded in objectification, but grounded in collaboration in objectification. With respect to the claim that assumed objectivity is weakly masculine, we should continue with our definitions. Through invoking those, we can get a string of biconditionals between (1), (2), and (3):

(1) Assumed objectivity is weakly masculine
(2) The norms of assumed objectivity are appropriate to a man's gender role
(3) Satisfying the norms of assumed objectivity would contribute to successful functioning in a man's gender role.

Furthermore, since playing the role of objectifier is part of a man's gender role, these will be true if satisfying any of the norms of assumed objectivity—epistemic neutrality, practical neutrality, or assumed aperspectivity—would contribute to successful functioning as an objectifier.

Haslanger argues that we have good reason to expect this to be the case under real world conditions of patriarchy. Under such conditions, men and women have very unequal access to power. Unequal access to power has material consequences, consequences in the behavior of men and women, and consequences in their ability to impose their will. Add to this the norms of assumed objectivity and this imposition will perpetuate itself, since

> those men who satisfy the norm of assumed objectivity will have reason to view women and treat women as they appear under the conditions of inequality—that is, as subordinate. These norms tell us to observe the differences and behave accordingly: see, women are subordinate (submissive, deferential, . . .), so treat them as subordinate (submissive, deferential, . . .). (Haslanger 2012, 73)

Thus, given that assumed objectivity is appropriate to the role of objectifier in this way, it is weakly masculine. Furthermore, while not strongly masculine—not grounded in the role of objectifier—assumed objectivity is grounded in the role of collaborator in objectification. That is to say, one who satisfies the norms of assumed objectivity will "view [a woman] and treat [a woman] as an object that has by nature properties which are a consequence of objectification" (Haslanger 2012, 74). In this way, assumed objectivity will aid in the conditions that allow for objectification, since "a collaborator shares with ... objectifiers a pattern of thought and action ... though in doing so she need not objectify women" (Haslanger 2012, 75).

Again, because of this possibility of promoting objectification, we should worry whether or not my promotion of logic falls prey to these concerns. The answer could easily be yes or no, as I agree with Haslanger that we need to do away with the norms of assumed objectivity but that "assumed objectivity does not capture a broad range of philosophical ideals of rationality" (Haslanger 2012, 81). The good news on this front is that Corcoran's accounts of logic and objectivity do not require the tenets of assumed objectivity.

To begin with, whereas assumed objectivity takes for granted that we start out with distanced and neutral perspectives through assumed aperspectivity, Corcoran's focus on logic is about recognizing the starting point of "human ignorance and fallibility" (Corcoran 1989b, 37). One of the best ways to do this is to recognize biases that are likely to go along with our own perspectives and to engage with different perspectives. Furthermore, objectivity requires cultivation, to get to a point where one can "make up one's mind in accord with the facts, whatever they may be, whether they fulfill or frustrate hopes" (Corcoran 1989b, 37). Finally, Corcoran denies an important presupposition of the logic of domination as well. There is no reason to pit logic and emotion against one another, since "being dispassionate does not exclude being compassionate" (Corcoran 1989b, 38).[17] Similarly, as John Mohawk said of the Peacemaker's outlook,

> An important principle is that all human beings have the potential for rational thought. Another is that with a judicious application of rational thought a society could be created in which human beings can create governments dedicated to the proposition that no human being should abuse another. (Mohawk 1986, xvi)[18]

Here, logic and emotion are deeply connected as a commitment to the importance of rational thought is connected to horror at the abuse of humans.

Despite the fact that we *can* promote logic, rationality, and objectivity in ways which are not gendered, it is important to remember that there has actually been a great deal of gendered work on these matters. Given this, we should be on the lookout for ways in which assumed objectivity or other problematically oppressive accounts of rationality might arise in analytic philosophy. In particular, the next chapter will look at assumed aperspectivity, how it was manifested in Stage 1, and how to use more contemporary work to solve it. Finally, in chapter 5, we will discuss an attempt to avoid such a position through logical empiricist epistemology and metaphysics.

In conclusion, I think that the future of logic, specifically, and analytic philosophy, generally, would best be served by seeing this future as wrapped up in bringing logic and ethics together. I believe this because the history of logic should make us pay homage to thinkers like Marcus, Prior, and Carnap who greatly encouraged this connection. Furthermore, reflections on the nature of logic given by Corcoran have made us recognize the extent to which logic serves the ethical ideals of cooperation and objectivity. Finally, I believe this because there are important lessons from nondeductive logic, which show that we easily *can* bring logic and ethics together. But, given that we *can* do this, why would we not encourage more of it?

NOTES

1. In all fairness, these misconceptions are perpetuated by analytic philosophers themselves.
2. "What is further remarkable about logic is that [since the time of Aristotle] it has also been unable to take a single step forward, and therefore seems to all appearance to be finished and complete." It would be most accurate to say that this is the way to use the time *after* Kant to ridicule this statement. We could also use the time *prior* to Kant to ridicule his statement's historical ignorance. Stoic logicians (n.b. Chryssipus), several prominent Islamic Golden Age polymaths (n.b. al-Farabi, Ibn Sina, Ibn al-Haytham, al-Ghazali, al-Razi, and Ibn Rushd), and a number of scholastic logicians and theologians (n.b. Ockham, Buridan) all made significant steps beyond Aristotle. What is important to notice about this is that Kant's ignorance here can largely be traced to his racism and Eurocentrism (cf. Park 2013, 90–95). I have plans to expand on the picture of history, logic, racism, and ethics which I have started to sketch here in future work. This will focus on the parts of the history of logic missed by Kant because of his Eurocentrism—Imhotep and Antef in Ancient Egypt, the School of Names and Mohists in Ancient China, Nagarjuna, the Nyaya, and Navya-Nyaya Schools in Ancient and Medieval India, as well as many throughout the Islamic Golden Age.
3. I take this to be the meeting point of an empiricist approach and a nonideal approach along the lines of Charles Mills (especially 1997, 2017).
4. Of course, this leaves out the contributions of Bernard Bolzano. That said, as the most comprehensive work on Bolzano's thinking points out, despite Bolzano's logical work anticipating Frege's, Tarski's, and Quine's, "important features of both have been neglected" (Lapointe 2011, 43).
5. It is important to recognize just how many parts of mathematics have been used for increasing logical rigor. Otherwise, we tend to not give credit where credit is due. This short list of such mathematical tools is notable in this way given that the first two entries give us our second opportunity to discuss underappreciated Islamic Golden Age thinkers. Our words "algebra" and "algorithm" are both forgotten homages to an early member of the Baghdad House of Wisdom, al-Khwarizmi. The extent to which these thinkers have been scrubbed from history is nothing short of dangerously Eurocentric. One such prominent example of this from our story comes

in the opening pages of Frege's *Grundlagen* (1950). Seemingly thinking that axiomatics is the only avenue for logical rigor, Frege ignorantly states "In arithmetic, if only because many of its methods and concepts originated in India, it has been the tradition to reason less strictly than in geometry, which was in the main developed by the Greeks." He would do well to remember the contributions of the Hindu-Arabic numerals—invented by various Hindu mathematicians, but systematically defended and popularized by al-Kindi and al-Khwarizmi—to the rigor of the study of arithmetic.

6. Given the topic of this chapter, I would be remiss if I didn't mention that many members of the Lvov-Warsaw School had deep concerns with ethics, society, and politics (cf. Brozek et al. 2017). While there are certainly greater gaps in the social justice aspect of the book, the greatest gap in the analytic philosophy side of things is the insufficient discussion we will have on the Lvov-Warsaw School. I am certainly partially responsible for this ignorance, but I suspect part of this has to do with latent antisemitism and anti-Slavism in the larger cultures that analytic philosophy has primarily developed in. As someone two generations removed from Ukrainian immigrants, I am particularly interested in rectifying this in future work.

7. Given that this overlaps the time period in which modal logic was revolutionized and what we will say here regarding modal logicians like Marcus and Prior, it is interesting to note that Henkin was a committed social activist, laboring "in much of his career to boost the number of women and underrepresented minorities in the upper echelons of mathematics" (Manzano 2015, 111).

8. None of this should be surprising, either. The Islamic Golden Age provided a great number of outlets for interest in an extremely large number of aspects of logic. Fiqh, the study of Islamic law as derived from the Qur'an and the sunnah, provided an opportunity for attention to analogical reasoning. The study of isnad, the chain of transmission used to verify the authenticity of purported hadith, allowed for study of the reasoning processes behind the citing of sources and peer review (Sardar 2012, 6). The taking of natural phenomena as ayat, signs of Allah, also could provide motivation to understand the reasoning processes that go into the scientific method.

9. For instance, see Pleitz (2013) and Rini (2013) for representative examples. It is also worth pointing out that Rini puts this work into action as well—saying in a Massey University press release about her role in celebrating women thinkers on World Philosophy Day "Over the past decade there have been numbers of stories around the world about how philosophy is a discipline that is not welcoming of women, with all sorts of problems about low participation and representation."

10. Note that this list is slightly different from the one discussed in chapter 1. This is because I have come up with the list in this chapter and its focus is logic, while Smith's (1995a, 1995b) focus was philosophy of language.

11. Ironically, the other omission that Soames admits is "the development of modern symbolic logic," which culminates in "the halting and painstaking development of modal logic and modal semantics by Carnap, C. I. Lewis, Marcus, Kripke, and others" (Soames 2003, 461–62).

12. The final thinker I claim the history of logic dictates that we pay more attention to is Carnap. For Carnap, a prima facie counter-example can be made against my

claim that more understanding of this revolution in logic will lead to connecting logic and ethics to a greater extent. Such an objection would involve pointing to Carnap's principle of tolerance, which has been put in slogan form as "in logic, there are no morals." On the surface, this seems very troubling for my view that a greater emphasis on Prior, Marcus, and Carnap will lead an inseparability of logic and morals. That said, this slogan formulation was just that, a slogan, and it was a rhetorical one at that. The official formulation of the principle involved encouraging everyone to be completely open and explicit about the axioms and inference rules they were using, to not judge a view until this was done, and to judge collectively when we do so. As Richard Creath has argued in his (2009), such a principle is ultimately about fairness, "the greater good of mankind," and a philosophical programme, which is concerned with "social progress" (Creath 2009, 209). We will discuss this more in chapter 5.

13. What is cruelly ironic about this state of affairs is that it was Islamic scientists and philosophers who did more than any other culture to advance our understanding of the induction and scientific method that hasty generalization bastardizes. It was Ibn al-Haytham who put forth the scientific method six centuries before Bacon. Such an overlook would not be so problematic if it were not part of a hugely Eurocentric telling of the history of philosophy or if Ibn al-Haytham were an enigma in the Islamic Golden Age. Nothing could be further from the truth, though. This time period was flush with extremely skilled experimentalists like Ibn Firnas in physics, al-Zarqali, Ibn Ridwan, and al-Battani in astronomy, al-Razi and Ibn al-Haytham in optics, Jabir ibn Hayyan, in chemistry, and al-Razi and Ibn Sina in medicine. For an informative introductory discussion of these matters, see (Masood 2009).

14. This is also evidenced by the fact that confirmation bias, another inductive fallacy, can be used to perpetuate oppression.

15. This definition can be found at https://www.dictionary.com/browse/prejudice (accessed June 22, 2019).

16. As Haudenosaunee scholar, John Mohawk argues, "Many professionals in this field operate on an expectation that rational thought is found only in the West" (Mohawk 1986, xv).

17. For instance, when I was receiving cancer treatment, it was extremely important to me to have medical professionals who were both dispassionate and compassionate with their patients. That is to say, it was very important to me that they were moved by the suffering of their patients (i.e., compassionate), but not moved in such a way that this would bias their findings (i.e., dispassionate). In other words, no matter how much they wanted me to avoid suffering, I did not want that to be a motivating factor in determining, for example, whether or not I needed further surgery.

18. Still further, "It was in that environment that [the Peacemaker] offered the idea that all human beings possess the power or rational thought and that in the belief in rational thought is to be found the power to create peace" (Mohawk 1986, xvi).

Part 3

RACE, GENDER, AND ANALYTIC PHILOSOPHY (THE MOVEMENT)

Chapter 3

Starting Points in Philosophy and Starting Points in the Analytic Tradition

§3.0 OVERVIEW OF THE CHAPTER

There are many disagreements over precisely when analytic philosophy begins—is it with Moore? Frege? Bolzano? Or somebody even earlier? With all of this disagreement, as a self-conscious *movement*, there is no doubt that analytic philosophy has begun by the time of Moore's and Russell's rejection of idealist monism in favor of a realist pluralism. Furthermore, Soames has argued that this first stage of the early analytic movement is most important for one of the two defining contributions of early analytic philosophy— "the recognition that philosophical speculation must be grounded in pre-philosophical thought" (Soames 2003a, xi). This chapter presents two types of concern for Moorean common sense as a way of filling out this idea of "pre-philosophical thought" as something along the lines of commonly and confidently held beliefs. In particular, standard problems from judgment aggregation theory show that sets of beliefs meeting this criterion are likely to be inconsistent and standard work from sociologists, political scientists, philosophers, and critical theorists show that giving a place of privilege to such beliefs is likely to perpetuate problematic biases and prejudices. Finally, Charles Mills' work on the connection between philosophy and practical applications to lived experience and Susan Stebbing's work on common sense and "how language is ordinarily used in human interaction" (Chapman 2013, 2), with their more socially engaged nature, are used to solve these problems.

§3.1 INTRODUCTION TO STAGE 1 OF EARLY ANALYTIC PHILOSOPHY

Whenever we engage in historical investigation of any sort, it is important to spend some time thinking about the starting point(s) for our narratives and analyses. A surprising number of problems can come from unreflective choices, uncritical choices, or insidiously motivated choices, of when and where to start a history. As Chimanada Ngozi Adichie, building off of Mourid Barghouti's famous passage from *I Saw Ramallah*,[1] says,

> If you want to dispossess a people, the simplest way to do it is to tell their story and to start with, "secondly." Start the story with the arrows of the Native Americans, and not with the arrival of the British, and you have an entirely different story. Start the story with the failure of the African state, and not with the colonial creation of the African state, and you have an entirely different story.[2]

Within the history of philosophy itself—though this could easily be said of intellectual and cultural history in the West, generally—there is the problem of starting the story with mid-first millennium BCE Greece. The extent to which such a story can be traced to explicitly racist arguments of German philosophers, historians, and anthropologists like Christoph Meiners, Wilhelm Tennemann, Dietrich Tiedemann, Immanuel Kant, and G. W. F. Hegel—and still perpetuates a seriously problematic Eurocentrism—has barely begun to be appreciated (see Gordon 2008; Park 2013; especially Introduction, chapter 1, chapter 4). There is evidence of a great deal of philosophy, religion, science, mathematics, and poetry for a couple thousand years prior to this in Africa and Asia. Furthermore, there is evidence of significant influence of these contributions on the beginnings and development of Greek philosophy and Western culture, generally. On top of that, even if one is going to restrict one's self to sixth to fourth century BCE thought, there is equally good reason to investigate the *Mahabharata*, *Ramayana*, *Torah*, as well as the thought of Lao Tzu, Zoroaster, Siddhartha Gautama, Mo Di, and Confucius as there is Socrates, Plato, and Aristotle.[3]

All of this means we must be very conscientious in our decision of where to start our story of the development of analytic philosophy. This is especially the case given that there is nonnegligible controversy over when analytic philosophy began. Many of the most popular recent histories written in English—for example, Soames (2003a, 2003b), Glock (2008), Hacker (1996), Schwartz (2012)—begin with Moore, Russell, or Moore and Russell.[4] That said, there are a number of prominent thinkers—n.b. Dummett (1978, 1993)—who have located the beginning of analytic thought in the works of

Frege (1879, 1884, 1892, 1893). Furthermore, Lapointe has also given arguments that, if we go back this far, we should at least go back to Bolzano—who also cannot be understood without understanding his responses to Kant's semantics, epistemology, metaphysics, logic, and ethics (Lapointe 2011, 2014). And, as I'm sure you have picked up on, if we include Kant, we have to go back to Leibniz's work on truth, his predicate-in-notion principle, etc.—as shown by Coffa (1991).

Because of all of this, we will start our story with Moore, Russell, and the fateful year of 1898. One simple reason for this is that, unlike Frege, Bolzano, and others, it is uncontroversial and widely known that these two are analytic philosophers—everybody agrees that analytic philosophy has begun by the time of Moore and Russell. Some just argue that it started even earlier (i.e., Moore, Russell, and 1898 constitute something of a greatest lower bound for uncontroversial analytic philosophy). Furthermore, it is uncontroversial that Moore and Russell had significant influence on each other, influenced many others philosophizing in like-minded ways around the world, and intended to start something of a new *movement* in philosophy. That is, unlike, for example, Frege and Bolzano, they were not intellectually isolated from an analytic movement during their own lives. Moore first studied philosophy on Russell's encouragement. Moore's initial work in philosophy then encouraged Russell to change his philosophical orientation away from British absolute idealism radically—a rejection taken to be characteristic of the early analytic movement. Since I am primarily interested in the social and political aspects of analytic philosophy, this makes Moore and Russell the natural starting points for my particular purposes.

Finally, there is a serendipitous historical fact about the early work of Moore and Russell that gives further reason to think their writings are an appropriate starting point for our historical investigation. Just as we needed to pay close attention to the starting point of our story, Moore and Russell spent a great deal of energy determining what our starting points in philosophical investigation should be. Part of this came from the fact that their interlocutors were making egregious mistakes on this front. Bradley, Hegel, Fichte, McTaggart, and other were coming to conclusions whose negations were to be taken as initially given premises on Moore's and Russell's pictures. So, this is where the disagreement needed to be investigated.

This too is where we shall begin our historical investigation—trying to understand the significance of Moore's and Russell's work on the starting points of philosophy as a starting point in the history of analytic philosophy. This is particularly important since the commonalities in issues identified, as well as the differences in responses to those issues, by Moore and Russell on these matters run throughout the whole of early analytic philosophy. As Dutilh Novaes and Geerdink have shown, there is a tension between the Moorean and the Russellian conceptions of analysis. Moore represents what could be described as an epistemically conservative conception of analysis, which accords default legitimacy to the common sense beliefs we start with; Russell represents a conception of analysis where there is more room for revision and transformation of these initial beliefs. We suggest that this tension runs through the history of analytic philosophy all the way up to present times, as exemplified by recent debates in philosophical methodology as well as by the debate involving Carnap and Strawson on explication in the mid-twentieth century. (Dutilh Novaes & Geerdink 2017, 70–71)

I will ultimately argue against a conservative, Moorean approach and for a revisionary (Russellian) approach, with revisions coming from Susan Stebbing, Charles Mills, Catarina Dutilh Novaes, Sally Haslanger, and Rudolf Carnap. We will proceed through this investigation with a section on each of the following:

(1) The basics and purposes of Moore's thoughts on common sense
(2) A logical problem for Moorean common sense
(3) An ethical problem for Moorean common sense
(4) Susan Stebbing on common sense and *Thinking to Some Purpose*
(5) Charles Mills on lived experience of oppression and exclusion
(6) Mills' and Stebbing's approaches and solutions to the two problems
(7) Conclusion and questions moving forward.

§3.2 MOORE ON COMMON SENSE

Again, while there are certainly those who would start elsewhere, there is nothing particularly new about starting investigations into the history of analytic philosophy with the work of G. E. Moore and Bertrand Russell. The question, then, is what it was about their work which led to this state of affairs. What turning points were manifested by the writings of Moore and Russell—what were they doing differently than others at the time?

They came onto the philosophical scene at the end of a century, which began in the wake of Kant's dominance—a dominance that then set in motion the tradition of German idealism. As this spread across the continent, a distinctive, British form of German idealism came about. This was most famously found in the works of F. H. Bradley, T. H. Green, and H. H. Joachim at Oxford, as well as J. M. E. McTaggart at Cambridge. While Moore was briefly swayed by his teacher McTaggart, the beginning of his mature philosophical system and significant influence was a reaction against this British absolute idealism in "The Refutation of Idealism."

Despite its title, this article begins only with trying to show that British idealists' arguments for their views from *esse est percipi* as premise are not successful. That said, through a series of overlapping publications over the next four decades, Moore eventually built this into a complete rejection of all the main tenets associated with British idealism. In particular, Moore advocates

(1) a division between the mind and its objects,
(2) a rejection of the view that reality is purely spiritual,
(3) a rejection of holism—the idea that there are no individual objects, but only a single absolute
(4) and a rejection of the doctrine of internal relations[5] which led to this holism.

And, while there were hints of it in "The Nature of Judgment," "The Refutation of Idealism," *Principia Ethica*, *Ethics*, and "Internal and External Relations," what Moore intends to replace idealism, holism, and the doctrine of internal relations with does not get published until his 1925, "A Defence of Common Sense." Furthermore, while this makes it clear that we should start philosophy with the deliverances of common sense, precisely what makes something common sense is never made quite clear.

Rather, what Moore does is start by noting that he will begin from what he takes to be a number of obvious truisms denied by the British idealists—for example, that he and the Earth have existed for a number of years, that he has a physical body, that he knows these things, that others know these things about themselves, and that he knows they know these things about themselves. That said, Moore himself acknowledges that abstracting from these particular examples to a general view of the starting points for philosophizing is quite difficult since "[t]he phrases 'Common Sense view of the world' or 'Common Sense beliefs' . . . are, of course, extraordinarily vague" (Moore 1925, 119).

All of this is highlighted to make it clear that getting precise about what Moore takes the proper starting points of philosophy to be and, antecedently, what he takes common sense to be are difficult tasks. Despite Moore's recognizing this himself, those working in the wake of Moore's influence have seemingly been more confident. That is to say, there are some dominant and standard ways of interpreting "common sense" in the field today. And, since we will primarily be concerned with Moorean common sense as a jumping off point, allowing us to generate desiderata for a successful theory of analysis, we will focus on this standard *reading* of what Moore meant by "common sense" more so than the question of what Moore *actually* meant.

This dominant interpretation seems to be most concerned with what Moore said at the very beginning of his work on these matters—that he was concerned with the fact that the British idealists believed "(1) that the universe is very different indeed from what it seems, and (2) that it has quite a large number of properties which it does not seem to have" (Moore 1903, 433). And, whose intellectual seemings did the British idealists violate? Moore's unqualified use of "us" and "we" in the passages after this, as well as his persistent concern with what is believed pre-theoretically, suggest that he is concerned with intellectual seemings of the general population.

We see interpretations of Moore along these lines even from his slightly younger contemporaries in passages such as,

> Moore did not commit himself to subscribing to every belief that might be held by a majority of his fellow citizens . . . he was concerned only to uphold three very general propositions, which he thought that nearly everybody took for granted. (Ayer 1982, 59)

While Ayer makes it clear that Moorean commonsense beliefs are not to be identified with those held by a sufficiently large portion of the general citizenry, he does suggest that they form the genus from which such commonsense beliefs will be pulled by some specific difference. In particular, it seems that not just everybody believing something, but that the belief is "taken for granted"—that it is believed in a certain way—which makes something a piece of Moorean common sense.

This way of reading Moore persists until today as well, as we can see in passages such as, "Moore's claim is that he is more certain of specific facts of common sense . . . than he is of any of the steps of the abstruse or involved philosophical arguments" (Schwartz 2012, 29). This reading is also bound to be replicated given that it is similar to the view advocated in the book becoming the standard text on analytic philosophy taught to advanced undergraduates in the anglophone philosophy world. Here, Soames argues that Moore takes commonsense beliefs to be "among those that all of us not only believe, but also feel certain that we know to be true" (Soames 2003, 3–4).

Given my goals, we will treat Moorean common sense along the lines of these standard readings of common sense, which take it to be a set of beliefs that every "ordinary" person, or at least a sufficiently large majority, would confidently profess to have. The standard tendency is also to extend this moniker to beliefs that we imagine an ordinary person *would* have *if* they were dealing with whatever issue we happen to be dealing with, even though ordinary people may tend to not have explicitly deliberated upon such matters. Often, we do this by comparison with beliefs they may have about other situations that we take to be similar in the essentials.

Because of this, the use of Moorean common sense is clearly connected to appeals to intuition. Given this, the extent to which common sense has been, and is still, influential in the history of analytic philosophy should become obvious. It is hard to go through a single journal issue without finding an elaborate thought experiment designed to pump this or that intuition. Fully aware of its influence and not happy with the sort of guessing game involved in this use of thought experiments, experimental philosophers have been engaging in empirical studies to determine the contents of common sense.[6] Their methodology shows a clear affinity for Moorean common sense as they do this by determining the statistical distribution of beliefs on particular matters by directly asking participants what their beliefs/intuitions are.

Aside from being the standard way of reading Moore, this characterization of common sense, "Moorean common sense" as I will call it (henceforth, MCS) does seem *close* to that which G. E. Moore had in mind in his principal elucidations of his philosophical system as well.[7] The closest he came to an explicit characterization of common sense had it consisting of "a whole long list of propositions, which may seem, at first sight, such obvious truisms as not to be worth stating" and which "each of us (meaning by "us," very many human beings of the class defined) has frequently known" (Moore 1925, 193–94). Given these comments, the operative characteristics of common sense for Moore seem to be acceptance by many and acceptance with a sense of obviousness (i.e., confidence). Thus, at the very least, our characterization of MCS is a criterion that all of his commonsense propositions, like that he has existed for some time, that the Earth has existed for some time before that, that there were others like him, that there were many other like them on the Earth for its history, etc., have in common nonaccidentally. Hence, MCS seems a reasonable candidate for the historically relevant sense of "common sense."

Again, though, since there are disputes over how to interpret "common sense" that we will simply not solve here, we will primarily focus on this conception of MCS as a point of comparison. That is to say, we will use it to develop potential problems, the solving of which, will serve as desiderata for a successful theory of commonsense analysis. In particular, we will follow the advice of the previous chapter instructing us to look at ways that logic and ethics come together when aiming at bringing the history of analytic philosophy together with issues concerning race, gender, and social justice. This is especially necessary given that the focus on logic has been considered as a potential hindrance to not only feminist analytic philosophy, as discussed in the previous chapter, but also antiracist analytic philosophy. Lewis Gordon, for example, remarks that, on Rodney Roberts' view, "Logic calls for a standard the core definition of which excludes Black folk" (Gordon 2008, 119). Thus, it would do dialectically significant work to have logical and ethical considerations driving our attempt at a race-conscious account of commonsense analysis.

§3.3 LOGICAL PROBLEM(S) FOR MOOREAN COMMON SENSE

There are several reasons that this conservative Moorean account of common sense should strike us as problematic upon further scrutiny. For starters, MCS is an unbelievably large and motley body of doctrine. It is hard to see how there would be much left for philosophers to do if we have to do justice to everything in this set of beliefs. Furthermore, as time passes, uniformity in beliefs and lowering of epistemic standards seem to be the norm. This means MCS—the set of sufficiently common and sufficiently confidently held beliefs—is ever bloating. Given this, at the very least, we need to come up with a principled way to be pickier. As far as I can tell, there are at least two different categories of reasons that should make us think that we need to shave away at this set—those based on combinations of logical, epistemic, and psychological considerations and those based on the ethical character of such beliefs.

We can begin to see why the first of these restrictions becomes necessary when we see that doing justice to the whole of MCS would tend to do away with intellectual surprise in philosophy. After all, it is not clear how surprise would arise if all we are doing is structuring beliefs that we all claim to already have and to be sure of. Not only would this lack of surprise run counter to many of our own experiences, it more importantly undermines a trend popular among the analytic tradition's founders and ignores facts about progress in the history of analytic philosophy. In particular,[8] the following currents came together during early analytic philosophy:

(1) Freudians were telling people that the most relevant factors to motivating human action were not quite what they appeared to be,
(2) quantum theorists were saying that causation and the nature of matter and energy were much different from what Newtonian physics claimed,
(3) biologists were replacing more standard Lamarckian processes with natural selection and genetic drift, and
(4) Wittgenstein, Russell, the logical empiricists, and Quine came to conclusions, which informed us that analysis using the tools of the new logic would show our language to function in a deep way much different from the way it seems to at the surface.

While it was probably most explicit in Russell's distinction between logical form and ordinary grammatical form, this tendency has never been far from the vanguard in analytic philosophy.

Building along this line, one should not forget the importance that the surprises of paradox have played in moving philosophical thought forward throughout the last 4,500 years. By the time of the Eleatics and the Chinese School of Names, philosophers were very explicitly using paradoxes and their solutions to spur progress. This emphasis for the analytic tradition becomes even more salient when considering the fact that Russell's Paradox, in particular, and the semantic paradoxes, in general, were vital to creating a base around which the analytic tradition could grow. This may have even approached a Kuhnian paradigm for problem solution.

Adopting Corcoran's definition of "paradox" as an argumentation, which starts from seemingly true premises and reaches a seemingly false conclusion by a seemingly valid chain of reasoning, we see that surprise comes in on both ends of a paradox (Corcoran 1989a). We feel surprise at the fact that a seemingly sound argument has a seemingly false conclusion, since it is impossible for an actually sound argument to have an actually false conclusion. That said, we also feel surprise when we solve the paradox and find one or more of the following—a seemingly true premise was actually false, the seemingly false conclusion was actually true, or the seemingly valid chain of reasoning actually contained a misstep. Because of all these considerations, we see that we need to be able to come to philosophical views, which refute some of the members of MCS.

Perhaps more worrisome, MCS is actually going to create such scenarios as MCS is almost certainly going to contain certain unsavory logical properties. In order to see this, consider the following example from judgment aggregation theory—the study of how to make a group judgment based on the beliefs and preferences of the individuals in that group. In particular, consider we are trying to determine the contents of MCS in the manner much like experimental philosophers do. For the sake of simplicity, imagine there are only three people to ask their opinion on three different propositions. Table 3.1 lists their responses.

If what we do in order to determine what belongs to common sense is merely collect and tally data on the de dicto beliefs of ordinary folk, as the proponent of MCS should encourage, then we will get the bottom row of this table. Unfortunately, this bottom row is inconsistent—there is no model on which two sentences can be true while the conjunction that connects them is false. Thus, we simply must have different processes for coming up with

Table 3.1 The Doctrinal Paradox

	P	Q	P & Q
Voter 1	TRUE	TRUE	TRUE
Voter 2	TRUE	FALSE	FALSE
Voter 3	FALSE	TRUE	FALSE
GROUP	TRUE	TRUE	FALSE

Author Created.

philosophically relevant starting points than those associated with MCS. Before we attempt to describe these processes, though, we should point out that we got this result, the doctrinal paradox, even while assuming that all of our agents are consistent (List 2012, 181–82). It seems very unlikely that the real world would pan out this way. It also happened by only including a minimal set of interrelated propositions. Surely we could only expect even worse results when adding in the complexity of the actual circumstances. Thus, MCS, understood as those beliefs that most people confidently profess to have or would tend to do so if probed, is simply not philosophically sacrosanct.

§3.4 ETHICAL PROBLEM(S) FOR MOOREAN COMMON SENSE

In addition to this logical problem of allowing for, and perhaps encouraging, inconsistent sets of beliefs, there are significant ethical challenges that can be raised against *individual* beliefs meeting the criterion of MCS. Put most simply, there is a significant potential for the encouragement of MCS to lead to the perpetuation of injustice and oppression. While this may seem a significant leap, I am not the first to recognize something like this fact. Dutilh Novaes and Geerdink point out that

> In criticizing our common sense knowledge, Russell thought we should go beyond the uncritical doxastic attitudes of our ancestors. He would famously use his scientific understanding of social issues to press for social change, on the basis of philosophical analysis. Russell was, for instance, an avid supporter of women's suffrage (Russell 1910b), sex outside marriage (Russell 1929), and against the continued existence of nuclear weapons (see, e.g. the Russell–Einstein Manifesto). (Dutilh Novaes & Geerdink, 84–85)

Haslanger too has argued that *conceptual* analysis, the type that Moore seems to encourage, runs into the problem that human societies bring ideology along with them. Ideologies often function without our knowledge, though—obscuring our own conceptual framework even to ourselves. As a result, such a priori analysis of our own concepts is likely to be misleading and nefarious wherever ideology is at play (Haslanger 2012, 383–86).

As Dutilh Novaes says while directly relating Haslanger's thoughts to the works of Moore and Russell, a conservative, Moorean reliance on common sense and intuition is problematic because "our ordinary understandings of social kinds tend to be ideology-ridden in such a way that they in fact perpetuate inequalities and hierarchies among men and women, white people and people of color" (Dutilh Novaes 2018, 14). That is to say, what may seem the deliverance of common sense, purely intuitive, or obvious is really the result of being socialized into a particular group of identities in a particular societal context. Given that almost all societal contexts that have actually existed have been oppressive, this is to say that MCS is likely to carry with it some of that oppressive baggage.

Here, we will focus on three different types of oppressive cognitions that seem to be encouraged by MCS to spell out this point in more detail. We will begin with implicit biases—dispositions to unreflectively and automatically make conceptual connections, or judgments, or engage in behaviors that reflect a prejudice of some sort. From there, we will look at hasty generalizations—the drawing of a conclusion about a target group based on a sample that is insufficient to tell us anything interesting about that target. Finally, we will end with the phenomenon of white ignorance—structural group-based miscognition that results from being socialized in a white supremacist societal context—something we can generalize analogs for with respect to each different dimension of dominance by people with certain social identities. We will take these one at a time.

To see how MCS relates to implicit bias, we must remember that these commonsense beliefs are supposed to be pre-theoretic and taken for granted by large groups of people. Encouraging such beliefs and the processes, which lead to them, seems to then encourage giving credence to unreflective and automatic cognitions. Put another way, as Cappelen has argued in his book on ridding analytic philosophy of appeals to intuition, Moore is one of the primary sources of analytic philosophers thinking that *intuitions* are the primary (source of) evidence for philosophers (Cappelen 2012, 23). Furthermore, since one of the prominent understandings of intuitions takes them to be beliefs generated by "processes that take place inside individuals without being controlled by them" (Mercier & Sperber 2009, 153), this would mean that Moore is responsible for encouraging beliefs generated in this way.[9] Implicit biases—biased beliefs, connections, attitudes, and feelings outside of our conscious awareness and control (Project Implicit)—are just that, though.

For instance, in some of the more recent studies of implicit bias, researchers have found that "[r]ace can bias people to see harmless objects as weapons when they are in the hands of black men" (Payne et al. 2018) in a way that they do not when in the hands of white people. Furthermore, when studying the behavior of early childhood educators, "[f]indings revealed that when expecting challenging behaviors teachers gazed longer at Black children, especially Black boys" (Gilliam et al. 2016, 1). Turning to gender and to a concrete example, Chimamanda Adichie discusses a case where she tipped a man—"I opened my bag, put my hand inside my bag to get my money, and I gave it to the man. And he, this man who was happy and grateful, took the money from me, and then looked across at Louis and said, 'Thank you, sah!'" (Adichie 2014, 15–16). Insofar as MCS encourages the type of cognitions that lead to these implicit biases, it seems that ending injustice and oppression would require discouraging MCS.

Of course, one of the persistent problems with combating implicit biases has been the extent to which people do not even realize they have them. That is to say, one can often have, for example, an implicit bias in favor of white people and against people of color while sincerely denying that they do—thus, falling far short of confident assertion. In this way, it seems that there can also be a significant disconnect between MCS and implicit biases. One of the ways in which implicit biases manifest themselves in explicit beliefs, though, is when these implicit biases encourage us to make hasty generalizations. This is important because hasty generalizations happen all over the place in our daily lives and in scary, abhorrent ways. As discussed in the previous chapter, if one watches Fox News long enough, they will eventually see somebody invoking something like the following argument:

P1: 19 Muslims perpetrated the September 11, 2001, terror attacks.
Conclusion: Muslims are terrorists.

As mentioned before, there are around 1.8 billion Muslims alive today. Again, this makes a sample of nineteen horribly insufficient for drawing conclusions about Muslims generally. In fact, this is very obviously a hasty generalization. So obvious that the existence of an implicit bias is needed to explain why anyone would be willing to accept something like it in the first place. Again, insofar as MCS seems to be in the same ballpark as these kinds of cognitions, we clearly ought not to encourage it.

Of course, one may object that philosophers—people trained in logic and spotting logical fallacies—are in a good position to not let their implicit biases manifest themselves in explicit beliefs reached by fallacies like hasty generalization, confirmation bias, and the like. While I am somewhat skeptical of philosophers' abilities to put such logical knowledge into practice, we can still make the general point behind the ethical problem for MCS even for someone who is not so skeptical. To see this, we must turn to the connection between MCS and the phenomenon of white ignorance. Most relevantly for our purposes, Charles Mills, the foremost theorist of white ignorance has pointed out that

> racialized causality can give rise to what I am calling white ignorance, straightforwardly for a racist cognizer, but also indirectly for a nonracist cognizer who may form mistaken beliefs (e.g., that after the abolition of slavery in the United States, blacks generally had opportunities equal to whites) because of the social

suppression of the pertinent knowledge, though without prejudice himself. (Mills 2017, 57)

Building off of this passage, we can see that cases of white ignorance, such as "that after the abolition of slavery in the United States, blacks generally had opportunities equal to whites," or that Christopher Columbus *discovered* the Americas in 1492, or that most Mexicans in the United States entered the country illegally are likely to also be instances of MCS. As they are the result of widespread, social, structural, institutional processes, they are likely to be common across populations. Furthermore, since the primary mechanism of the perpetuation of such pieces of white ignorance is the suppression of any potential evidence to the contrary, these beliefs will likely be held confidently. Hence, such pieces of white ignorance are likely to meet the criterion for being instances of MCS.

Before moving on, it is important to note that it is not only the content of MCS intuitions, but also the *form* of epistemic process MCS encourages that could make philosophy unjustly exclusionary. That is to say, it is not just that automatic, common, and confident beliefs can end up being horribly racist, sexist, etc., it is also the case that encouraging people to think that they must rely on such automatic cognitions to be a good philosopher can itself be ableist. Interestingly, this would happen even if there were no ableist ignorance, implicit biases, or stereotypes. In particular, this view of MCS and its role in philosophy would mean that someone with a mental health issue like obsessive-compulsive disorder (henceforth, OCD) would likely need to remove themselves from philosophy if they were to promote their mental health. Given the more serious oppression seen in the previous paragraphs, this seems further reason to think that a conservative MCS analysis is not what we ought to be after.

To see that MCS and healthy approaches to OCD are often at odds, note that OCD is characterized by the existence of obsessions—intrusive, repetitive, unwanted thoughts—and compulsions—behaviors aimed at minimizing distress—which result in impairment or decreased quality of life (American Psychiatric Association 2013). Some of the most useful OCD management tools include exposure and response prevention, meditation, and mindfulness (Abramowitz 1996; Hershfield & Nicely 2017; Tang et al. 2015). What these all have in common is something along the lines of recognizing that an automatic cognition, even if it is intense and persistent, need not be something that is to be given much of any sort of credence. That is to say, if people with OCD are hoping to treat their symptoms, they cannot give general weight to their intuitions. One might suggest that the common portion of MCS would mean that this could be dealt with by checking what others' beliefs are on the matter. That said, this form of reassurance seeking is extremely common and detrimental for people with OCD (Kobori & Salkovskis 2013).

Again, all of this leads us to the conclusion that, in order to ensure that philosophy does not contribute to the rampant injustice and oppression in the world, we must come up with a different way of philosophizing than simply analyzing and systematizing MCS. MCS simply has too many potential connections to oppressive cognitions like implicit biases, hasty generalizations, and white ignorance to be a primary source of evidence in philosophy. This is particularly relevant given that philosophy itself has clearly fallen prey to issues like this. The earlier mentioned popular, but mistaken, belief that philosophy was created out of whole cloth in Ancient Greece is a clear case of MCS *and* white ignorance. Thus, if Moore was on to something important with his particular manner of refuting British idealism, it will have to be spelled out in some other way. It is to this project that we will now turn, and we will do so by bringing in the work of Susan Stebbing and Charles Mills.

§3.5 SUSAN STEBBING ON COMMON SENSE AND *THINKING TO SOME PURPOSE*

Given these significant problems for the logical coherence of sets of beliefs meeting the criterion of MCS and the unethical potential for individual such beliefs to perpetuate injustice, analytic philosophy will need to ground itself in something other than MCS. Given that Moore's influence on the analytic tradition has been far from an uncritical one, it will be of use to look at some work influenced by, but not beholden to, MCS. Remember, Dutilh Novaes has argued that, in addition to Moore's *conservative* approach to common sense, many have also taken *revisionary* approaches to common sense. The crucial difference between the approaches can be gleaned via the following questions, with the conservative approaches answering yes to the first question and revisionary approaches like Russell's, Carnap's, and Haslanger's answering yes to the second question:[10]

> When engaging in philosophical analysis, are we trying to faithfully capture commonsensical concepts, which thereby become clarified and systematized but otherwise remain intact? Or do we openly seek to transform and improve on these concepts? (Dutilh Novaes 2018, 2)

While the influence of MCS on Russell, Wittgenstein, Malcolm, Black, and many others has been well documented, I will focus here on one of Moore's lesser-known influences. In particular, we will discuss Susan Stebbing's revisionary take on the role of common sense in a larger system of doing philosophy.

While Stebbing is primarily known only to a small group of specialists today, this was not always the case during her lifetime or even the decades after. Living from 1885 to 1943, Stebbing was once one of the most prominent analytic philosophers in the world. She wrote the first textbook on the new logic and analytic philosophy (Stebbing 1930), in addition to being one of the founders of *Analysis*. She also served as the president of the Aristotelian Society in 1933 and 1934 and held the same position for the Mind Association in 1934 and 1935. Beatrice Edgell is the only woman to have held either one of these positions prior to Stebbing. Additionally, Stebbing invited Carnap to England and wrote reviews of his works, introducing Carnap to Russell and logical empiricism to the larger Anglophone world through works like Stebbing (1933, 1935, 1936).

Particularly important to our concerns, Stebbing was both a strong proponent of common sense and arguably the most prolific public philosopher from the early analytic tradition outside of Russell. Also of great importance to this discussion is that, despite her strong influence by Moore and the importance she placed on common sense, she was not a proponent of what we have been calling MCS. Furthermore, we will see that this was connected to her public, social, and political engagement. Because of this, we turn to her own work on a practically oriented and publically engaged common sense.

To see both the influence of Moore on Stebbing and the subtle, but important, ways in which her focus differed from his, we can begin simply with the title of the first book-length work on her philosophy—Siobhan Chapman's *Susan Stebbing and the Language of Common Sense*. While Chapman rightly sees Stebbing's interest in common sense being important enough to be in the book's title, she also seems to be suggesting that her focus is not on MCS *beliefs*, but on commonsense *language* and, in particular, "how language is ordinarily used in human interaction" (Chapman 2013, 2).[11] That is, rather than an interest in commonly and confidently held beliefs, Stebbing is concerned with paying "[a]ttention to the language in which philosophical discussion is conducted, and respect for the ways in which people ordinarily use language to make sense of and describe the world around them, . . . themes running through Moore's philosophy" (Chapman 2013, 18). Chapman sums this up by arguing that Stebbing was concerned to "urge the necessary links between philosophical outlook and manner of living" (Chapman 2013, 7).

Most interesting for our purposes, Stebbing gives a justification for this move away from MCS beliefs very similar to issues we have considered already in a very prominent place in her work. In the preface of arguably her most important work, *Thinking to Some Purpose*, Stebbing says "I am convinced of the urgent need for a democratic people to think clearly without the distortions due to unconscious bias and unrecognized ignorance" (Stebbing 1939, 9). Later in the book, Stebbing points out that our commonly and confidently held beliefs (i.e., MCS) can go wrong for both personal and social reasons, since "[o]ur fears and hopes, our ignorance, our loyalties, these lead us to entertain prejudices which are an effective bar to thinking a problem out" (Stebbing 1939, 39) and "[t]here is a fundamental difference between holding a belief into which we have been persuaded and holding a belief as the outcome of a reasoned argument. It is upon persuasion that the propagandist relies" (Stebbing 1939, 81).

Because of all of this, we must not simply acquiesce to MCS beliefs and try to understand them better. We must critically engage with them and subject them to logical scrutiny to see if they can really be justified. Connecting to this, "Stebbing was committed to carrying logic's requirements of rational argument and valid reasoning over to the actual problems of human existence" (Chapman 2013, 7). This is perhaps best put by Stebbing when she says, "our unwillingness to make definite to ourselves what it is we believe to be worth the seeking" is one of the causes of the fact that "in no other century have so many human beings—men, women, and children—suffered pain, anguish of heart, bitterness of spirit, despair, and unnecessary death" (Stebbing 1941, vii–viii).

For all of these advances on MCS that we can garner from Susan Stebbing's work, it still had significant problems in the areas upon which we wish to improve. For example, despite her valiant efforts to avoid the "distortions due to unconscious bias," some of Stebbing's bigger mistakes involve an unconscious Eurocentrism. Take for example the discussion Stebbing gives of the second Italo-Ethiopian War—an illegal, imperial war that led to roughly 1 million deaths, including several hundred thousand civilians. She conducts her discussion by saying she will "consider, finally, possible differences in the point of view of, say, an Italian, an Englishman, a Frenchman, an American, with regard to the Italo-Abyssinian War" (Stebbing 1939, 25). Notice that, in discussing a variety of perspectives on a war fought on Ethiopian soil by Ethiopians over the fate of Ethiopia, Stebbing does not consider an Ethiopian perspective at all. This is surely a wildly Eurocentric way of looking at the matter and is the exact type of thought process that has led to disasters like the Sykes-Picot Agreement, Nigerian borders that cut across, but also artificially bring together, the historical lands of Igbo, Hausa, Yoruba, and many other peoples, among many other colonial instances. So, if we wish to get to a socially just picture of analysis, we will need to build in antidotes to such mistakes.

§3.6 CHARLES MILLS ON LIVED EXPERIENCE OF OPPRESSION AND EXCLUSION

Given that Stebbing's work constituted an advance over MCS, but that it still struggled with respect to the ethical problem for MCS and did so with respect to an implicit Eurocentrism, we want to look to a prominent thinker who has dealt both with issues surrounding common sense and combating Eurocentrism in our philosophizing. Here, I believe there is no better choice than the work of Charles Mills, which is a continuation of standpoint theory in the vein of Marx or Harding (1986).

One of Mills' seminal works begins by pointing out that there is an unjust demographic as well as conceptual whiteness in philosophy and that "the result is a silence—a silence not of tacit inclusion but rather of exclusion: the black experience is not subsumed under these philosophical abstractions, despite their putative generality" (Mills 1998, 3). Given this, we should be worried about looking at unreflective and common beliefs (i.e., MCS) of philosophers—a group with very unrepresentative standpoints—because for example, "if whites spontaneously generalize and universalize from their uncontested moral personhood, [many] moral realities will remain largely invisible to them" (Mills 1998, 16). While Mills is primarily concerned with this spontaneous generalization in moral, social, and political philosophy, there is no reason we should be happy with it anywhere in philosophy. Hence, this demographic and conceptual whiteness that Mills brings up gives us further reason to be concerned with MCS.

That said, Mills is certainly interested in some of the same types of concerns as Moore as well. For instance, like Moore, he too is concerned with the fact that a philosophy that takes seriously the problem of other minds is misunderstanding the proper starting points of philosophy. Here, he says,

> If your daily existence is largely defined by oppression, by forced intercourse with the world, it is not going to occur to you that doubt about your oppressor's existence could in any way be a serious or pressing philosophical problem; this idea will simply seem frivolous, a perk of social privilege. (Mills 1998, 8)

This sounds like something a woke Moore would love. In a separate chapter, Mills takes on another Moorean target, that of skepticism, when he says "Hume pointed out long ago that whatever skeptical iconoclasm with respect to everyday beliefs philosophers may indulge in privately" this is lost immediately upon returning to the social world (Mills 1998, 22). Of course, the conservative lessons that Moore and others have taken from this way of thinking are, rightfully, not going to be endorsed by Mills. Alluding to Wittgenstein's conservative approach to analysis, Mills says that "African-American/black philosophy would see itself as antipodal to a philosophy that, in one famous formulation, 'leaves everything as it is'" (Mills 1998, 17).

So, how do we be concerned with these Moorean targets without leaving everything as it is? Again, like Stebbing, Mills' work reminds us that our focus on common sense should not be on commonsense *beliefs*, but on everyday interactions, goals, experiences, and ideals. For instance, in continuing the discussion of skepticism as Hume mentioned earlier, Mills argues that the problem seems to be that such philosophizing "ha[s] no practical implications for the actual beliefs and behavior either of the nonphilosophical population at large or even of the philosophers themselves" (Mills 1998, 22). Instead, then, we need to focus on philosophical problems, questions, issues, and theories that "are by no means scholastic riddles to occupy an idle hour but burningly practical issues, problems that really are deeply troubling" (Mills 1998, 17).

That said, whereas Stebbing runs into problems of Eurocentrism on this front, Mills avoids this by recognizing the importance of different standpoints and perspectives on lived experiences, purposes, and goals. Generalizing from the earlier quoted point about the problem of other minds, Mills points out that this consideration of oppressed and privileged perspectives can be useful in metaphysics in pointing out that "the starting point needs to challenge this metaphysical complacency, to show that the white existential condition, the Cartesian predicament is 'white' to begin with and is quite unrepresentative" (Mills 1998, 10). Furthermore, such considerations of different standpoints can be useful in epistemology since systems of oppression lead to differential experiences for oppressed and oppressors such that "hegemonic groups characteristically have experiences that foster illusory perceptions about society's functioning, while subordinate groups characteristically have experiences that (at least potentially) give rise to more adequate conceptualizations" (Mills 1998, 28).

Connected to these issues, Mills has argued that we can often avoid this parochialism and problematic generalization by looking to historical circumstances and how they have impacted different communities. That is, we can avoid problematic abstraction by not assuming that the world has been ideal or similar to the way we have experienced it. Rather, we should take the actual historical reality as our starting point for philosophizing. In a number of works, Mills has discussed this in relation to ideal theory vs. nonideal or naturalized theory. We will return to this question in a number of the chapters that follow (see chapter 7 especially). For now, we turn to the implications of what we have looked at so far has for MCS and starting points for philosophizing.

§3.7 MILLS' AND STEBBING'S APPROACHES AND SOLUTIONS TO THE TWO PROBLEMS

At this point, we want to bring together Moore's insights with Stebbing's and Mills' amendments into at least a suggestion for a general strategy for starting a philosophical debate or conversation. Following Moore, we will encourage beginning with our commonsense beliefs (and the way we discuss them) about a subject matter upon which we intend to philosophize. Using Dutilh Novaes' terminology, we should take a revisionary and critical eye toward MCS, rather than a conservative approach, though. Sometimes we *may* clarify and systematize our MCS beliefs and concepts, but many times these will be deficient and in need of revision to improve upon them. Following Stebbing, this revisionary approach to critical analysis should be guided by goals, purposes, and ideals from everyday, ordinary, practical life. Finally, building off of Mills, we should do what we can to verify that these practical revisions are not dependent on our privileged vantage points, but livable across the population. If we wanted to put this into something like an overly simplified algorithm for starting a philosophical dialectic, we might have something like the following for a politically revisionary critical analysis:[12]

(1) We should begin by looking at MCS beliefs.
(2) We should take a critical eye toward MCS and be prepared to revise such beliefs.
(3) We should be prepared to revise MCS in relation to pre-philosophical experiences, actions, and purposes.
(4) We should be concerned with making our answers liveable across the population —not just from our own positions, which might be privileged (and should do so by learning from standpoint theorists the best way to do so).

Now that we have seen the tools from Stebbing and Mills, which will be used to solve logical and ethical problems for MCS, all that remains is to directly address how they come together in an explicit counter to these arguments against MCS. To do this, we must remember the logical and ethical problems and formulate them in terms of explicit, numbered premise-conclusion format arguments with chains of reasoning and premises to be challenged. For the logical problem, we will use:

P1: If we ought to take MCS as our ultimate evidence in philosophy, then we ought to aggregate over human populations' judgments in order to help determine our philosophical views (from the definition of "Moorean common sense").

P2: If we ought to aggregate over human populations' judgments in order to help determine our philosophical views, then it is permissible to ground our philosophizing in inconsistent sets of beliefs (from the Doctrinal Paradox).
SC: If we ought to take MCS as our ultimate evidence in philosophy then it is permissible to ground our philosophizing in inconsistent sets of beliefs. (Hypothetical syllogism with P1 and P2).
P3: It is not permissible to ground our philosophizing in inconsistent sets of beliefs.
CONCLUSION: We should not take MCS to be our ultimate evidence in philosophy. (Modus tollens with SC and P3)

For the ethical problem, we will use the following:

P1: If we ought to start our philosophizing with MCS, then we ought to ground our philosophizing in unreflective and automatic beliefs (from the definition of "Moorean common sense").
P2: If we ought to ground our philosophizing in unreflective and automatic beliefs, then it is permissible to ground our philosophizing in beliefs that result from implicit biases, hasty generalizations, white ignorance, etc. (from the discussion in §3.4).
SC: If we ought to start our philosophizing with MCS, then it is permissible to ground our philosophizing in beliefs that result from implicit biases, hasty generalizations, white ignorance, etc. (Hypothetical syllogism with P1 and P2)
P3: It is not permissible to ground our philosophizing in beliefs that result from implicit biases, hasty generalizations, white ignorance, etc.
CONCLUSION: We should not start our philosophizing with MCS. (Modus tollens with SC and P3).

With these arguments in mind, our current project will be complete with counterarguments to each of them.

As stated earlier, one of the most important steps in Stebbing's and Mills' getting beyond MCS was to always be practical and oriented toward our everyday lives. That is to say, rather than Soames' focus on pre-philosophical *thought*, Stebbing encouraged us to always ground our philosophizing in pre-philosophical goals, experiences, actions, and practicalities. This means that the way we are interpreting "common" from "common sense" is in terms of the everyday, practical, and not just philosophical, rather than something about beliefs present in the majority of some population. This is what removes the need for relying on the results of judgment aggregation as an essential step in what we might call politically revisionary critical analysis. Hence, P1 of the logical problem is false on this view and we need not worry about the Doctrinal Paradox or ending up with inconsistent sets of philosophical views.

A counterargument based on politically revisionary critical analysis is as straightforward for the ethical problem as well. On this view, the reason to consider MCS is not to rely upon it as our ultimate evidence, but to expose precisely those places where we may have fallen prey to implicit biases, hasty generalizations, oppressive ignorance, etc. That is to say, on this view, P1 from the second argument is false because it does not encourage us to ground our philosophical views in automatic and unreflective beliefs, but rather to expose our automatic and unreflective beliefs to critical scrutiny.

Now, obviously, much more needs to be said about exactly how we do that and, especially, how we do that in ways that do not simply fall prey to further manifestations of implicit bias and the like. Part of this will certainly be understanding something about ourselves as cognizers and empirical results about ourselves as cognizers. That is to say, we will need to naturalize our epistemic practices to some extent. Furthermore, since such empirical studies tend to find that our epistemic weaknesses often have to do with our social positions, it will be important to recognize the extent to which philosophy is a social activity. We must not simply be solitary, a priori philosophers. We must engage with others and, in particular, we must engage with others who do not occupy relatively similar social positions. Exactly how to do this will be discussed in greater detail in the chapters that follow. For now, it is sufficient to recognize that, for politically revisionary critical analysis, P1 from the ethical problem is false.

§3.8 CONCLUSIONS AND QUESTIONS MOVING FORWARD

In conclusion, we can now recognize some ways in which we can fruitfully bring together investigation into the starting points in philosophy, the history of analytic philosophy, and social justice. At the outset of a distinctive and self-conscious analytic *movement* in philosophy, things began with Moore and Russell's revolt against British speculative holist idealism, in favor of common sense and empirical findings. Despite there being agreement on something like this throughout the analytic tradition, there has been an underlying dispute as to whether or not commonsense analysis should be, what Dutilh Novaes called, conservative or revisionary. Moore's initial offering of commonsense analysis as capturing and better understanding our commonly and confidently held beliefs began the conservative side. Russell's belief that "the point of philosophy is to start with something so simple as not to seem worth stating, and to end with something so paradoxical that no one will believe it" (Russell 1918, 178) set the terrain from the revisionary side. A generation later, Stebbing and Carnap would develop the revisionary, Russellian side, while thinkers like Strawson and Wittgenstein developed the conservative side. Today, we see variations of the revisionary approach in prominent thinkers such as Bright, Haslanger, Mills, and Dutilh Novaes.

In this chapter, we hoped to develop a picture of common sense inspired by these politically and socially motivated revisionary takes on commonsense analysis. Furthermore, the approach was developed with an eye toward solving what we called the logical and ethical problems for MCS. This was achieved by an account that held that the *common* portion of common sense should be about everyday, practical matters for all people, rather than aggregating over the beliefs of all people. In short, we should never accept something when philosophizing that we would not be willing and able to implement in the rest of our lives. To do this, we should always look to the lived experiences and purposes relevant to the area being investigated. We should not take our own experiences to be sacrosanct, though. Remember that we can and should revise beliefs based off of them sometimes—especially in light of the lived experiences of those with different backgrounds than our own.

Of course, this is just an introductory sketch in need of much more development. We saw that some particular avenues of promising development could be looking into ideal language and ordinary language approaches to analysis, ideal and nonideal theory approaches to social and political philosophy, as well as armchair and naturalized approaches to epistemology. These will be taken up in subsequent chapters.

NOTES

1. "Start your story with 'Secondly', and the arrows of the Red Indians are the original criminals and the guns of white men are entirely the victim. It is enough to start with 'Secondly', for the anger of the black man against the white to be barbarous. Start with 'Secondly', and Gandhi becomes responsible for the tragedies of the British." (Barghouti 2003, 178)

2. This quotation comes from Adichie's well-known TED talk, "The Danger of a Single Story," which can be found at https://www.ted.com/talks/chimamanda_adichie_the_danger_of_a_single_story/.

3. Unfortunately, sufficiently engaging with these facts is outside of the scope of this book on more recent historical matters. For those interested in investigating them further, see the works of Martin Bernal, Cheikh Anta Diop, Feng Youlan, Lewis Gordon, Peter K. J. Park, Sarvepalli Radhakrishnan, Chancellor Williams, and Jiyuan Yu, among others. For those interested in criticism of this line of work, see the writings of Mary Lefkowitz.

4. Again, I highlight the fact that these are all written in English to make it clear that this is a failure of the book, which comes from my standpoint as a monoglot English speaker.

5. The doctrine of internal relations is the view that there are no contingent or extrinsic relations. That is to say, for all objects, x and y, if xRy, then necessarily xRy. Moore argues against this view by distinguishing between the necessity of a conditional and the necessity of the consequent of a conditional, which often get expressed ambiguously in ordinary language (Moore 1919).

6. It is important to note that much of this work by experimental philosophers is intended to debunk common sense, rather than endorse it. This is largely immaterial to my purposes, though, as I'm merely concerned with what many experimental philosophers take common sense to be, rather than whether or not they find it theoretically important.

7. These are to be found in Moore (1925, 1939). One thing that should be kept in mind here is that I think there is a pretty serious disconnect between what lots of analytic philosophers *do* and what they *say* they are doing (Moore and a number of his followers are particularly bad about this). Some of the time I'm criticizing the practice, other times I'm criticizing the theory about how to practice.

8. This connection was first suggested to me by John Kearns in passing, but I think there is much truth to be unearthed in it.

9. Importantly, this is one of the places that I think Moore would disagree with the way in which his own work has been taken. That said, my primary concern is with how Moore has actually been read and how people actually think of intuitions in the field. Furthermore, this reading is certainly still influential in the field. Consider, for example, "My working account of the ordinary meaning of 'intuition' is: immediate judgment, without reasoning or inference. One might well put this briefly by saying that 'intuition' means unreflective judgment." (Devitt 2015, 674)

10. Dutilh Novaes devotes special attention to impressively detailing the similarities and differences between Carnapian explication and Haslangerian ameliorative analysis. In particular, when trying to understand the fruitfulness criterion of a good Carnapian explication, we see that "fruitfulness may also be understood in *political* terms, i.e. in terms of promoting much-needed social reform and liberation from obscurantism" (Dutilh Novaes 2018, 7). Similarly, with respect to Haslanger's ameliorative analyses, these "are from the beginning motivated by practical purposes, and thus start off with revisionary proclivities" (Dutilh Novaes 2018, 12). That said, "the negative component of *ideology critique*, which is crucial in the ameliorative method, does not seem to have a natural counterpart in Carnapian explication, at least not in its classical formulation" (Dutilh Novaes 2018, 18).

11. For an interesting take on these two different ways of taking Moore or, perhaps, two different aspects of Moore's philosophy, it is worth reading Ambrose (1960).

12. This is simply a way of beginning to systematize what I have meant when saying elsewhere that I define "philosophy" as the rigorous and systematic investigation into those questions and issues that people across disciplines and ways of life normally take for granted.

Chapter 4

Post-Tractarian Critique of Metaphysics and Ethics

§4.0 OVERVIEW OF THE CHAPTER

One of the most distinctive aspects of the second stage of early analytic philosophy, where Wittgenstein's and Russell's works on logical atomism dominated, was their radical critique of metaphysics and ethics. This trend, which lasted at least into the third stage of logical empiricism, has also been taken to undermine the potential of a critical analytic philosophy—that is, analytic work that contributes to critique and betterment of society. Because of that, it is important to see how the *Tractatus Logico-Philosophicus* could fit into my overall picture of the history of early analytic philosophy.

 Here, I argue that these philosophers' attitudes toward metaphysics and ethics have been greatly misunderstood in the larger discipline of philosophy. In particular, I believe that Wittgenstein's *Tractatus Logico-Philosophicus* started a trend of viewing metaphysics as something of *disguised* ethics—though this phrasing would have been completely anathema to him. I illustrate this general view by showing how it can be applied to Liam Kofi Bright's account of the logical empiricists' views on the metaphysics of race (voluntarist racial eliminativism) and their ethico-political motivations (ending racist divisiveness and promoting internationalist politics). Finally, particular problems with the logical empiricists' metaphysics of race are discussed to illustrate problems with the idea of metaphysics as disguised ethics generally.

§4.1 INTRODUCTION TO STAGE 2 OF EARLY ANALYTIC PHILOSOPHY

As discussed in previous chapters, from 1898 through the first decade of the twentieth century, G. E. Moore and Bertrand Russell set in motion a new movement in philosophy—the analytic tradition of philosophizing. In this earliest stage, the approach largely involved particular applications of this movement's new logical and linguistic methods and tools, which themselves remained largely implicit. Moore and Russell tackled perennial problems, but did so one at a time—providing novel arguments for nonskeptical realist pluralism over idealist monism, a new solution for the problem of negative existentials, and a defense of logicism as a way to understand long-standing issues in the epistemology and metaphysics of mathematics. This first stage came to fruition with 1912's *The Problems of Philosophy*, which has been called "one of the first concrete expressions of analytic philosophy" (Russell 2004, vii) and the final volume of Russell and Whitehead's most prominent attempt at logicism, *Principia Mathematica*, in 1913.

From there, the analytic tradition took a number of different turns. Not only did World War I break out in 1914 and have profound impacts on the social and cultural backdrop for analytic philosophizing, the second half of the 1910s and the first half of the 1920s also saw a move from piecemeal solutions to problems in metaphysics, epistemology, logic, and the philosophy of language to attempts to develop an overarching framework for analysis. Finally, this time frame signaled a shift from Moore and Russell as the analytic torchbearers to Russell and Wittgenstein as the primary analytic philosophers of note.

Importantly, this shift to building grand systems of philosophizing in the analytic tradition and the rise of Wittgenstein were essentially connected. That is, this second stage of early analytic philosophy can be characterized as the time of the rise of Russell's and Wittgenstein's systems of logical atomism. While one can run into issues overly assimilating Wittgenstein's and Russell's logical atomisms—after all, Russell self-styled his system this way and Wittgenstein seems to have never applied it to his own work—there is certainly enough similarity between the two for it to be worth talking about them as two species of the same genus.[1]

Both systems are concerned with the nature of representation and what a language must be like to have the potential to accurately represent the world—that is, to express truths. They both answer this in a two-tiered way, arguing that what it is for an atomic sentence to represent the world involves sharing the same logical form as the fact it represents, with molecular sentences' truth-conditions being recursively defined in terms of atomic sentences.[2] These meaningful atomic sentences consist of linguistic units combined in ways isomorphic to combinations of things in the world. This strict picture of meaning had a clear place for the sentences of scientific discourse, and odd places for logic and mathematics. On the other hand, at least for Wittgenstein, it held as meaningless or nonsensical many sentences of traditional metaphysics, theology, poetry, and, most importantly for our purposes, ethics and politics.

This brings us to the challenging aspect of Stage 2, and, arguably, the greatest challenge to my entire project. While I would imagine many would be surprised by directly connecting social justice and Stage 1 of the history of analytic philosophy, there are at least some who have started to work on such matters (e.g., Dutilh Novaes, Stebbing, Chapman) and few would actively argue they cannot possibly be connected. Many would very happily argue that there cannot be such a connection made with Stage 2 and work on its associated logical atomisms, though. After all, Wittgenstein held at this time that

> Hence also there can be no ethical propositions. Propositions cannot express anything higher. (Wittgenstein 1922, 6.42)

And

> The right method of philosophy would be this. To say nothing except what can be said, i.e. the propositions of natural science, i.e. something that has nothing to do with philosophy: and then always, when someone else wished to say something metaphysical, to demonstrate to him that he had given no meaning to certain signs in his propositions. This method would be unsatisfying to the other—he would not have the feeling that we were teaching him philosophy—but it would be the only strictly correct method. (Wittgenstein 1922, 6.54)

As a result, many philosophers of different persuasions and varied levels of allegiance to analytic philosophy have expressed skepticism at the possibility of Wittgenstein's and Russell's developments of logical atomism having any connection to politics, society, ethics, or anything relating to matters of values at all. For instance, Glock believes that Stage 2 is the start of some trends that made it so he had to begin his chapter on "Ethics and Politics" in relation to the history of analytic philosophy with arguments against "the idea that analytic philosophy is characterized by the exclusion of moral philosophy and political theory" and the belief "that analytic philosophy shirks ethical and political commitments and hence inclines to being apolitical and conservative" (Glock 2008, 179). The fact that people have these beliefs that Glock argues against could not have come from their readings of anything earlier than Stage 2. After all, Stage 1 was set in motion by Moore's rebellion and "ethical considerations loom large in Moore's rebellion against Idealism" (Glock 2008, 181). Furthermore, Moore was most famous throughout the cultural world at large for his *Principia Ethica*, but "Post World War I, his meta-ethical and ethical ideas were taken up not by the analytic avant-garde, but rather by 'old-fashioned' traditionalist philosophers like Ross and Pritchard" as well as the writers associated with the Bloomsbury Group (Glock 2008, 181).

So, again, Russell's and Wittgenstein's systems centered around an account of the relationship between language and the world as well as "a very powerful test" that "purports to state the conditions that must be fulfilled in order for a sentence to be meaningful" (Soames 2003a, 235). As famous and influential as this test of intelligibility was throughout the history of analytic philosophy, it also constitutes the source of the single greatest challenge to my primary theses. This is because of the large group of statements taken to fall on the nonsense side of this test's division. In particular, all statements of value are taken to be nonsense on this view. This would seem to make any statements concerning justice to be nonsense on this view as well. Coming up with how we can bring together considerations of social justice and Stage 2 of early analytic philosophy given this challenging relationship between logical atomism and ethics will occupy the remainder of this chapter. We will proceed through this investigation in the following order:

(1) An overview of logical atomism, generally
(2) An overview of logical atomism in relation to ethics and nonsense, specifically
(3) My particular interpretation of Wittgenstein on ethics, metaphysics, and nonsense—metaphysics as disguised ethics
(4) Liam Kofi Bright on voluntary racial eliminativism
(5) Voluntary racial eliminativism as an instance of metaphysics as disguised ethics
(6) Problems with voluntary racial eliminativism and the problems with metaphysics as disguised ethics that they display
(7) Conclusions and questions moving forward.

§4.2 THE STANDARD READINGS OF TRACTARIAN METAPHYSICS AND ETHICS

While both Russell's and Wittgenstein's logical atomisms were extremely influential during Stage 2, I will here focus on Wittgenstein's development of logical atomism, which culminated in the *Tractatus Logico-Philosophicus*. Aside from the fact that the *Tractatus* had greater influence at the time and is still engaged with more today, I take this focus to be justified by just how much writing Russell did on ethics, politics, and justice. This was framed as a chapter embracing a significant challenge. Focusing on Russell's work makes my task much easier and much less of a challenge. Even though Stage 2 was not his most ethically and politically active period, Russell still wrote *Justice in War-Time, Principles of Social Reconstruction, Political Ideals, Roads to Freedom: Socialism, Anarchism and Syndicalism, The Practice and Theory of Bolshevism, Free Thought and Official Propaganda, The Problem of China, The Prospects of Industrial Civilization* (with Dora Russell), *How to Be Free and Happy*, as well as *Education and the Good Life* and served a prison sentence for protesting World War I during this time.

Furthermore, I do not claim that *Russell's* level of commitment to social justice and advocacy was common throughout the history of early analytic philosophy. He was certainly an exceptional figure on this front. So, again, focusing on his work is not the best way to support my overall project. Instead of focusing on this figure who many have recognized was committed to rationality and objectivity as part of a commitment to ethics, politics, and social justice, we will focus on Wittgenstein—a thinker (and influences of his) who has been taken to be positively destructive of ethical thinking, theorizing, and living.[3]

Wittgenstein's atomism, being an absolutely central part of analytic philosophy, has both logical and linguistic views central to the overall system. As Glock has argued, Wittgenstein's *Tractatus* was first motivated by the fact that he felt he needed to provide a philosophical foundation for—an account of the nature of—the new logical techniques and truths that Frege and Russell had systematized (Glock 2008, 34). Furthermore, as Wittgenstein himself says, the book's "whole meaning could be summed up somewhat as follows: What can be said at all can be said clearly; and whereof one cannot speak thereof one must be silent" (Wittgenstein 1922, Preface). Because of this, to get clear on Wittgenstein's early views on ethics, we must understand his views on logic and the philosophy of language from the *Tractatus* and how they ultimately have consequences for ethics. Hence, we turn to giving an account of the main pieces of Wittgenstein's philosophy of logic and language at this point.

The *Tractatus* philosophy of language begins from the Kantian question of how it is possible that language represents reality—what are the preconditions necessary for this to be the case? Famously, Wittgenstein's answer to this question was first inspired by a real-life example he came across in a magazine. As Georg Henrik von Wright recounts it:

> There is a story of how the idea of language as a picture of reality occurred to Wittgenstein. It was in the autumn of 1914 on the Eastern Front, Wittgenstein was reading, in a magazine about a lawsuit in Paris concerning an automobile

accident. At the trial a miniature model of the accident was presented before the court. The model here served as a proposition, that is, as a description of a possible state of affairs. It has this function owing to a correspondence between the parts of the model (the miniature-houses, -cars, -people) and things (houses, cars, people) in reality. (von Wright 2001, 8)

As Wittgenstein himself put things at the time that he was responding to this experience, "[i]n the proposition a world is as it were put together experimentally. (As when in the law-court in Paris a motor-car accident is represented by means of dolls, etc.)" And, by the time it made it into the *Tractatus*, we are told that "[t]he proposition is a picture of reality. The proposition is a model of the reality as we think it is" (Wittgenstein 1922, 4.01). From this, we get the basic idea behind Wittgenstein's early thinking on meaning and sense, that when a sentence represents a particular state of affairs, it is because they share a *form*. That is to say, when a sentence pictures a state of affairs, there is an isomorphism between them—to each element of the sentence, there corresponds an element of the state of affairs playing the same role in the combination.

To fill out this picture, we need to say something about the elements of the domain and co-domain of this isomorphism. On the linguistic side, elementary or atomic sentences are said to be combinations of names. These names have a meaning insofar as they correspond to, or stand for, some simple object in reality. Just as the names are combined in a particular way to form a sentence, the sentence has sense by representing or picturing the world as containing a state of affairs consisting of a corresponding combination of the simple objects named by the words in that sentence. Wittgenstein sums this up, "The general form of a proposition is: This is how things stand" (*TLP* 4.5). Because of this, sentences have a fundamentally bipolar nature. That is to say, they are true if they picture the world, if they say things stand, as it actually is and false if they do not—giving us the principle of bivalence.

This is how the meaning and truth values of atomic sentences work. To complete the *Tractatus* account of sense, we must also look into more complex sentences, which allow for a further account of the law of excluded middle and the law of noncontradiction. Sentences that are not atomic are called "molecular." Sticking with the analytic nature of logical atomism, molecular sentences are defined in terms of containing a logical constant which, rather than standing for some object, merely expresses a truth function of some atomic sentences (and truth functions of them). Furthermore, molecular sentences' sense and truth-conditions are defined in terms of the senses of atomic sentences. Since molecular sentences contain logical constants, like "and," "or," "not," "if . . . , then . . . ," "neither . . . nor . . . ," "~," "∨," "&," "N" (as used by Wittgenstein in the *Tractatus*), which allow us to create truth functions of atomic sentences, they can be defined in terms of truth tables like figure 4.1.

Getting to the most important aspect of Wittgenstein's early philosophy, once we have such truth functions, an interesting possibility arises. In particular, there is the possibility of degenerate combinations of atomic sentences where truth or falsity is guaranteed rather than contingent on the way the world is. This is where Wittgenstein's distinctive philosophy of logic comes in. For Wittgenstein, all necessity is logical necessity, which is a result of the rules of symbolism. Truth tables always give us a way of testing for necessity, contingency, and impossibility. For example, the truth-table in figure 4.2

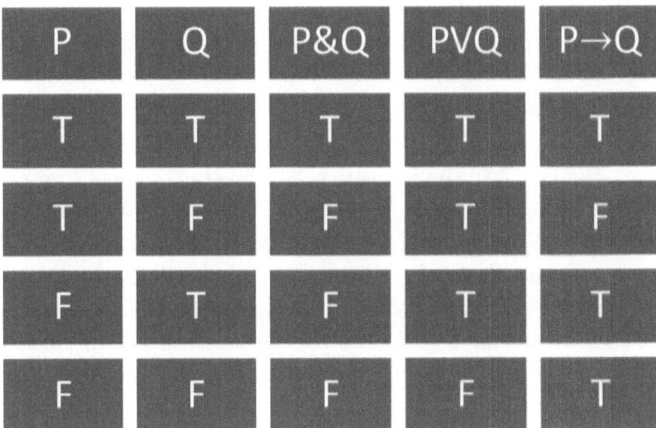

Figure 4.1 **Truth Tables Defining Logical Constants.** Author Created.

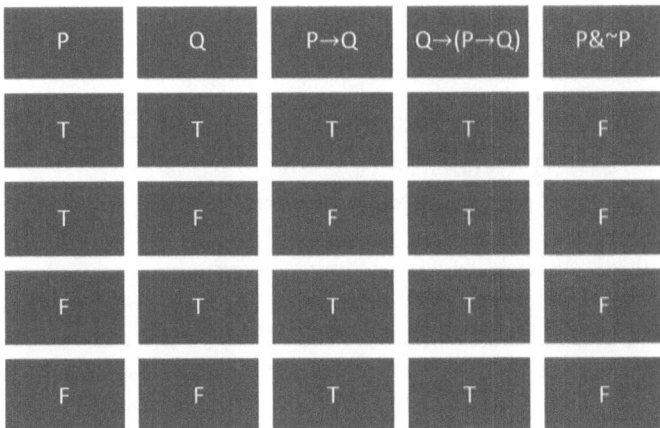

Figure 4.2 **Truth Tables Testing Logical Truths.** Author Created.

shows us that for any two distinct atomic sentences, P and Q, $P \rightarrow Q$ will be contingent, $Q \rightarrow (P \rightarrow Q)$ will be necessary, and $P \& \sim P$ will be impossible.

This philosophy of logic and language come together with a way to specify all sentences' relation to sense. Atomic sentences have sense and picture some contingent state of affairs. Molecular sentences do not picture some complex state of affairs because the logical constants are not names of abstract, logical objects. Rather, they have sense by being truth functions of atomic sentences with sense. The complement class of sentences with sense is not unified and introduces an area for some Wittgensteinian terms of art. Some molecular sentences are combined in such a way that they are *sinnlos*, senseless, rather than *unsinn*, nonsense. These are the tautologies and the contradictions. Finally, what does not fall into those categories is nonsense/unsinn. Getting to the most operative view of the *Tractatus* needing to be discussed given my goals, this category of nonsense includes metaphysics, ethics, aesthetics, theology, and politics.

This follows because sentences of ethics, like all other sentences according to the *Tractatus* test of intelligibility, will be either (a) contingent, bipolar propositions of natural science (sinn), (b) necessary propositions that are tautologous (sinnlos), (c) impossible propositions that are contradictory, or (d) nonsense (unsinn). Ethical sentences are traditionally thought to not be contingent—nobody would say that, if the world were just a little different, then oppression would be a good thing.[4] "Oppression is evil" also does not seem to be something which would be shown to be a tautology or contradiction through truth-table calculations. Hence, (d)—that ethics is nonsense seems to be the conclusion. For those statements concerning politics which are not straightforwardly empirical, we seem to be in the same situation. Perhaps even more surprising, this also seems to be the verdict for all of the philosophy of the *Tractatus*, itself. While all of this requires some significant working out, it is not difficult to see why many would take this to be a serious problem for the primary theses of this book.

§4.3 STANDARD READINGS AS A MAJOR CHALLENGE TO THE BOOK

Again, if this is the right way of reading Wittgenstein—that sentences about ethics, politics, and matters of value are all nonsense—then this seems to cause a major issue for my primary theses. I'm trying to argue that not only is there much more to be gained from further connecting matters of social justice and the history of analytic philosophy than is currently done, but that there is also historical precedent for this in each one of the stages of the early analytic movement. This is all despite the fact that Soames has argued that "in general, philosophy done in the analytic tradition aims at truth and knowledge, as opposed to moral or spiritual improvement" (Soames 2003a, xiv). If ethics, politics, and justice all consist of nonsense, then it seems that they cannot be very important and Soames would be right that Wittgenstein and those influenced by him are not concerned with moral and spiritual improvement in the way they philosophize. This would then constitute quite weighty evidence against my theses.

The situation for my project is made worse by the fact that Soames is not alone in saying things like this at all. Although Glock ultimately argues against it, he admits that the fact "that analytic philosophy sticks out by virtue (or by vice) of ignoring the areas of moral philosophy and political theory . . . may strike connoisseurs of the current scene as absurd, [but] this idea is not entirely without foundation" (Glock 2008, 180). Furthermore, he seems to think that this foundation starts with Stage 2, as Moore's *Principia Ethica* and *Ethics* of Stage 1 make this characterization completely implausible for that time. After Schwartz complains that the early Wittgenstein and many of those influenced by his work "dismissed ethics from the area of serious philosophical enquiry," he argues that they *must* be mistaken because "one can live, I suppose, without any views about metaphysics [but] one cannot avoid having urgent views about what is right and wrong, morally good and evil" (Schwartz 2012, 264–65). Those from outside the analytic tradition tend to agree, with Simon Critchley claiming that, unlike analytic philosophy, "so much philosophy in the continental tradition . . . attempt[s] to produce a critical consciousness of the present with an emancipatory intent" (Critchley 2001, 111).

This is not just later historians of philosophy reflecting back on a previous time saying things like this, either. Actors from the history of early analytic philosophy like P. F. Strawson have said things such as, "more or less systematic reflection on the human condition" is to be contrasted with what analytic philosophy does (Strawson 1992, 2). The contemporaneous view from those outside of the analytic tradition was even more disturbing, with Max Horkheimer claiming that those greatest influenced by Wittgenstein's *Tractatus*, the logical positivists, are connected "to the existence of totalitarian states" through their ignoring ethics and political philosophy, which leads to fear of social upheaval (Horkheimer 1937, 140). A nice summary of the type of view chronicled here is given by Alice Crary when she says "Some commentators argue that Wittgenstein's work is deeply conservative and locate its putatively conservative character in a tendency to undermine the critical modes of thought required to make sense of demands for progressive change" (Crary 2000, 118). Or, more concisely, there is a decent bit of agreement that "it is very unclear how a book consisting of nonsense could have an ethical point" (Cahill 2004, 34).

Of course, it is important to remember that Wittgenstein's work is not particularly transparent at times and is very difficult to interpret. This is particularly so with respect to his views on ethics, as well as sense and nonsense—the two operative areas under discussion. Looking more closely at Wittgenstein exegetes, rather than broader historians of analytic philosophy, the picture on what Wittgenstein meant by holding that ethics was nonsense becomes cloudier. Part of this distinction between the two camps comes from Wittgenstein exegesis paying much closer attention to how Wittgenstein's unpublished works and their development can help us to understand his published work.[5] And, while Wittgenstein's two major publications, *Tractatus Logico-Philosophicus* and *Philosophical Investigations*, did not directly address much of ethics, politics, aesthetics, and culture, this is significantly less true for his *Nachlass*. Though it is not the only work published from his *Nachlass* on such matters, the most significant attention to them is in *Culture and Value*. Von Wright's preface to this work perfectly exemplifies the uncomfortable nature of the scholarship on the state of ethics for Wittgenstein. Von Wright begins by saying of this work on matters of value that

> In the manuscript material left by Wittgenstein there are numerous notes which do not belong directly with his philosophical works although they are scattered amongst the philosophical texts. (Wittgenstein 1980, Preface)

After this implication that value theory and philosophy are separate and disconnected for Wittgenstein, von Wright complicates this by saying "[i]t is not always possible to separate them sharply from the philosophical text," before going even further to say "these notes can be properly understood and appreciated only against the background of Wittgenstein's philosophy and, furthermore, that they make a contribution to our understanding of that philosophy" (Wittgenstein 1980, Preface).

As alluded to earlier, there are also many different interpretations of Wittgenstein's early philosophy of language and logic in relation to sense and nonsense. Again, these will be important to understanding Wittgenstein's views on ethics, as it seems to be central to his view that ethics is nonsense. The most standardly taught interpretation is the *illuminating nonsense* reading of G. E. M. Anscombe and P. M. S. Hacker. Developed later and becoming more popular as an alternative to the dominant view recently, Cora Diamond and James Conant have developed an *austere* or *resolute* reading of, what have come to be known as, the New Wittgensteinians (Crary 2000).[6] While each of these has an importantly different way of interpreting Wittgenstein's claim that ethics is nonsense, we will see that each one of them starts to paint a much more friendly picture for my main claims while still leaving some open questions.

On the standard reading begun by Anscombe and developed in most detail by the work of Hacker, understanding Wittgenstein's early view that philosophy, ethics, and the like are nonsense requires understanding that Wittgenstein believed there to be multiple different kinds of nonsense. Anscombe first discusses this in relation to Wittgenstein's picture theory of meaning, when she says, "there was a residue that would never fit in with it; these he dismissed as nonsensical: perhaps simply nonsensical, perhaps attempts to say the inexpressible" (Anscombe 1963, 79). Therefore, on the one hand, there is simple nonsense along the lines of outright gibberish—strings like "jate ope thwoppymat," which contain terms that have been given no meaning and "red tall seven Carmelo," which combine meaningful terms in meaningless ways. On the other hand, according to Anscombe and Hacker, there is also illuminating nonsense—attempts to say something that only fail because what they attempt to say is inexpressible.

Connecting this to matters of ethics, value, and living one's life, Anscombe says that Wittgenstein "[s]peaks of people 'to whom the meaning of life has become clear'. But he says of them that they have not been able to say it" (Anscombe 1963, 170). This seems to gesture at the essence of the illuminating nonsense reading—the *Tractatus* shows important things even if they cannot be said. Summing this up, Hacker says, "That there are things that cannot be put into words, but which *make themselves manifest* (*Tractatus* 6.522) is a leitmotif running through the whole of the *Tractatus*" (Hacker 2000, 353). Such an interpretation of Wittgenstein's work—where nonsense can be illuminating and, thus, that calling something "nonsense" need not be pejorative—seems to significantly help with my aims. In particular, this helps because such a view holds that ethics is, itself, illuminating nonsense. It is important independent of its expressing a sense. Now, the obvious question would be how *can* ethics be illuminating? While answering this question is outside the scope of this chapter, it is included to begin to muddy the waters given the near-universal agreement from the preceding views that Wittgenstein's early work is wholly destructive of ethics.

Again, the primary contender to the illuminating nonsense reading today is the *austere* reading of Diamond and Conant. According to Diamond, this is the view that "[n]onsense is nonsense; there is no division of nonsense" (Diamond 2000, 153). That is to say, all nonsense is of the same kind according to the austere reading and, like anything that lies outside the bounds of sense, ethics is simply gibberish for Wittgenstein. Here, the only difference between a supposedly ethical sentence like "it is wrong to treat certain groups of people unfairly" or a supposedly metaphysical sentence like "the world is all that is the case" (Wittgenstein 1922, 1) on the one hand and 'jate ope thwoppymat' on the other, is that nobody even *thinks* they're saying anything illuminating with the last.

Much of this austere reading is built off of a particular interpretation of Wittgenstein's view of the specific nonsense found in the *Tractatus* and his famous metaphor of the *Tractatus* as ladder that we must throw away after having gotten up it in the remark: "[m]y propositions serve as elucidations in this way: anyone who understands *me* finally recognizes *them* as nonsensical" (Wittgenstein 1922, 6.54).[7] The added emphases are intended to highlight the view of the austere reading that Wittgenstein does not think there is anything even close to understanding what these nonsense statements say or show. At best, there is understanding a *person* who is inclined to utter nonsense sentences and who has "at most the illusion of understanding them" (Diamond 2000, 150).

Building off of this austere reading, Michael Kremer gives "the very interesting suggestion that one of Wittgenstein's fundamental goals in that book was to expose as illusory all attempts for ultimate justification in logic, metaphysics, and of course, ethics" (Cahill 2004, 46). To understand this illusion, we must go through something like the pages of the *Tractatus*, to try to imagine the pull that would make somebody inclined to utter its sentences, even though they are simply nonsense. After all, "[i]f I could not as it were see your nonsense as sense, imaginatively let myself feel its attractiveness, I could not understand you" (Diamond 2000, 158). So, on Diamond's view, part of the point of the *Tractatus* is to get us to see the importance of this ethical imagination. Again, this seems to give us a way of reading Wittgenstein on which it is not at all clear that my primary theses are in as much trouble as the scholars we started this section with would have us believe.

§4.4 THE SOLUTION THROUGH THE METAPHYSICS AS DISGUISED ETHICS READING

While either the illuminating nonsense or austere, simple nonsense readings of Wittgenstein being correct would block the conclusion that Wittgenstein is not concerned with ethics, they both leave it unclear why Wittgenstein would have been so motivated and still discussed ethics so little. If the nonsense of ethics can be illuminating, then why not engage with this type of nonsense more? He did, after all, try to utter a great deal of illuminating nonsense in the form of metaphysics of logic and language.[8] On the other hand, if we should try to imaginatively engage with those who are inclined to utter simple nonsense thinking that it has sense, why not engage in such ways in the *Tractatus* more?

So, if my main argument is to be accepted, having a response to this worry (that the Wittgensteinian view that ethics is nonsense means there is no room for moral, political, or social improvement to be serious or important to our philosophical outlook) is essential. The way I will attempt to do this will involve building off of a suggestion from Matt Chick and Matt LaVine that there is a group of analytic philosophers for whom "metaphysics may be nothing more than disguised ethics" (Chick & LaVine 2014, 142).[9] In other words, the view is that these thinkers believed we can express, convey, or encourage ethical outlooks without actually uttering sentences containing any terms traditionally taken to be necessary for an ethical claim.

This metaphysics as disguised ethics view was held on to by a number of different analytic philosophers for a number of different reasons. Some were simply so skeptical of any traditional systems of ethics, politics, and religion that they believed getting people to stop thinking about and theorizing about ethics altogether would actually put us in a preferable position with respect to ethics. If all ethical theorizing has had to offer are divisiveness, coercion, and subjection of the many to the few, then we could actually be in a better world without ethical theories at all. And, if that is the case, getting people to talk and theorize about something other than ethics is perhaps the best move. As Russell put it around this period,

> The evils of the world are due to moral defects quite as much as to lack of intelligence. But the human race has not hitherto discovered any method of eradicating moral defects. . . . Intelligence, on the contrary, is easily improved by methods known to every competent educator. Therefore, until some method of teaching virtue has been discovered, progress will have to be sought by improvement of intelligence rather than of morals. (Russell 1935, 127)

Getting more to the namesake for this section—metaphysics as disguised ethics—some others have thought that we could get ethical points across by talking about something other than ethics entirely. That is to say, adopting, for example, certain metaphysical theories would be taken to bear a significant psychological or epistemic relation to a particular ethical viewpoint, even if not strictly entailing it.[10] In other words, one would start with some particular ethical goal in mind, see that there is a metaphysical theory uniquely positioned among the considered alternatives thought to be consistent with our other evidence that leads to that ethical goal as consequence, and conclude that metaphysical view. This is not to say that the metaphysical view would be adopted simply because it was part of a true conditional with the desired ethical viewpoint as consequent. One would still consider the battery of evidence and theoretical virtues they find relevant, but just add ethical outlooks as part of this evidence.[11]

Given that this might seem to be extremely implausible, we should look at how I see it operating in Wittgenstein's work in the *Tractatus*. For starters, we must remember that despite not discussing ethics a good deal, Wittgenstein famously said to Ludwig von Ficker that the point of the work was ethical and that what is important is precisely "all that I have not written" (McGuiness 1971, 16). And, as Severin Schroeder puts it, "[a]lthough Wittgenstein has written very little on ethics, it is probably true to say that no philosopher of the twentieth century was so constantly and seriously concerned with moral issues as he was" (Schroeder 2006, 99). This initially confusing state of affairs would be explained by the metaphysics as disguised ethics reading. After all, he is primarily giving a metaphysics of language and logic in the book. If Wittgenstein was honest and correct about his work, then the book is primarily about promoting a certain ethical perspective. This would mean that he thought the best way to promote an ethical perspective is through a discussion of metaphysics.

So, the question then is how could some of the metaphysical work in the *Tractatus* contribute to Wittgenstein's ethical views? For this, we need to know something about Wittgenstein's ethical views. Following Schroeder (2006), I believe that Wittgenstein's most central view concerning ethics at this time was his moral solipsism—his belief that ethics is not about external connection/persuasion or objective, rational foundation, but rather being answerable only to one's true self, one's true nature. Such an unfailing commitment to one's own character seems to have partly come from his own biography. As a child, Wittgenstein was "eager to please and constantly worrying about the impression he would make on others," but later on "decided to fight against it and at least not be influenced by it in his behavior any more" (Schroeder 2006, 11). As Wittgenstein himself would put his moral solipsism, "just improve yourself, that is all you can do to improve the world" (Monk 1990, 17). Piecing all of this together, Schroeder convincingly argues that

> Wittgenstein's moral individualism explains why ethics is almost absent from his philosophical writings. Since morality has to be an expression of one's natural character, a profitable discussion of moral questions require that one know each other well. (Schroeder 2006, 14)

How, then, does Wittgenstein's *Tractatus* convey or encourage moral solipsism? Again, according to the *Tractatus* account of language and logic, all the things we can talk about are contingent states of affairs, each one of which is of equal value. This means that it could not be the case that some such contingent facts are action-guiding and others not, which would need to be the case for there to be ethical facts. Providing a theory that allows people to see that there can be no ethical facts expressed by language will turn their ethical attention from an external world to their internal selves. This allows for Wittgenstein's preferred relation to the ethical, which "we must not try to state, but must contemplate without words" (Anscombe 1963, 19). Here,

Wittgenstein's *Tractatus* seems to have a metaphysics that encourages his ethics without much attention being paid to talking (or even trying to talk) about ethics.

So, if the metaphysics as disguised ethics view is correct, Stage 2, logical atomism, and the avoidance of discussion of ethical matters need not be challenges to the primary theses of this book. If the metaphysics as disguised ethics view is right, then there is no reason to believe that there was a large gap in philosophy intended to better the living of our lives. Of course, none of this is to say that Wittgenstein or others following him were *justified* in holding such a view. It is simply to say that Wittgenstein calling ethics nonsense does not mean that ethics, politics, and justice are absent from these philosophical theories or irrelevant to their evaluation. In order to see this, we will look at how the metaphysics as disguised ethics view works in practice and build to a criticism of the view by looking at a specific application of it in the metaphysics of race. Because Wittgenstein failed to give many specific views in his writings, we will turn to one of the greatest influences of the *Tractatus*—namely, the logical empiricists.

§4.5 BRIGHT ON THE LOGICAL EMPIRICISTS ON RACE

Since we are primarily concerned with thinking about this metaphysics as disguised ethics view in relation to the book's overall theses on the potential for connections between social justice and the history of analytic philosophy, we will look at the logical empiricists in relation to views on race, specifically. Before identifying these connections, though, we must first get clear on those views independently. For this, we will turn to Liam Kofi Bright's groundbreaking work from "Logical Empiricists on Race" (Bright 2017)—one of a number of Bright's pieces that show him to be among the very best philosophers anywhere in the world exemplifying the politically revisionary critical analytic approach I have advocated (along with Dutilh Novaes, Haslanger, Kukla, and Mills among others). In this piece, Bright looks at the works of eight different logical empiricists over a span of almost forty years in order to argue that there is a somewhat unified, coherent position in the metaphysics of race running through these works—that of voluntary racial eliminativism.

In order to see the significance of voluntary racial eliminativism, it will be helpful to give a brief sketch of the logical space that the metaphysics of race begins from. Being a subdiscipline of metaphysics, it will naturally focus on questions concerning existence and essence. In particular, the focus is on what, if anything, the essence of races are—what *kind* of thing is a race—and do those kinds of things exist in the actual world? There are thought to be three standard types of positions in the metaphysics of race, which can be distinguished by their answers to these two questions (Haslanger 2012, 299–302; Glasgow and Woodward 2015, 449–52; Hardimon 2017, 2–11). Race naturalists hold that races do exist and that their essence is of the type that the natural sciences are best suited for studying them. Race eliminativists hold that races would be naturalistic if they existed, but all of our best genetics since Lewontin (1972) shows that such naturalistic divisions between racial groups do not actually exist. Finally, social constructionists agree with naturalists in holding that races exist and agree with the eliminativist that our best science shows they cannot be naturalistic. Rather, constructionists believe that races are best studies by the social sciences, since they are brought into existence by social processes.

Returning to the logical empiricists' views on race, Bright gives convincing arguments that the logical empiricists subscribed to a particular version of racial eliminativism—one where "human racial taxonomy is an empirically meaningful mode of classifying persons that we should refrain from deploying" (Bright 2017, 9). This is called a *voluntary* race eliminativism because, seeing the way that racial taxonomy and divisions have been utilized historically, one should *choose* to stop using them. That is to say, being prior to Lewontin (1972) and Rosenberg et al. (2002), the eliminativism of logical empiricism did not rely on empirical evidence that there is no good reason to believe that naturalistic distinctions between racial groups exist, as modern forms of eliminativism do (e.g., Appiah 1996; Zack 2002). Rather, this earlier, voluntaristic form of racial eliminativism relied on philosophical arguments. Given what is so often taught of Wittgenstein and logical empiricism, we might expect this to come in the form of an argument that racial predicates are meaningless or nonsense. That said, as the Bright quote earlier shows, this is distinctly not what we get. The logical empiricists' believed that human racial taxonomy was meaningful, but thought they could give good reasons for us to voluntarily choose to refrain from using it.

In order to see why the logical empiricists disapproved of using racial terms, Bright shows that we must look at their views on racial *explanations*. A racial explanation for Bright and the logical empiricists "purports to explain phenomena in a way that involves either referring directly to the racial categorisation of those involved, or by claiming that certain features of those involved track racial categorization" (Bright 2017, 9). For example, somebody arguing that a particular person loves rap because they are black and all black people love rap would be invoking a (clearly spurious) racial explanation.

There seemed to be descriptive and evaluative motivations that the logical empiricists had for thinking we ought to avoid such racial explanations. In fact, Bright looks at what we can glean from six different descriptive passages and two normative passages involving racial explanations in the works of various logical empiricists. Coming up with a summary of these passages, Bright explains that "Waismann, Carnap, and Neurath all suggest that racial theory as they discuss it is biological . . . [and] . . . all either refrain from endorsing or openly oppose the racial explanations they consider" (Bright 2017, 11). Importantly for my view, this opposition to racial explanations was connected to the fact that "[t]he logical empiricists frequently expressed hostility to ethnic or racial prejudice, and support for political acts which promoted more equitable racial relations" (Bright 2017, 13). Since they had not experienced much in the way of racial explanations other than those that connected to racial prejudice, they thought the appropriate political act was to think we should avoid racial explanations and, thus, racial taxonomy altogether.

While the empiricists' writings are not without unrecognized racial prejudice themselves (cf. Bright 2017 on Schlick), this commitment to political acts of antiracism and racial liberation did not ring hollow for them either. As has been recognized more and more, Carnap became active in the black civil rights movement in Los Angeles in the 1960s (Bright 2017; Sarkar 1992). Perusing the files that the FBI kept on Carnap due to his political activities thought to make him a Communist sympathizer over decades reveal that they were watching his activities connected to antiracism more and more toward the end of his life. Carnap also gave some advice, which could arguably be useful today—"the poor white Americans and the blacks should get together then they would have more political power" (Gimbel 2013; Bright 2017).

Slightly less well known were the activities of Kurt Lewin, a member of the Berlin Society for Empirical Philosophy. A social psychologist, Lewin has been "[c]redited with founding modern social psychology, [and] laid the foundations for what is now called sensitivity training as a way to combat religious and racial prejudices" (Creath 2017). Furthermore, one of the reasons these thinkers were so concerned with respect for science was its cooperative nature, believing that logical empiricism allies itself with "movements which strive for meaningful forms of personal and collective life, of education, and of external organization in general. . . . It is an orientation which acknowledges the bonds that tie men together, but at the same time strives for free development of the individual" (Carnap 1967, xvii–xviii). Since they believed their antiracism to follow from this desire to acknowledge the bonds that tie people together, they thought avoiding racial taxonomy, a tool of division, was the appropriate action.

With the specifics and basic justifications for the logical empiricists' voluntary racial eliminativism in hand, it is time to turn to seeing how it exemplifies, what I have called, the metaphysics as disguised ethics thesis. Remember, voluntary racial eliminativism is the view that "human racial taxonomy is an empirically meaningful mode of classifying persons that we should refrain from deploying" (Bright 2017, 9). That is to say, voluntary racial eliminativism is a view about what linguistic frameworks to use—namely, that we ought to avoid the framework of races. This is an answer to an *external question*, in the language of Carnap (1950), the closest thing to metaphysics that many of the logical empiricists would allow for. Furthermore—as Carnap takes all external questions to be essentially value-laden, having virtues such as practicality, fruitfulness, and expedience—the justification for this view is, unsurprisingly, ethical and political in nature. The logical empiricists thought that ridding ourselves of the framework that allows for racist views to be expressed and racist policies to be promulgated, especially those of the Nazis, would help us reach the aim of eradicating these manifestations of racism. That is to say, the logical empiricists' voluntary racial eliminativism was a clear example of metaphysics as disguised ethics.

§4.6 PROBLEMS WITH THE LOGICAL EMPIRICISTS' METAPHYSICS AND ETHICS OF RACE

Now that we have sketched the actual view and how it exemplifies the metaphysics as disguised ethics thesis, we can finally critically evaluate the former as a way to gesture at problems with the latter, as well as what we might learn from them both. Put most simply, while voluntary racial eliminativism comes from a good place, it simply does not accomplish what it is intended to do. In fact, it seems to contribute to the politically problematic myth that the West is post-racial or even post-racist.[12] Yes, it would be great if race were not so relevant to the way that people's lives, opportunities, and experiences were structured. That said, to simply choose to not discuss race is not going to make that the case. We cannot wish material inequalities and injustices away simply by changing one aspect of our linguistic behavior. We will have to address those inequalities, understand them, and change our practices and institutions in such a way that they finally start to undermine those inequities. Of course, nothing I am saying here is particularly new in antiracist, feminist, Marxist, and queer movements across the academy.

In the intersection of psychology and education research, Beverly Daniel Tatum has made a multipronged case for the necessity of having a conversation in terms of racial predicates and investigating racial explanations. Legal cases, societal trends, and academic work from the previous several decades led her to ask "can we talk about race? Are we allowed to do so? . . . do we know how?" (Tatum 2007, xi–xiii). Unfortunately, the history since this time (including the striking down in *Shelby County v. Holder* of portions of the Voting Rights Act, which require looking at voting laws' racial impacts and former Attorney General, Jeff Sessions, rescinding guidance that colleges be free to consider race in admissions decisions) only seems to verify Tatum's hypothesis that we live "in a society that does not encourage—indeed actively discourages—talk about race" (Tatum 2007, xiii). In the intersection between philosophy and biology, Michael Hardimon encourages us to defend compatibilism—"the view that there is a place for both a social and a biological . . . concept of race in medical research" (Hardimon 2017, 150). Such concepts of race and their discussion in medical contexts is thought necessary to deal with the facts that, for example, "substantial racial disparities in health exist . . . a biological expression of social inequality" (Hardimon 2017, 154) and there are some diseases, for example, cystic fibrosis and Tay Sach's, which are "most prevalent within single continental-level racial groups" (Hardimon 2017, 156). In the intersection of politics and sociology, Angela Davis argues that the reason stereotypes that connect people of color to criminalization persist in our society is our failing to ask questions like "why [has there] not been up until now a serious effort to understand the impact of racism on institutions and on individual attitudes" (Davis 2016, 34).

Furthermore, there is nothing unique about race on this front, either. Feminism has always involved a push to discuss things that people had remained silent on. For example, think of the rallying cry of "the personal is political," which has been ever-present since the second wave feminist movement came onto the scene. This was meant to signal that encouraging people to consign certain matters to the private sphere and not discuss them in public was itself an insidious political action. Most recently, the #MeToo movement has been raising awareness regarding, and coordinating opposition to, the silence and lack of discussion surrounding regular sexual assault, harassment, and violence. In the LGBTQAI+ community, there has been a similar push to discuss different identities and labels for them that people refrain from deploying and subsequent silence regarding them and their issues. Julia Serano, for instance, has made the case that "not having a word to describe people who are marginalized by [a heteronormative] double standard makes it difficult, if not impossible, for sexual and gender minorities to organize and carry out activism to challenge this double standard" (Serano 2013, 14). With respect to socioeconomic status, similar calls to not refrain from discussions on matters of pay, wealth, and poverty have been encouraged for moral reasons. For instance, despite its being considered polite to not, we must discuss our salaries with colleagues to help avoid pay inequities.

What Tatum, Hardimon, Davis, and Serano have in common is a call for more, not less, discussion of those identities, which have led to marginalization and oppression. In doing so, they push against an overly individualist understanding of oppression and injustice. Color-blind attempts at racial equity and claims that we do not need to talk about race in a supposedly post-racial world seem to involve thinking that oppression emerges entirely from individual attitudes and beliefs. So, if you do not even give people the conceptual tools to form those attitudes and beliefs, then we can do away with oppression.

That said, with more sophisticated understandings of oppression in the last handful of decades, much more attention has been paid to institutional and structural manifestations of oppression. Carole Pateman, for instance, argues convincingly that there are implicit contracts governing the behavior of the whole of society that are systematically exploiting women to the benefit of men (Pateman 1988). The crucial point here is that this creates the possibility for these structures and practices to continue the oppression *even after the removal of all individual racist, sexist, classist, ableist, etc. attitudes and beliefs*. This is perhaps most vividly expressed in the title of Eduardo Bonilla-Silva's famous 2003 book *Racism Without Racists: Color-blind Racism and the Persistence of Racial Inequality in America*.

So, the failure to recognize the fact that oppression takes both individual and institutional forms seems to be one problem lurking behind the metaphysics as disguised ethics view. In order to get to further significant criticisms we can raise against this view, it will be helpful to remember some of its motivations and what it has going for it. This will allow us to see that part of the problem with this view is that it does not take its own premises to their logical conclusion. Remember, part of the basis for this view is that traditional and dominant systems of ethics and politics often do such a bad job that we would be better off without talking about ethics as we traditionally have. If this were the case, though, it seems like we would not be in a position where we could afford completely avoiding traditional ethics. If these systems are as problematic as some held and they have been so influential, then there will be a great deal of problematic thinking and beliefs among the community. These will need to be critically examined and this can only be done by engaging with traditional ethical theories and their hold on us. This will need to be done in relation to standard ethical statements to repair the associated thinking. In other words, even if one grants that all traditional ethics has been mistaken or misdirected, there is no need to grant that we should stop explicitly discussing ethics.

This is not the only internal critique we can give of the metaphysics as disguised ethics view, either. To see another related criticism, we must first reintroduce Haslanger's account of ideology. According to Haslanger, in addition to conscious and intentional beliefs, "ideology includes habits of thought, unconscious patterns of responses, and inarticulate background assumptions." These cognitive frameworks "functio[n] as the background that we assimilate and enact in order to navigate our social world" (Haslanger 2012, 18). While these are necessary for us to be a part of a community and engage in social life on Haslanger's view, ideologies can be very dangerous and dominant ideologies have been a significant factor in the perpetuation of unjust institutions and political systems.

Unfortunately, this seems to happen in precisely those cases where the metaphysics as disguised ethics view is followed, where the ideology has become hegemonic—that is, when "ideology is invisible to us" (Haslanger 2012, 19). For example, Haslanger tells us:

> No doubt some of the police officers, sheriffs, judges, and members of juries who violate citizens' rights are, as individuals, sexist, racist and classist. There are also serious problems with the laws that govern the American educational system and other state and non-state institutions. However, at the heart of these patterns of racial injustice is a structure of social relations that is ideologically sustained in spite of legislative, judicial and individual efforts to change it. (Haslanger 2017, 152)

Since such "[e]ntrenched ideologies are resilient and are barriers to social change, even in the face of legal interventions," we must encourage social justice by talking about it and bringing it to light, contra the metaphysics as disguised ethics view (Haslanger 2017, 149). For this reason, a significant goal of ideology critique is simply to bring ideology into view as ideology (Haslanger 2012, 19). This can form one part of the two-step process involved in Haslanger's approach to critical analysis of society, of institutions, and of social practices. The first step is descriptive and involves stating the empirical facts about whatever practice is under consideration "in a way that highlights those features that are relevant to normative evaluation" (Haslanger 2012, 16). The second step is to bring ethical and normative terms to bear on the practice in an explicit evaluation.

Importantly, while they are comfortable with the second, explicitly normative, step, Haslanger argues that to this day the first step—the descriptive step—tends to be ignored (Haslanger 2012, 16). This seems to be something that Wittgenstein and some following his thinking believed in their metaphysics as disguised ethics view. For instance, Carnap says logical empiricists shared "the view that all deliberate action presupposes knowledge of the world, that the scientific method is the best method of acquiring knowledge and that therefore science must be regarded as one of the most valuable instruments for the improvement of life" (Carnap 1963, 83).[13] Given this, focusing on the descriptive would be a way to drive this point home—especially since these theorists tended to really want people to recognize the difference between description and evaluation (many were noncognitivists about evaluative terms, after all). While I understand where such a response would come from, as we have seen throughout this section, it seems to have simply gone too far in the other direction. Try as we might, philosophy simply cannot do without description *and* evaluation.

§4.7 CONCLUSIONS AND PREVIEW OF THE REST OF THE BOOK

In conclusion, after analytic philosophy began with a commonsense reaction to British absolute idealism, it moved into a second stage dominated by Russell's and Wittgenstein's grand systems of logical atomism. While there is much that is unclear about Wittgenstein's *Tractatus Logico-Philosophicus*, logical atomism, and Stage 2 of early analytic philosophy, I hope to have shown that it is clearly incorrect to say that they were dismissive of ethics and politics or unconcerned with their philosophy being connected to the way one lives one's life. Quite the opposite is true, in fact. On either of the most popular specialist readings of the *Tractatus*—the illuminating nonsense or austere readings—ethical views are absolutely central to what Wittgenstein was trying to accomplish. On my own reading, the metaphysics as disguised ethics view, this disconnect between generalist and specialist readings of Wittgenstein can be explained by the fact that Wittgenstein thought the best way to encourage his own outlook on ethics was by discussing its complement class (i.e., everything but ethics).

While there is much about Wittgenstein's approach to ethics that was unique, this idea of encouraging ethical and political views through discussion of things other than ethics and politics was present elsewhere in the history of early analytic philosophy. For instance, we saw a prominent manifestation of it in the logical empiricists' voluntary racial eliminativism—racial eliminativism being a metaphysical view that was adopted due to vehement disapproval of the motivations, which have historically led to the use of racial taxonomy and explanations. Investigating this instantiation of it allowed us to not only fill out the metaphysics as disguised ethics view, but also allowed us to see why it is not workable, even if motivated by reasonable concerns. Yes, much traditional ethics has been very poorly done. Yes, to their detriment, philosophers have tended to ignore the important task of accurately describing the actual world. Yes, we must be equally concerned with living our ethical views as discussing the theory and meta-ethical views behind them.

That said, ignoring discussion and theorizing about ethics is a significant overreaction. We cannot fix the mistakes of traditional ethical theorizing without discussing those very theories. We cannot show just how important accurate, relevant description is without showing the difference it can make in evaluation. We cannot see the full impacts of our lived ethical views, persuade others to follow them, or improve upon them without significant and dedicated discussion of them. It is to these tasks that we will turn in the remaining chapters.

NOTES

1. As should already be clear by now, I will not be concerned with putting things the way Wittgenstein would have liked. Rather, I'm much more concerned with Stage 2 as a whole and his role in it.

2. This glosses over some of the metaphysical complexities that Russell associated with molecular sentences. Since Russell will not be our focus of this chapter, I leave these issues undiscussed.

3. It should be noted that even those with completely contrary evaluations of the political nature of analytic philosophy and those who wish to steer it in the exact opposite direction as me have had similar things to say here (cf. Sesardic 2016, 7–11).

4. In an interesting paper on different ways of thinking that philosophy has a linguistic basis, Wittgenstein's student, editor, collaborator, and sufferer of his misogynist rage, Alice Ambrose, gives something like this as a reason for thinking that all philosophical claims are not empirical and, thus, not factual. In particular, she argues that, since philosophers have no laboratories and conduct no experiments, they come to opposite conclusions from the same facts, and they focus on what is possible rather than actual, philosophical claims cannot be factual. Despite this similarity to Wittgenstein, Ambrose ultimately gets to a different meta-philosophy, where philosophers make linguistic proposals. Interestingly, despite similarities, Ambrose also contrasts her views with the logical empiricists (Ambrose 1952).

5. This literature also places much more emphasis on the cultural and societal contexts in which Wittgenstein found himself. For instance, many have made something of the fact that the *Tractatus* was referred to by Wittgenstein's family as "Uncle Ludwig's little book on ethics."

6. Given the fact that Crary's work forms part of an interpretive school, which helps to support my claims with respect to the work of Wittgenstein, it is important to note that she would argue against my primary theses with respect to the larger analytic tradition. In a very interesting recent article, Crary argues that analytic feminism is destructive to truly feminist projects given its methodological conservatism (Crary 2018). For Crary, one is a methodological conservative iff they believe that "the only responsible posture for considering social phenomena is an ethically neutral one" (Crary 2018). While I agree that the project of feminism requires both the political radicalism that bell hooks argues for, but also the methodological radicalism that Crary argues for, I would simply argue that there is room for analytic methodological radicalism. Chapters 2, 3, 6, and the conclusion are an attempt to develop some of the seeds of just such a method built off of the idea that there is a significant and overlooked distinction between objectivity and neutrality.

7. Importantly, this is only one edge of the "frame" of the book that austere readers place a great emphasis on in coming up with their view. The beginning of

the book, the preface, is also given heavy interpretive weight. Given that our goal is not to understand the justification for or evaluate the austere reading, but simply to understand what the view is and what consequences it has for Wittgenstein's thinking on ethics and my primary theses, we will not discuss this aspect of Diamond's development of the view.

8. Yet again, this is not the way Wittgenstein would have put this. I mean "metaphysics" only in the sense of responding to questions about existence and essence.

9. Importantly, this is not the only suggestion we could take to challenge the conclusion from the standard reading. Another student of Wittgenstein's, Margaret MacDonald, considers a reading of political discourse on which, even though different political philosophies do not differ in any factual content, they differ with respect to practical and psychological consequences. This is because "philosophical remarks resemble poetic imagery rather than scientific analogy" (MacDonald 1940, 101). Unfortunately, this has not gotten much attention because MacDonald is another one of the women who has been written out of the history of early analytic philosophy.

10. This is not to say that there cannot be logical relations between ethical statements and descriptive statements. For a critical discussion of these matters in the history of analytic philosophy, see chapter 2 of this book.

11. For further development of a view along these lines, see (LaVine 2016b, 3601–604).

12. It is also important to notice that the problems discussed in chapter 3—implicit bias, prejudice, white ignorance—mean that, even if the West were post-racial, there would still be a significant need to address structural racism.

13. Relevant to this discussion, but more appropriate for chapter 5, is Carnap's remark: "For [Neurath] the strongest motive for [physicalism] was the fact that, during the last hundred years, materialism was usually connected with progressive ideas in political and social matters, while idealism was associated with reactionary attitudes" (Carnap 1963, 51).

Chapter 5

Logical Empiricism and the Scientific Worldview

§5.0 OVERVIEW OF THE CHAPTER

The most vastly misunderstood stage of early analytic philosophy was the third—the one dominated by the logical empiricists (but shared by Cambridge analysts, critical rationalists, and the Lvov-Warsaw School).[1] As previously alluded to, these thinkers are often dismissed in terms of ethics and politics with statements like "the logical positivists 'eliminated' normative ethics much as they had 'eliminated' metaphysics. . . . One can live, I suppose, without any views about metaphysics. One cannot avoid having urgent views about what is right and wrong, morally good and evil" (Schwartz 2012, 264–65). Contra this standard line, I will argue that the overarching framework of the logical empiricists across the world—the scientific worldview—had ethical and political motivations throughout.

Here, I will build off of recent work by Thomas Uebel and others who argue that the logical empiricists had a "political philosophy of science" (Uebel 2005, 2010). Finally, this is shown to be less of an aberration than it might have seemed as other major figures of this stage who were only associates of the logical empiricists (n.b. Susan Stebbing) and those who set themselves in direct opposition to them (n.b. Karl Popper) had similarly political philosophies of science. To again juxtapose with Soames' take on these matters, the view will not be that analytic philosophers of this stage "aim[ed] at truth and knowledge, as opposed to moral and spiritual improvement," but rather they aimed at truth, knowledge, clarity, and rigor in argumentation as one particularly important avenue toward moral and spiritual improvement.

§5.1 INTRODUCTION TO STAGE 3 OF EARLY ANALYTIC PHILOSOPHY AND POLITICAL PHILOSOPHIES

Stage 3 is an interesting case to discuss in relation to the major theses of this book, especially right after Stage 2. Part of the difficulty in discussing the logical atomism of Stage 2 in relation to issues of values, ethics, politics, justice, power, and oppression was that so little has been said on these matters one way or the other. That said, with respect to the dominant force of Stage 3, logical empiricism, we run into difficulty in the exact opposite direction. A great deal has been said about the political intent and emancipatory potential of certain currents in, and strands of, logical empiricism—especially with respect to what has been called the "Left Wing of the Vienna Circle" (henceforth, LVC). For this reason, there is a sense in which this chapter ought to be the easiest of the book.

That said, because of the existence of this literature, there is also more work arguing *against* the kinds of claims I am making with respect to Stage 3 than any other. For this reason, this chapter also creates a unique challenge for my primary theses. Given all of this, it will be important to be more careful and precise about who and what we are talking about, as well as exactly what claims are being made about them in this chapter. As a starting point, we will use the debate between Thomas Uebel and Sarah Richardson over whether or not LVC's scientific worldview constituted a political philosophy of science (clarified by Amy Wuest to a "social" philosophy of science), which sets out the issues and structures the dialectic best. Then, Audrey Yap, Liam Kofi Bright, and Catarina Dutilh Novaes solve the problems brought up.

As mentioned in the introduction, I take Stage 3 to be bounded by 1926 on the early side and roughly 1940 on the later side. This was the time period between the dominance of Wittgenstein's and Russell's logical atomisms and the onset of World War II—before ordinary language philosophy dominated in the postwar years following the destruction Nazism brought to Stage 3 social structures. Obviously, the Vienna and Berlin Circles played a large role during this stage. Carnap's joining the University of Vienna in 1926 allowed the Vienna Circle to be fully constituted in its mature and most influential form. Along with Neurath and Hahn, Carnap would coauthor the group's manifesto in 1929, laying out the scientific worldview, which would characterize as much common ground as could be found among a group of unique and innovative thinkers.

It was also during the 1930s that the unified movement around this scientific worldview would make itself most greatly known through publications and congresses—perhaps most notably the International Congresses for the Unity of Science and the *International Encyclopedia of Unified Science*.

Given the influence that these had, their connection to the scientific worldview, and the caricature of a single-minded, monolithic logical empiricist movement, it is important to note that these were also planned, attended, and contributed to, by those outside of the logical empiricist movement. For instance, Cambridge analysts were well represented by Susan Stebbing, who sat on the congresses' Organizing Committee and the *Encyclopedia*'s Advisory Committee. Furthermore, longtime critic of the logical empiricists and proponent of critical rationalism, Karl Popper, also took part in a number of these conferences and published his famous *Logik der Forschung* in one of the logical empiricists' monograph series. Given the obviously political and public nature of Stebbing's and Popper's work, we will come back to these connections later in this chapter.

Despite the aforementioned existence of a nuanced and interesting debate in the specialist literature, the logical empiricists are much more controversial and drastically misunderstood in philosophical and cultural circles, generally. In fact, I can imagine some who would be willing to grant a great deal of what has been said in the previous chapters, but who would also hold that there is still a core trend within analytic philosophy, which consists of logic-chopping, formal semantics, and generally scientistic philosophy that shuns normative, practical, and public work and traces itself back to the logical empiricists and their idols. But, if nothing else is done in this chapter, I hope to show that this is clearly mistaken.[2]

To begin that work, we should start with the claim that the logical empiricists were not concerned with practical, political, and moral matters. Interestingly, this claim about the empiricists has been repeatedly refuted over the past quarter century by Bright (2017, 2018), Clough (2003), Crary (2006), Creath (2009), Douglas (2003), Friedman (1999), O'Neill (2003), Romizi (2012), Uebel (2005, 2010), and Wuest (2015), among others. Of course, close attention to the logical empiricist movement would lead one to expect nothing else. Bertrand Russell—a man who ran for public office, served prison terms for civil disobedience, organized worldwide social movements, and wrote books on marriage, mysticism, religion, mathematical logic, epistemology, and metaphysics was their professed worldview guru. Furthermore, on the very first page of the first volume of the *International Encyclopedia of Unified Science*, Neurath states the movement was united by a "hope that science will help to ameliorate personal and social life" (Neurath 1938, 1). And, as has been noted many times by the scholars listed earlier, in the midst of the Vienna Circle's manifesto, we read lines like "the Vienna Circle believes that in collaborating with the Ernst Mach Society it fulfills a demand of the day: we have to fashion intellectual tools for everyday life, for the daily life of the scholar, but also for the daily life of all those who in some way join us in working at the conscious re-shaping of life" (Carnap, Hahn, & Neurath 1929 (1973), 305).

I am acutely aware of the dangers of a biographical fallacy here—a philosopher's life need not entail anything about their work. Recognizing this, I will make a stronger, more direct case for their work as political later in this chapter. Here, I only mean to suggest that if we look at the lives of these people, we see many reasons to believe the empiricists to be champions of leftist, liberal, and progressive movements. This seems reason to at least investigate further—the thought being that it would be odd if their lives were *so* completely disconnected from their works. To list just a handful of examples relevant to this suggestion—Neurath was an official of the short-lived Bavarian Socialist Republic. Ayer was the president of the Homosexual Law Reform Society and helped lead the APA away from segregated states after being moved by the horrific disrespect showed to William Fontaine at the 1948 Eastern meeting in Charlottesville, Virginia. Carnap's activities surrounding international peace, civil rights, and due process were threatening enough to the American political establishment for the FBI to have dozens of pages documenting them. Women philosophers and scholars were also invited, engaged, and encouraged at a time when this was even more unique than it is today—Maria Reichenbach, Olga Hahn-Neurath, Marie (Reidemeister) Neurath, Rose Rand, Izydora Dąmbska, Janina Hosiasson, Maria Kokoszyńska, and Susan Stebbing (more on her to come) having strong ties to the group (Brozek 2017). Many of them faced the horrors of the Nazis to boot. At a minimum, their lives, suggest a need for philosophical work that is practical, political, and public. In what follows, I argue that they, indeed, provided it themselves and that we can learn from this work today.

In doing so, I will build off of Thomas Uebel's work on the aforementioned LVC. In today's usage, which has precedent that will be discussed later, the LVC consisted of Vienna Circle members Rudolf Carnap, Philipp Frank, Hans Hahn, and Otto Neurath. As Uebel argues about the term for the group, "[p]rominently, but not primarily, it was suggested by their shared political beliefs" (Uebel 2004, 249). Importantly, so as to keep the specter of the biographical fallacy in mind, "it was also meant to indicate . . . their shared philosophical doctrines and approaches to philosophical problems as evidenced in the discussions of the Circle" (Uebel 2004, 249).

So, the LVC was clearly a group of philosophers who shared political and philosophical views. What we need to discuss is whether or not this was happenstance or if there was an important connection between these shared political and philosophical views. In a follow-up paper, Uebel argues that there is such a connection and, in fact, the LVC developed a political philosophy of science (henceforth, LVC-POL). Pitting this against dominant narratives of logical empiricism, while acknowledging part of where this came from, he says "[t]here once existed another form of logical empiricism that was critical and politically engaged in just the way that, it still seems, Reichenbach's was not" (Uebel 2005, 755). Furthermore, such a view had already been put forth several years prior when Sharyn Clough said,

> Within the Vienna Circle, the search for objective criteria for truth and rational grounds for demarcating science from non-science was at least partly a critical response to European fascism and anti-semitism [sic], especially as these fueled Nazi persecution of Jewish scientists. (Clough 2003, 3)

Again, acknowledging the existence of a much more developed literature on LVC than other parts of early analytic philosophy, we will engage with the most sophisticated portions of this literature and then branch out to what this says about the Vienna Circle, logical empiricism, and Stage 3 more generally. Toward these ends, we will proceed in the following manner:

(1) A section on what I take to be the best arguments against LVC-POL from Sarah Richardson
(2) A section responding to the normative portions of Richardson's work
(3) A section responding to the historical portions of Richardson's work
(4) A section developing a proposal for a logical empiricist inspired critical epistemology and metaphysics.

§5.2 SARAH RICHARDSON'S ARGUMENTS AGAINST LVC-POL

In my mind, Sarah Richardson provides the best arguments challenging the type of critical analytic work among the leaders of Stage 3 that I am going to encourage and argue has been encouraged historically. In a series of two articles, Richardson argues against two theses analogous to my general theses from this book, but which are specific to the LVC. Much like my two primary claims for the whole of early analytic philosophy, one of Richardson's counterarguments is historical and one is normative. In particular, Richardson's (2009a) historical work "argue[s] that while some members of the Vienna Circle saw their work, and science, as politically important, they did not develop a 'political philosophy of science'" (Richardson 2009a, 14). On the normative side, Richardson (2009b) argues that "[the historians' model for an LVC-inspired political philosophy of science] is inadequate to today's best descriptive and normative accounts of science and politics" (Richardson 2009b, 172–73).

If either, or both, of these arguments is convincing, then my primary set of claims would have significantly less justification. Even though I claim that Susan Stebbing (and Cambridge analysis) as well as Karl Popper (and critical rationalism) have been given insufficient credit for their work, the logical empiricists are clearly central to Stage 3. If I cannot justifiably claim to have made a case that LVC and Stage 3 give further credence to my claims that there is much to be gained by bringing together inquiry into social justice and inquiry into, as well as the use of, analytic philosophy and that there is actually some significant historical precedent for this, the book will be considerably worse off for that. Because of this, we will spend the rest of the section developing Richardson's views and turn to evaluating them in the following sections.

Richardson on the Historical Aspects of LVC-POL

Again, Richardson (2009a) focuses on the historical claim that there is not a political philosophy of science to be found among the LVC. The structure of the argument looks something like the following:

P1: Carnap does not provide a political philosophy of science and Neurath does not provide a political philosophy of science.
P2: LVC consists of Carnap, Frank, Hahn, and Neurath.
P3: If Carnap and Neurath do not provide a political philosophy of science, then none of Carnap, Frank, Hahn, and Neurath did.SC: None of Carnap, Frank, Hahn, and Neurath had a political philosophy of science. (Modus Ponens, P1, P3)
CONCLUSION: There was no political philosophy of science among the LVC (i.e., ~LVC-POL). (Leibniz's Law, P2, SC)

Since P2 is simply making clear what the thinkers in the dialectic mean by LVC, we will just need to say something about P1 and P3 in order to complete Richardson's (2009a) argument. Since P3 is never directly discussed, the thought seems to be that Carnap and Neurath are representative enough to be telling of the whole LVC. Given that Carnap is normally thought of as the theoretical face and Neurath the social face of the group, this is not an implausible place to start.[3]

This leaves P1 as the premise we need to put most of our focus on. Three sections of Richardson (2009a) are dedicated to providing historical and textual evidence for P1. One section (§3) is dedicated to evidence that applies to both Carnap and Neurath, one section is focused on Carnap (§4), and one is dedicated to Neurath (§5). The first is rather straightforward and is primarily focused on countering LVC historians offering the Vienna Circle's manifesto and the context of Red Vienna as evidence for LVC-POL, since "careful attention to context legislates against this simple reading" (Richardson 2009a, 16). That is to say, simply because there was involvement and intersection between Vienna Circle members and their writings, on the one hand, and the Social Democrats after the fall of the Austro-Hungarian Empire on the other, that does not mean LVC-POL is true. After all, Richardson argues that "the LVC's association with Red Vienna only amounts to a vague affinity with a paternalistic socialist party reform programme" (Uebel 2010, 215). Furthermore, associating with political processes is not sufficient to establish a specifically political *philosophy* of science, since they "shared with present-day socialism not a particular set of values, but a commitment to a scientific model of intersubjective, collective work proceeding on rational principles" (Richardson 2009a, 16).

With respect to Carnap more specifically, Richardson argues that, despite his commitment to political causes and activism throughout his life, "Carnap was a firm political neutralist, however, in his philosophical work" (Richardson 2009a, 17). Furthermore, this was not accidental, either, as Carnap's noncognitivism actually required that he have a "neutralist stance on the question of science, politics, and philosophy of science" (Richardson 2009a, 17). Second, despite LVC sharing a general outlook on politics and the role of science therein, Carnap makes clear that "[t]his belief in the urgent political importance of the advancement of science, however, was a backdrop of the Vienna Circle's work and not integrated into its philosophical project" (Richardson 2009a, 17). Third, Carnap was unwilling to consider some of the ways in which Neurath tried to interject the political into philosophical work. This is most famously evidenced by their back and forth during the well-known protocol sentence debate. Finally, the end of Carnap's intellectual autobiography (Carnap 1963), the place where Carnap most directly discusses the role of politics in philosophy "makes it clear that the question of *philosophy's* engagement with politics and questions of value was either a blind spot for Carnap or a deep and unresolved tension in his own philosophy" (Richardson 2009a, 18).

Despite the fact that Richardson admits "Neurath was more openly and actively political in his philosophical writings than Carnap," she still does not think that he provides evidence for LVC-POL (Richardson 2009a, 19). Furthermore, when looking into all the myriad ways that LVC historians try to say that Neurath anticipated later criticisms of standardly understood logical empiricism, "the historiography faces tensions and difficulties in moving between a reconstruction of Neurath's philosophical positions from his extant written work and a reconstruction of his actual role within the social and institutional reality of the Vienna Circle" (Richardson 2009a, 19). Such careful historical attention is necessary since "[i]n his early work, he was not party-political and in many cases explicitly disavowed socialist politics" (Richardson 2009a, 19). Rather, he thought of himself primarily as involved in social engineering, which he took to be best exemplified by eugenics.

Furthermore, even when he became more directly involved in politics, "Neurath maintained his self-conception as a neutral social engineer when he became active in public administration" (Richardson 2009a, 20). On top of that, we have every reason to expect that this is what Neurath would have held at least through most of the 1920s, because he accepted the Weberian conception of social science as value-relevant, while still being value-neutral. That is to say, while social science would have to deal with values in the content it studied, the social scientist need not bring values into the study of those values. Finally, even when Neurath seems to become more socially and politically concerned with his Marxism and unified science pushes, "Neurath's locution on the topic of the political content of logical empiricism and unified science, unfortunately, comprise intermittent, inconsistent, and ambiguous commentary over several decades" (Richardson 2009a, 22). Thus, Neurath does not develop a political philosophy of science, nor does Carnap, and we have reason to reject LVC-POL.

Richardson on the Normative Aspects of LVC-POL

From here, Part 2 of Richardson's work moves from the purely historical question over the truth of LVC-POL to normative issues by taking a "look at the claim that there are productive enrichments to be gained from the engagement of feminist philosophy of science with the history of the LVC" (Richardson 2009b, 167). Continuing the trouble for my primary theses, her verdict on this front is that there is lots of reason to believe that LVC and feminist epistemology and philosophy of science (henceforth, FEPS) engagement will yield no fruitful philosophical inquiry. After all, she holds that LVC-POL is false and that, when engaged in politics, the LVC members were in wildly different contexts than FEPS. Furthermore, such engagements have not just been factually mistaken, but morally problematic as, for example, "Don Howard's (2003, 2006) discussion of feminist philosophy of science exemplifies [a] complex of acknowledgment, appropriation, and marginalization of feminist work in LVC scholarship" (Richardson 2009b, 167). Despite this appropriation and marginalization of FEPS, Richardson believes LVC-POL and LVC historians have been very warmly received by analytic philosophers and some feminists. Feeling these last two points are at such odds with another, Richardson (2009b) argues that an explanation is in order along the lines that "LVC historiography operates as a new disciplinary history reflecting anxieties within analytic philosophy of science" (Richardson 2009b, 167). Given that Richardson and I disagree on the amount of uptake LVC-POL has received, but that I agree some of its uptake has been about problematic anxieties, we will focus primarily on her initial assertion of a lack of productive engagements and argument for it.

Putting all of this together, the structure of this second, normative argument looks something like the following:

P1: If there are situations in which productive philosophical work can be gained from engagement between work on LVC and FEPS, then either there are links between them, common ground between them, analogies between them, or it is harmless to engage them.
P2: There are no links, common ground, or analogies between the LVC and FEPS.
P3: Engagements between LVC and FEPS scholarship have been harmful.
SC: It is not true that there are either links between LVC and FEPS, common ground between them, analogies between them, or it is harmless to engage them. (P2, P3, And-Introduction, De Morgan's Laws)
CONCLUSION: There are no situations in which productive philosophical work can be gained from engagement between work on LVC and FEPS. (P1, SC, Modus Tollens)

Notably, P2, P3, and C are all explicitly stated in Richardson (2009b). Furthermore, P1 is a perfectly reasonable implicit premise. In fact, I think it would be reasonable to abide by the even stricter constraint that productive engagement between LVC and FEPS would require such links *and* harmless engagement. That said, the disjunctive consequent rather than a conjunction makes Richardson's development of both P2 and P3 stronger. Hence, these two premises ought to be our focus for developing and then critiquing Richardson's argument.

With respect to P2, Richardson holds that overzealousness for finding commonalities with FEPS has led LVC historians to confirmation biases in their claims of common ground. In particular, LVC historians have overlooked significant differences between LVC and FEPS thinking, both in terms of content and societal context (Richardson 2009b, 170). As for the institutional contexts, LVC consisted of several thinkers in a pre-disciplinary knowledge community without sophisticated, programmatic coherence, while FEPS is part of a large, international body of scholarship with values and social justice in relation to science as primary focus. In this context, FEPS is then dedicated to political/academic projects like "improving the status of women in the science professions; . . . critiquing sexist science; and . . . building both practical and theoretical models for better science" (Richardson 2009b, 171). With these very context-dependent projects in mind, FEPS has a naturalistic focus on science as different local, plural knowledge practices, rather than the LVC's ideal theory focus on "abstract method, universal language, or codified practice" (Richardson 2009b, 171). Hence, we have significant reason to doubt what LVC historians have offered in response to P2.

Shifting to P3, Richardson argues that missing these points of disconnect is so significant that it constitutes not just a historical or factual error, but causes significant ethical problems as well. In particular, LVC historians "fail to acknowledge the streams, circulations, and sources of FEPS" and, in doing so, "reinscrib[e] the view of feminist work as marginal, illegible, and unrigorous" (Richardson 2009b, 172). This seems to be achieved by arguing that FEPS should be given legitimacy only in terms of how similar it is to LVC scholarship or "properly philosophical" work. This has the doubly problematic impact of suggesting that nothing needs to change about philosophy when FEPS does line up with LVC and that it is the work in FEPS, which needs to change when they do not line up. So, despite their own intentions, LVC historians have caused harm to FEPS when they try to engage LVC and FEPS.

§5.3 RESPONDING TO RICHARDSON 2009B

Before I get to the details of my critique of Richardson (2009a, 2009b), it will be instructive to make clear my overall evaluation of them and relationship to them. While I do not agree with her final conclusions in either paper, I do believe that she does very important work and gets a lot right along the way to them. So, while I think Richardson is incorrect that there are no productive engagements between LVC and FEPS, I do believe she has put significant *constraints* on what is needed for a just, as well as theoretically and historically sound engagement. I am not the first to think something like this either, as Amy Wuest argues that "on one reading of Richardson's paper, she encourages historians of philosophy of science to use some of the work done by feminists in order to better achieve their political ambitions" (Wuest 2015, 72).

Richardson (2009b) also recognizes something like this in the concluding paragraph of the two papers, saying

> LVC scholarship must appropriately figure the relevant empirical and theoretical work in fields such as feminist and ethnic studies if it is to avoid the reentrenching of old disciplinary borders, insularities, and narratives that have been hostile to these projects. (Richardson 2009b, 173)

So, in particular, these constraints include that we must not appropriate, marginalize, mainstream, or moderate FEPS. Importantly, as Richardson makes clear, these are not empty constraints and have been violated by some LVC historians. For instance, Don Howard argues that theses like LVC-POL "might make possible our welcoming our feminist colleagues into the mainstream" (Howard 2006, 12). Furthermore, "LVC scholars suggest that the LVC model prescribes a political engagement that is uniquely moderate and middle ground" (Richardson 2009b, 169). Here, I cannot possibly agree with Richardson enough. My own interest in LVC, LVC-POL, and Stage 3 in relation to social justice has nothing to do with mainstreaming or moderating FEPS. Rather, my hope is for the converse—to radicalize LVC and the field generally.

So, despite the fact that this and the next section will consist of counters to Richardson's (2009a, 2009b) conclusions, it is important to note that there is a great deal of agreement between us as well. For instance, even though I want to argue for the importance of critical analytic projects, I agree that nonanalytic and nonphilosophical approaches are equally important. In particular, interdisciplinary work, work that is not constrained by disciplinary traditions, and work that recognizes the lack of distinctiveness of analytic approaches is extremely important. Even more specifically, I agree that "descriptive philosophy of science must appreciate the particular context of an area of science and engage with sociological, ethnographic, and historical analysis of a field of science" (Richardson 2009b, 171). Finally, I agree that after such engagement, "[e]thically and empirically, it is no longer possible to think of science as only a liberatory force or ideal way of knowing" (Richardson 2009b, 173).

Given all of these sights of agreement, one may wonder why I am so keen to counter her final conclusions. A large part of this has to do with how strong of conclusions her papers get to. On the normative side, she gives a negative existential that there are *zero* productive engagements between LVC and FEPS to be had. On the historical side, "LVC-POL-theorists . . . are charged, in short, with anachronisms that would make amateurs blush" (Uebel 2010, 215). Because of this, all that needs to be done is show one potentially fruitful engagement between LVC and FEPS and one genuine historical connection to that engagement. As was done in the previous chapter, I will look to the work of Liam Kofi Bright, which will be followed by a brief discussion of reasons to expect more such fruitful engagements to exist.

As we discussed in the previous chapter, Bright has argued that:

> The logical empiricists often discussed racial explanations, and never painted them in a positive light. They also shared a commitment to undermining racial divisions in so far as they were a basis for divisive political policy. There is a consistent view of the nature of human racial categorisation which could unify and explain the logical empiricists reactions to racial explanations with their general epistemological principles, and which could be motivated by their shared political commitments. To summarise this view: racial categorisation is a challenge to be overcome. (Bright 2017, 17)

That is, Bright has given good reason to believe that there are productive engagements between LVC and critical theories of race. While this certainly does not guarantee there are productive engagements between LVC and FEPS, it gives us reason to investigate the possibility. Upon that further investigation, we find such engagements between LVC and FEPS—as Bright (2018) does this with respect to standpoint epistemology, in particular. As we discussed in chapter 3, "[s]tandpoint theories claim to represent the world from a particular socially situated perspective that can lay a claim to epistemic privilege or authority" (Anderson 2015). In Bright (2018), this staple (though not universal view) of FEPS is argued to go hand in hand with empiricism. Along the way, contrary to what would be expected if accepting P2 of Richardson's second argument, Bright specifically argues that LVC members give an argument very similar to his.

Bright's argument here starts with a basic position common to all forms of empiricism—namely, that experience is the primary source of knowledge. Given this, an empiricist should hold that a person who has had more experiences of a particular phenomenon and thought about those experiences will have more knowledge about that phenomenon. This means that epistemic privilege, expertise, and authority on a particular phenomenon will track experience with that phenomenon. So, in particular, with respect to power relations, injustice, oppression, marginalization, and the like, the greater experience that people with marginalized social identities have with respect to these will provide them epistemic privilege and authority. That is, given that experience is socially situated and that knowledge tracks experience for the empiricist, empiricists should hold that knowledge is similarly socially situated—just what the standpoint epistemologist holds.

As Bright puts it, "in a society with divisions of labour and social roles that track demographic categories then what experiences and incentives to learn you have will track ... group membership" (Bright 2018). Importantly for our project of showing productive engagements between LVC and FEPS, Bright sees a similar argument in section 4 of the Vienna Circle's manifesto. Here, the LVC members suggest that the experiences of those who suffer from capitalist modes of production are those likely to recognize that the scientific world-conception "serves life." As they put it, "So it is that in many countries the masses now reject these doctrines much more consciously than ever before, and along with their socialist attitudes tend to lean towards a down-to-earth empiricist view" (Carnap, Hahn, & Neurath 1929 (1973), 317).

Not only does Bright give significant connections between LVC, critical theories of race, and FEPS, in further work (Bright et al. 2016) he does so in ways that get beyond one of the biggest issues Richardson saw for LVC-POL—that "The Old Left model ... failed to recognize how class oppressions are distributed differentially across race and gender" (Richardson

2009b, 173). As those at all familiar with academic work on social identities from the last three-plus decades will recognize, this is to say that Richardson is concerned that LVC has no way to recognize *intersectional* phenomena. While this may be true of the LVC members themselves, Bright et al. (2016) shows that their work can be put to use in causally interpreting intersectionality theory. In this paper, Bright and coauthors are concerned to join in debates concerning how to put intersectionality theory to work in social science. This is important given that it is contrary to the reasons Richardson gave for P3 from her second argument. On the one hand, some opponents of intersectionality theory have argued that it is problematic because it cannot generate quantifiable causal predictions. On the other, some proponents of intersectionality theory have argued that, by the very nature of intersectional analyses, they do not lend themselves to such quantified generalizations.

Interestingly, Bright et al. came up with a way to allay both of these groups' concerns. In particular, they argue that there are ways to use quantitative methods to causally interpret intersectionality theory, while encouraging a pluralist approach that does not discourage qualitative methods. Importantly for our purposes, they do so using one of Carnap's favored methods—that of explication—saying "[o]ur analysis will address social scientists' concerns about applying intersectionality analysis by providing causal explications of some key claims in the intersectionality literature" (Bright et al. 2016, 62). In particular, they argue that claims of intersectional analysis can be given at least two different explications, which admit of causal interpretation open to quantifiable testing—what they call "non-additive" and "switch" intersectionality.

In the first case, "some causal effects of belonging to multiple identity categories are stronger than one might have predicted from information about the causal effect of belonging to each identity category considered separately" (Bright et al. 2016, 63). For instance, it may be the case that differential pay associated with being a woman of color is greater than one would expect from adding the differential pay associated with being a white woman and associated with being a man of color. In the case of switch intersectionality, "[s]uch claims describe causal relationships that are (de)activated only for individuals who occupy the intersection of certain identity positions" (Bright et al. 2016, 63). This seems to be the kind of case that Kimberle Crenshaw had in mind when first introducing the term "intersectionality" (Crenshaw 1991). There, she was concerned to describe a type of discrimination faced by women of color looking for work in a field that hired women, but only white women, and hired people of color, but only men of color. This work, using tools from Carnap, is extremely important to critical work because "our framework could help address criticisms that have been leveled at intersectionality theory" (Bright et al. 2016, 65) and "much conflicting advice as to how best to test the claims of intersectionality analysis in the social scientific literature" (Bright et al. 2016, 61).

In addition to this work, which shows productive engagements between LVC and FEPS, it is also important to remember a similar such engagement that we discussed in chapter 3 from Catarina Dutilh Novaes. There, we saw that Dutilh Novaes has convincingly argued there were important connections between Russellian revisionary analysis, Carnapian explication, and Haslangerian ameliorative analysis. Inspired by this, the new suggestion I will make in §5.5 will be trying to connect logical empiricist work to Haslanger's (and MacKinnon's) work on assumed objectivity, which we discussed in chapter 2. Before we move on from this discussion, though, it should also be mentioned that there are logical empiricists outside of the LVC for which such productive engagements with FEPS have been made as well. Heather Douglas, for example, has argued that Carl Hempel's work on inductive risk "serves as a useful analytical tool both within feminist critiques of science and in socially relevant science generally" (Douglas 2003, 302). In particular, she argues that researchers abiding by Hempel's strictures would have preempted sexist work on supposed innate difference in mathematical ability between men and women (Douglas 2003, 290–97).

§5.4 RESPONDING TO RICHARDSON (2009A)

So, again, rather than showing that there are no productive engagements between LVC and FEPS, I believe that Richardson (2009b) has shown that there are significant constraints on such engagements. Furthermore, I believe that the work of Bright and Dutilh Novaes show that these constraints can be met. With this out of the way, I want to turn to the historical matter of just how faithful their work is to the LVC members themselves. Remember, Richardson (2009a) argued that works like these would have to be reaching, since LVC-POL is false to begin with. In particular, we should not believe LVC-POL given that neither Carnap nor Neurath had political philosophies of science. Furthermore, she argued for this with historical and textual evidence that applied to Carnap, that applied to Neurath, and that applied to them both. We will look at these pieces of evidence one at a time, but first we will look at whether this evidence would actually provide sufficient justification for the conclusion.

Remember, LVC consisted of not just Carnap and Neurath, but also Philipp Frank and Hans Hahn. Because of that, it is important to point out that it could be something of a hasty generalization to think that if Carnap and Neurath did not have political philosophies of science, then no LVC members had political philosophies of science (i.e., P3 may have been reached by problematic reasoning). In fact, looking into recent work on Frank's thinking, we find much of what Richardson seems to suggest would not be found. For instance, Amy Wuest has convincingly argued about Richardson's work that "[w]hile each argument offers important insights, I ultimately conclude that 'social' (as opposed to 'political') engagement is a more useful and less problematic way of understanding the nature of Frank's contributions" (Wuest 2015, 62) and Frank's work does "invite and encourage value-laden discussions in a manner that Richardson does not acknowledge (where the values in question are not just epistemic)" (Wuest 2015, 102).

In one of her more striking examples, Wuest points out that

> Frank was deeply concerned with the role played by philosophical systems in the apparent legitimation of authority in central Europe. To better combat those systems, Frank decided that it was important to understand them empirically. Following Frank's immigration to the United States, his work would be deeply motivated by these final experiences in Europe. . . . The intellectual focus of his work had changed. His targets would be Thomism, Dialectical Materialism, and Nazism. . . . Eschewing technical work, Frank approached these questions from the perspective of the Scientific Conception of the World. (Wuest 2015, 53–54)

For this and other reasons, "Frank's work centered on two major pursuits: the development of the Unity of Science Institute and a fuller realization of his ambition to bring the philosophy of science into close contact with social/political concerns" (Wuest 2015, 76).[4]

Countering Richardson's Historical and Textual Evidence on LVC

So, even if Richardson's P1 about Carnap and Neurath not having political philosophies of science was completely correct, it is not clear that her conclusion would follow. That said, it seems to me that there is good reason to challenge this view about Carnap and Neurath. Again, Richardson (2009a) supports this premise with evidence about Carnap, evidence about Neurath, and evidence which would apply to both Carnap and Neurath. We'll call these into question one at a time.

Beginning with Richardson's view that Carnap did not have a political philosophy of science, she focuses on the fact that Carnap was, to borrow a phrase from Wuest, simply a philosopher who happened to be political (Wuest 2015, 63). This is better for Carnap, though, since his ethical noncognitivism required him to be a staunch neutralist in his philosophy (of science). Not only was this his general view, though, he actively applied this in his discussions with Neurath. Whereas Neurath was willing to allow his political views and preference for intersubjective cooperation to influence his favoring a physicalist take in the protocol sentence debate, Carnap was supposedly not as comfortable. All of this, Richardson tells us, means that Carnap did not have a political philosophy of science and did not allow for values to come into philosophizing or scientific work.

First, while there are some senses in which Carnap was a "neutralist," he was not in any way that precludes values coming into scientific philosophy. As Uebel (2005, 2010) points out, Carnap breaks the philosophy of science into the logic of science and the pragmatics of science. If there is a way in which Carnap was a neutralist, it is only with respect to the logic of science and not the pragmatics of science.[5] In particular, "[d]ealing with the role of social factors in scientific practice due to the underdetermination of theory, LVC-POL is of course implemented by the pragmatics of science" (Uebel 2010, 217).

Furthermore, while Uebel shows that Carnap's neutralism need not be evidence against LVC-POL, I think he may still have conceded too much here. Even in the sense in which Carnap is a neutralist with respect to the logic of science, it is not by precluding social and political values. To see this, remember that Carnap's views here are driven by his principle of tolerance—"In logic, there are no morals. Everyone is at liberty to build up his own logic, i.e. his own form of language as he wishes" and "It is not our business to set up prohibitions, but to arrive at conventions" (Carnap 1937, §17). This tolerance is actually itself driven very heavily by Carnap's values.

As Richard Creath has argued, such a principle is ultimately about fairness, "the greater good of mankind," and a philosophical program which is concerned with "social progress" (Creath 2009, 209). That said, even if this is an implausible reading of Carnap's own views, it is a perfectly plausible way to apply them. (Remember, I am mostly concerned with LVC for the benefits it can have for FEPS and kindred developments.) As Audrey Yap has shown, whether or not Carnap would have wanted this to be the case, there are important ways in which his principle of tolerance can be quite helpful to feminist projects. Building off of Michael Friedman's work on Carnap's tolerance, Yap argues that "[t]he assumption under which both [Friedman's description and feminist critiques of language] operate is that observations, and the languages in which those observations are articulated, are not neutral" (Yap 2010, 447). Furthermore, "[t]his implies that if sexist principles are encoded in our language, then our observations about the world will also most likely be sexist" (Yap 2010, 448). Turning to the other subdiscipline that my earlier chapters argued is central to analytic philosophy "[i]f logical analysis can give us another way to uncover some of our problematic basic assumptions, all the better to help us determine the potentially radical changes that might correct them" (Yap 2010, 451).

With Richardson's evidence against Carnap discussed, we should be able to find it somewhat easier to defend Neurath as one having a political philosophy of science. Of course, we should not mistake this with always defending the content of that political philosophy of science. For instance, Uebel (2010) tried to contextualize the fact brought up by Richardson (2009a) that Neurath was once interested in eugenics by saying "by the time of World War I, Neurath has lost interest in it because he realized that it was of no use for transformation of society . . . required to alleviate the misery of the largest part of the population" (Uebel 2010, 218). Here, I think it is best to simply make it clear that this is a place where Neurath erred. This is a different case from Richardson's pointing out that Neurath seeing himself as an unpolitical, neutral expert at social engineering would provide evidence against LVC-POL, rather than reason to disavow some of that political philosophy of science, though.

On this front, I believe Uebel does give the right response—focusing on the fact "that 'unpolitical' has a somewhat technical meaning in Neurath's hands" (Uebel 2010, 218). Like Richardson, Uebel believes that the right way to understand Neurath's meaning here is to relate it to Max Weber's work. That said, rather than Weberian value-neutrality, Uebel argues that we need to understand Neurath's being unpolitical in terms of Weberian value-freedom (Uebel 2010, 219). Value-freedom is about recognizing that science ought not to engage in offering unconditional value statements, rather than about avoiding value statements altogether (i.e., value-neutrality). Similarly, Richardson misses Neurath's political philosophy of science by too quickly equating objectivity and neutrality. As discussed in chapter 2, some pictures of objectivity are problematic for feminist work through a mistakenly assumed neutrality, but not all such accounts need to be this way. In §5.5, we will further discuss a way in which logical empiricist views could be put to use to undermine the problematically gendered account of assumed objectivity.

Finally, against the idea that being affiliated with the SDAP in Red Vienna provides some background for thinking that both Carnap and Neurath provide evidence for LVC-POL, Richardson says that "the LVC's association with Red Vienna only amounts to a vague affinity with a paternalistic socialist party reform programme" (Uebel 2010, 215). The idea here seems to be that, because SDAP was paternalistic, so too were the members of the LVC. This might be the greatest mischaracterization from Richardson's work. At least as I see the logical empiricists, they were grouped around the scientific worldview because of the potential it held for cooperation among equals. In this way, I see the Vienna Circle as more like the Haudenosaunee Confederacy than the National Academy of Sciences. They were committed to an epistemic egalitarianism based on "the way of reason, righteousness, and peace"

(Wallace 1986, 34). And, as Donata Romizi puts it, understanding LVC philosophy of science requires that we "conceive of philosophy of science as being also a form of practice, as the expression of an attitude, as a way of acting in the world" (Romizi 2012, 208).

When looked at this way, we see that paternalism and elitism are completely anathema to LVC. This is perhaps best seen in the role that the Vienna Circle members and their associates played in education movements. Bertrand Russell tried to educate the public for more than seventy years and founded a school of his own with Dora Russell. Neurath, himself, is perhaps most widely known for his work on the pictorial language, Isotype. The whole point of Isotype was to be able to get information out to the masses and in ways which would allow for readers to make up their own minds. As Uebel points out, this is part and parcel of "Richardson's neglect of the close connection between the Vienna Circle and the adult education movement in Vienna" (Uebel 2010, 216). Frank also put great energy into putting the scientific worldview to work in education movements. According to Wuest, "Frank's interest in education proves to be an early example of socially engaged philosophy of science. At Harvard, Frank contributed to James B. Conant's education proposals by envisioning them as a foundation that would enable students to become citizens and to more fully participate in democracies" (Wuest 2015, 61). Kurt Lewin laid the foundations for sensitivity training to combat prejudices. Izydora Dąmbska taught at grammar schools and at an underground university during World War II (Brozek 2018). Karl Popper was a secondary school teacher. Much of Susan Stebbing's career was aimed at getting clear thinking out beyond the confines of academia and "the elite." She worked with the British Institute of Adult Education, the B.B.C., and the Kingsley Lodge School for Girls, among others (Chapman 2013).

Putting Logical Empiricism in the Larger Context of Stage 3

As we start to branch out further from LVC, I think it is important to go outward to Stage 3 as a whole. In this way, we can give a context that makes LVC-POL more plausible, since Stage 3, generally, saw a great number of political philosophies of science. Hence, if we are to convince those skeptical of LVC-POL, then it will be useful to show that the oft-quoted remarks of these canonical figures form part and parcel of a larger, entrenched trend toward viewing political philosophy at that time in a particular way. In particular, it will be helpful to look to other prominent figures of S3 connected to and associated with the logical empiricists.

For this, we will start by returning to the work of the far-too-often overlooked, Susan Stebbing. Again, while Stebbing is discussed very little today, she was one of the single most important philosophers of the 1930s and

1940s—being the closest thing to a common link between logical atomism, logical empiricism, Cambridge analysis, and ordinary language philosophy other than Wittgenstein. This makes understanding her views in relation to these matters indispensable to understanding the larger context of S3. This should be unsurprising given the important institutional roles she played at the time—cofounding *Analysis* as well as presiding over the Aristotelian Society and the Mind Association. Again, Stebbing even wrote the first textbook on logic for training analytic philosophers (Beaney 2006).

Most important for our purposes, though, was that she was the main point of contact between the Cambridge analysts (and Anglophone philosophy generally) on the one hand and logical empiricism on the other—the main players in the third stage of early analytic philosophy. In March of 1933, she gave the lecture "Logical Positivism and Analysis," which ultimately distinguished between, but intimately linked together the Cambridge School and Circles in Vienna, Berlin, and Poland. The next year she invited Carnap to give lectures in Britain and meet Ayer and Russell for the first time. The following year she glowingly reviewed four of Carnap's works (e.g., "I think there can be no doubt that [*Logical Syntax of Language*] is a work of outstanding merit and importance" (Stebbing 1935, 510)). The year after that she positively reviewed Ayer's *Language, Truth, and Logic*. Stebbing was also the lone woman on the advisory committee for Neurath's *International Encyclopedia of Unified Science*.

Most important to our present unorthodox purposes is the fact that Stebbing, in addition to being an associate of the logical empiricists, capped off this work of the 1930s with a brilliant piece of political (and very public) philosophy, *Thinking to Some Purpose*. Surprising to many I'm sure, I would argue that the work stands as a striking example of many of the features that purportedly gave John Rawls his originality and made him the "revival" of political philosophy. Glock, for instance, would have you believe this unlikely, saying "Rawls's . . . *A Theory of Justice* was a compelling trendsetter" in that "it marked the rise of political theory, hitherto neglected" by those who would not get "beyond conceptual analysis" (Glock 2008, 59). As Stebbing made clear in the earlier works mentioned, she "maintain[s] that . . . the proper method of metaphysics is the method of analysis" and "we cannot secure reliable foundations unless we recognize that analysis is indispensable to metaphysical inquiry" (Stebbing 1933, 94). Hence, Stebbing was not trying to get "beyond conceptual analysis" at all.

That said, contrary to Glock's presumptions, the preface of Stebbing (1939) makes clear that it is meant to be a contribution to practical and political philosophy—stating that the book grew out of the "urgent need for a democratic people to think clearly without the distortions due to unconscious bias and unrecognized ignorance" (Stebbing 1939, 9). Of interest to those concerned with the current public philosophy movement, the book's genesis was Stebbing's lifelong belief that philosophy has an important role in adult education and was supposed to be delivered as a BBC lecture series. Furthermore, the book contains chapters on propaganda, democracy, freedom, and moderates as well as discussions on abstractions, ambiguity, arguments, Bacon, Broad, vicious circles, conditionals, contradictions, De Morgan, excluded middle, fallacies, logic, prejudice, rationality, rationalization, Russell, and syllogisms. And, coming in at 250 pages, it is a comprehensive work of both philosophical and political thought.

Aside from these ways in which we can read Stebbing's (1939) as a piece of squarely analytic public and political philosophy, there are direct connections between this work and the Rawlsian corpus. One of the staples of Rawls' work from Rawls (1971) onward was his difference principle—"social and economic inequalities are to be arranged so that they are: to the greatest benefit of the least advantaged" (Rawls 1971, 302). In fact, not only has this principle been echoed over and again, Rawls' particular justification for it is equally canonical—since "goods and benefits of society are a joint product of everyone," it follows that "people can be expected to agree to a division of goods that is unequal only if everyone is better off because of the unequal distribution" (Schwartz 2012, 291). While they are not as well developed, the seeds of this idea can be found in Stebbing (1939). Here, in a discussion of arguments over the justification of a society that allows poverty to be a perpetual state for some while others have excesses, Stebbing argues that such a justification would need to appeal equally to "your case and mine" regardless of "my own interests peculiarly important to me" (Stebbing 1939, 53). In other words, such a situation is only justified if it can be justified to anyone, the least advantaged included, regardless of idiosyncrasies of position. Furthermore, this comes in the middle of a chapter which, in stressing that "a safeguard against [prejudice and special pleading] is to change *you* into *I*" in the premises of our arguments, gives a practical maxim that would follow from accepting the importance of Rawls' veil of ignorance (Stebbing 1939, 50).

Furthermore, Stebbing's work is not just an isolated example by any stretch. To see just how much of a trend in S3 is missed by the proponents of the Rawlsian myth,[6] it should be noted that it was not just the logical empiricists and their associates like Susan Stebbing who connected philosophical analysis to publicly and politically engaged work. People who set their entire projects in opposition to logical empiricism, Wittgenstein, and the Vienna Circle did so as well. Here, the obvious case is Karl Popper, who vehemently opposed verificationism and replaced it with critical rationalist falsificationism.[7] Helpful to our purposes is the fact that these semantic, epistemological, and methodological differences were taken by Popper to have significant consequences for our thinking about society and politics. Popper's work in both *The Poverty of Historicism* and *The Open Society and Its Enemies* greatly connects work on falsification and the philosophy of science to political, public, and social concerns. Here, Popper argues that dire political mistakes, such as totalitarianism, and mass confusion result from historicism—an approach to the social sciences, which assumes that good sociology must rationally predict sweeping impending developments of human behavior (i.e., the future course of history) and must do so via methods fundamentally different from the natural sciences (Popper 1957, ix–xi). Hence, no matter where we look in S3, we can find complications for the Rawlsian myth and for the final conclusion of Richardson (2009a).

§5.5 ASSUMED OBJECTIVITY, EPISTEMIC EGALITARIANISM, ANALYTICITY

While this chapter has been focused on history, I am primarily concerned with these matters for their benefits for FEPS, critical theories of race, queer theory, and so on. That is, I am concerned with Stage 3 because I think there are a lot of ways in which logical empiricism and others can be beneficial to such work. That said, like Bright (2019) and Yap (2010), this is not because I think all, or even the majority of, such views are correct. Rather, when it comes to the logical empiricists, I feel like Bright says he feels about Carnap—namely, "when it comes to the philosophical positions he spent most time developing, I do not actually agree much with Carnap on substance," but he "seems to have been a basically quite admirable human being" and "when I see a new Carnap piece to read I tend to be excited, since I anticipate getting . . . [a] sort of fruitful error" (Bright 2019). Because of this, I want to end with one further example from the logical empiricists, which I believe could be helpful to critical theories of many social identities.

So as to make this as substantive as possible, I will choose an example I imagine would be unexpected by many and that covers as much of logical empiricism as possible. This is difficult since, contrary to what was thought throughout the latter twentieth century, there was not a great deal of doctrinal similarity running throughout the Vienna and Berlin Circles and their associates around the world. One such view, though, was a rejection of the synthetic a priori and much of what came with it in Kant. In just the third sentence of the Stanford Encyclopedia entry on the Vienna Circle, Uebel points out that "[t]hey denied that any principle or claim was synthetic *a priori*" (Uebel 2016). Later in the piece, this is generalized beyond the Vienna Circle to part of a "standard logical empiricist story." Creath, too, in his entry on logical empiricism says that "from fairly early on there was widespread agreement among the logical empiricists that there was no synthetic a priori" (Creath 2017).

The claim I want to investigate here is that a rejection of the synthetic a priori can be connected to politically motivated epistemological and ontological views. On the epistemic front, the logical empiricists were concerned about the supposed source of the synthetic a priori in intuition—something that would make public and rational dispute resolution impossible. Avoiding this was achieved by arguing that, for example, logic and mathematics were analytic a priori and "[t]hus defanged of appeals to rational intuition, the contribution of pure reason to human knowledge . . . was thought easily integrated into the empiricist framework" (Uebel 2016). This was then generalized into a view where the analytic/synthetic, a priori/a posteriori, and necessary/contingent distinctions lined up perfectly. Finally, the analytic/synthetic distinction was thought to have priority here, with analyticity being the source of (whatever was reasonable in) a priority and necessity.

While holding that "analytic," "necessary," and "a priori" are necessarily coextensive is no longer plausible, I do think that an epistemology and ontology of modality, which places analyticity at center stage and does so for political reasons is quite worthwhile to investigate. And, while there has been much written on the epistemology of modality over the past century, political relevance is a facet that hasn't been sufficiently appreciated. This is a problem specifically for epistemologies of modality that have an evidential place for intuitions—views that have become extremely commonplace since Kripke's *Naming and Necessity*, which claimed to rely heavily on intuitions.[8] As Herman Cappelen has noted, "the claim that contemporary analytic philosophers rely extensively on intuitions as evidence is almost universally accepted in current metaphilosophical debates and it figures prominently in our self-conception as analytic philosophers" (Cappelen 2012, 1). Of course, as the rest of Cappelen's relevantly named *Philosophy Without Intuitions* shows, not all of this writing has been in favor of intuition-friendly epistemologies. Still, even in these critical works, little discussion has been made of not only the *social and political* implications of an intuition-driven epistemology of modality, but also the social and political sources of intuitions themselves.

Most notably, I believe that various accounts of the synthetic a priori and necessary a posteriori and the role of intuition of essences in our knowing such types of facts seem to lend themselves to what we might call an *epistemic hierarchy*—a belief that some are inherently better knowers than others. Most basically, I believe that the essentially private and contested nature of armchair intuitions hinders the public dispute resolution, which is integral for an epistemic egalitarianism free of epistemic hierarchy. I want to end by outlining an attempt to develop an epistemology of modality, which keeps these concerns in mind throughout as a way to suggest one more potential avenue for productive engagement between LVC-inspired work and FEPS.[9] Before that, I want to quickly outline the reasons for the ontological aspects of this view.

To get to this work in ontology, we will actually begin with some epistemological work from Haslanger. Remember from chapters 2 and 3, she lays out a position for criticism that she calls "assumed objectivity" and which is defined by adopting each of the following norms: (1) epistemic neutrality (where regularities are always taken to be signs of a thing's nature), (2) practical neutrality (where decision-making is dependent on things' natures), and (3) assumed aperspectivity (where observed regularities are assumed to not have any connection to observers) (Haslanger 2012, 71–72). While we focused on problems with assumed aperspectivity before, here we will focus on how we could drop epistemic and practical neutrality while still holding on to a thinner notion of objectivity, which is neither masculine nor collaborative in masculinity, as assumed objectivity is. This is done because both epistemic and practical neutrality rely on the metaphysically loaded notion of a mind-independent *nature* or *essence* of an object. Since both of these can be explicated in terms of necessity (e.g., the property expressed by "P" is part of the nature/essence of an object denoted by "o" iff $\Box P(o)$), the logical empiricists' attempts to reduce necessity to analyticity are again relevant. Given that they wanted this to be a part of a conventionalism which denied the existence of mind-independent natures or essences, such a view would be another way to deny the problematically gendered assumed objectivity.

We turn now to the fully epistemic problem associated with the idea that we have intuitions which give us knowledge of these mind-independent essences. For the purposes of this chapter, I will take intuitions to be defined as follows:

DEF'N: *Intuition* is a (faculty) mode of apprehending propositions that does not rely on sensory experience, linguistic training, or inference.

An intuition then is any particular manifestation of this general faculty and *intuitionism* will be the view that intuition exists and delivers something positive in terms of epistemology. While there are many different versions of intuitionism on this broad definition, as well as many who would deny it, it is still an enormously influential view unto itself and one that deserves critical scrutiny.[10]

Furthermore, it is a view that has played a wholly central role in the work of two of the most influential thinkers on the epistemology of modality from the history of Western philosophy—namely, Kant with respect to his epistemology of the synthetic (necessary) a priori, and Kripke, with respect to his epistemology of the necessary a posteriori. Kripke, for instance, says striking things like:

> Of course, some *philosophers* think that something's having intuitive content is very inconclusive evidence in favor of it. I think it is very heavy evidence in favor of anything, myself. I really don't know, in a way, what more conclusive evidence one can have for anything, *ultimately* speaking. (Kripke 1980, 42)

And

> My main remark is that we have a direct intuition of the rigidity of names. (Kripke 1980, 14)

This is the primary form of intuitionism I wish to combat in this chapter—largely because I hold that to rely on intuitions (especially in one's epistemology of modality) is socially and politically problematic.

Unfortunately, this has not been recognized to a great extent in the mainstream literature. That said, there is a decent amount of literature on, what Charles Mills has called, "alternative epistemologies," which is relevant to this fact.[11] In particular, alternative antiracist epistemologies have chronicled issues like a widespread unwillingness to consider other perspectives, which leads to "systematic historical amnesia about the achievements of African civilizations" (Mills 1998, 23). They have also shown that this involves misinterpretation of one's own background, where

> racialized causality can give rise to what I am calling white ignorance, straightforwardly for a racist cognizer but also indirectly for a non-racist cognizer who may form mistaken beliefs (e.g., that after the abolition of slavery in the United States, blacks generally had opportunities equal to whites) because of the social suppression of the pertinent knowledge. (Mills 2017, 57)

Furthermore, the relationship between these internal and external perspectives is managed by "hegemonic ideologies [that] help to sustain a particular interpretation of what is happening and to denigrate other viewpoints" (Mills 1998, 29). Similarly, Marxist alternative epistemologies have shown that "we should look for structurally generated misperceptions that arise out of the social system" (Mills 1998, 25).

Most directly relevant to an intuitionistic epistemology of *modality*, feminist alternative epistemologies have noted that

> Traditional efforts to justify what we now view as racist and sexist institutions have portrayed women and people of color as "different," and often explicitly

"inferior," *by nature*. In these contexts there is an unmistakable pattern of projecting onto women and people of color, as their "nature" or as "natural," features that are instead (if manifested at all) a product of social forces. (Haslanger 2012, 148–49).

Furthermore, this has meant that many feminists have spent a great deal of time unearthing the assumptions built into pictures that posit a women's nature and "it has been a primary goal of feminist theory to challenge the givenness, naturalness, and stability of [such] picture[s]" (Haslanger 2012, 150).

What all of these alternative epistemologies have in common is the recognition that many of our immediate inclinations to believe are conditioned by our positions within unjust, oppressive social systems. Given that intuitions would seem to be some of the beliefs that flow out of these inclinations, this work would seem to show that we should be skeptical of any view that assigns a positive epistemic value to such intuitions. This is especially the case given that Mills has argued that "white ignorance is best thought of as a cognitive tendency—an inclination, a doxastic disposition—which is not insuperable" (Mills 2017, 59–60). That is to say, we can get beyond these unjust intuitions if we continue to openly reflect, investigate, listen to testimony, and so on. So, we should not be happy to stop an investigation when we stumble upon an intuition. Rather, this should be the beginning of a deconstructive investigative process.

Second, and more crucially for my argument here, is that by relying on intuitions, one somewhat blocks the ability to publicly challenge them. It is more difficult to challenge someone's belief if we allow intuitions as evidence, rather than explicit arguments. By not being subject to public and empirical verifiability, the offering of intuitions can actually harm public discourse. In other words, it seems that not being strict about verifiability allows the door to open for truly problematic and *private* intuitions to enter into *public* discourse. Public discourse, as has been variously claimed by thinkers from Kant to Wollstonecraft to Rawls to Sen, should abide by constraints of public reason. That is, when justifying our beliefs to others, we should, as a matter of treating all as free and equal, only use reasons justifiable, verifiable, or acceptable to all. But, there is no method of public dispute resolution when one's intuition-delivered judgments conflict with another's. And, to go on believing something via intuition in such a situation is to inherently trust one's intuition over another's. That is to say, it is to take one to be an inherently better knower than another—it is to deny epistemic egalitarianism and accept an epistemic hierarchy. This, I believe, is simply unacceptable.

So, to summarize, I believe that there are at least two distinct social and political worries connected to intuitionistic epistemologies of modality, which have been underappreciated. One of these is an empirical worry and the other theoretical. For the former, those beliefs identified as intuitions are very often the result of, or at least significantly conditioned by, social structures, many of which might be unjust in their own rights. Even if this were not the case, though, there would be significant social damage done by intuitionism to the potential of robust public reason. Private intuitions are simply not public enough to satisfy such requirements and, without this public access allowing for verification procedures, to believe one's intuitions trump somebody else's is to not treat all knowers as free and equal. I will be looking to sketch an epistemology of modality motivated by these worries.

An Updated Political Theory of Analyticity

So, I hold that this is one of the sources of the logical empiricists' doctrines on analyticity—the belief that we must not allow intuition or pure reason as a source of knowledge or justified belief because of how it would disrupt public methods of dispute resolution, an important component of public reason. A doctrine of analyticity was central to this project because the synthetic (necessary) a priori was the traditional source of Kant's claiming we had knowledge from pure intuition. The logical empiricists understood the *analytic* a priori just fine—analytic truths come from our meaning conventions, some of our meaning conventions can be accessed a priori, and so, some of our knowledge of analytic truths will be a priori. Hence, an epistemology free of intuition seemed to require an account free of only the synthetic a priori.

Unfortunately, the most influential logical empiricist strategy for achieving this identified the extensions of "analytic," "necessary," and "a priori" on the one hand, and "synthetic," "contingent," and "a posteriori" on the other. This left their rejection of intuitionism and the associated epistemology of modality vulnerable to Kripke's discovery of the necessary a posteriori and contingent a priori. What would a *contemporary* epistemology of modality that is attentive to the public reason related dangers of intuitions look like, then? I believe it needs to:

(1) Ground knowledge of necessary truths in something other than intuition
(2) Ground a priori knowledge in something other than intuition
(3) Explain how there can still be necessary a posteriori and contingent a priori knowledge

Here, I build toward showing how a linguistic (i.e., analytic) account of necessity and a priority (i.e., an account that satisfies desiderata (1) and (2)) could be achieved with contemporary accounts of analyticity replacing those of the logical empiricists. In particular, I will build off of the recent work of Paul Boghossian and Gillian Russell on the analytic/synthetic distinction (henceforth, A/S).

Boghossian's most significant contribution to the discussion has been a separation between quite distinct notions of analyticity at play in the traditional literature on A/S. According to Boghossian, one of these, the metaphysical notion, is the source of what he calls the "analytic theory of necessity" (henceforth, ATN)—the logical empiricist's doctrine that there is a linguistic explanation of all necessary truths (i.e., the logical empiricist solution to (1) above) (Boghossian 1996, 366). And the other, the epistemic notion, is the source of the "analytic theory of the a priori" (henceforth, ATA)—the logical empiricist's view that there is a linguistic explanation of a priori knowledge (i.e., the logical empiricist solution to (2) above) (Boghossian 1996, 364).

While Boghossian unfortunately never gives us explicit definitions, which state precisely what he intends to be included in ATN and ATA, we can infer some possibilities from comments such as

> It was, therefore, an important threat to the analytic theory of the a priori to find Quine arguing, in one of the most celebrated articles of the century, that the a priority of no sentence could be explained by appeal to its Frege-analyticity, because no sentence of a natural language could be Frege-analytic. (Boghossian 1996, 369)

Here we see that Boghossian holds that, since any sentence's a priority being *explained* by its analyticity requires that *it actually be* analytic, ATN and ATA require at the very least holding that there are analytic sentences and that

(ATN) All necessary propositions are expressed by sentences that are analytic.
(ATA) All a priori knowledge is of propositions grasped (i.e., entertained and understood) via sentences that are analytic.

Given that the prevailing view since Kripke (1980) came onto the scene has been that there are necessary a posteriori and (perhaps) contingent a priori truths, that there would be such a distinction between the source of necessity and the source of a priority should have some prima facie plausibility.

Furthermore, this feeling is only bolstered by the clarity and distinctness of the definitions Boghossian does give to these two notions:

DEF'N: A sentence, S, is *metaphysically-analytic* iff S is true and S "owes its truth value completely to its meaning, and not at all to 'the facts'." (Boghossian 1996, 363)
DEF'N: A sentence, S, is *epistemically-analytic* iff "mere grasp of **S**'s meaning ... suffices for ... being justified in holding **S** true." (Boghossian 1996, 363)

On the face of it, Boghossian is right to call these distinct notions. Metaphysical analyticity (henceforth, MA) yields truth and is a property determined by the truthmakers and ontological status of certain sentences. Epistemic analyticity (henceforth, EA), on the other hand, yields knowledge and is a property determined by the type of warrant available for certain sentences. While there could ultimately be a connection between a sentence's truthmaker and the type of warrant available for belief in what that sentence expresses via some principle along the lines of, one knows a truth iff they have epistemic access to its truthmaker, this would be a significant discovery, not the triviality it would be if these were two different explications of the same notion.

While he spends most of his time dealing with the EA/MA distinction, Boghossian does take time to separate this distinction from the ATA/ATN distinction. But, while he thinks they are ultimately not the same, Boghossian does claim that there is a tight connection between these distinctions. In particular, he holds that ATA would fall along with EA (if it did) and ATN, in fact, falls along with MA. Less metaphorically, he thinks that each of the following conditionals is true:

(EA-ATA) If there are no EA sentences, then there can be no ATA.
(MA-ATN) If there are no MA sentences, then there can be no ATN.

From what I can tell, though, this way of viewing things misses part of the point of Boghossian's own work. Once we have got two different notions of analyticity, won't there be two different interpretations of ATA and ATN? That is, once we have got two readings of "analytic" there will be two different readings of an assertion made with the sentence "all a priori truths are analytic," namely,

(ATA1) All a priori knowledge is grasped via sentences which are EA.
(ATA2) All a priori knowledge is grasped via sentences which are MA.

Furthermore, somebody claiming that all necessary truths are analytic could be claiming either of the following:

(ATN1) All necessary truths are expressed by sentences that are EA.
(ATN2) All necessary truths are expressed by sentences that are MA.

In other words, just as Boghossian feels one of the main points of his paper is that "the two notions of analyticity are distinct and that the analytic theory of the a priori needs only the epistemological notion" (Boghossian 1996, 363), I believe that his paper has also shown that the analytic theory of necessity needs only the epistemological notion as well. Furthermore, while there would seem to be something of a concession in, for example, the logical empiricist's denying ATN2, a further defense of ATN1 in addition to Boghossian's thorough defense of ATA1 would seem to justify a new linguistic and anti-intuitionistic philosophy of sorts. In order to see this, consider the following argument such a theorist could give:

P1: All philosophical truths are either necessary or a priori.
P2: All a priori knowledge is of propositions expressed by analytic sentences. (ATA1)
P3: All necessary propositions are expressed by analytic sentences. (ATN1)
CONCLUSION: All philosophical truths are analytic.

This is obviously all unbelievably sketchy and speculative at this point—this chapter having done very little to motivate belief in any of the premises. It is just meant to show another reason that ATN should not be dropped as quickly as Boghossian has. Interestingly enough, Gillian Russell has perhaps shown a further disambiguation that needs to be made in thinking about ATN, which she discusses under the heading "Linguistic Doctrine of Necessary Truth" (or "L-DONT" for short) (Russell 2010). Here, she points out that, once we remember that all that was being sought was a linguistic explanation of *necessity*, one could drop the requirement that ATN requires that all necessary truths are analytic or that all necessary truths were made true by linguistic convention and move to the "weaker claim . . . that all necessary truths have their modal status as a result of our linguistic conventions" (Russell 2010, 269). This could be made perfectly consistent with, for example, the Meaning-Truth Truism (often held to be a problem for theories of A/S),

(MT) S is true iff there exists some proposition, p, such that: S means that p and p, and a denial of MA by claiming something along the lines of:
(ATN3) While necessary truths are not all analytic and are all true independently of our linguistic conventions, their status as necessary is a result of our linguistic conventions regarding the sentences expressing those language-independent truths.

Precisely how this would be cashed out is beyond the scope of this chapter, but its mere possibility shows that even if Boghossian's attempted refutation of MA is successful, more needs to be done to undermine ATN.[12]

Furthermore, I believe that Boghossian's work shows that one need not drop a neo-logical empiricism or adopt intuitionism because of the necessary a posteriori or the contingent a priori (i.e., that (3) mentioned earlier can be accommodated as well). One need only drop the identification of the extensions of "analytic," "necessary," and "a priori" (n.b. the view that all analytic truths express necessary propositions and are known a priori) and adopt some combination of

(1) There exist instances of EA.
(2) There exist instances of MA.
(3) ATA is true.
(4) ATN is true.

With multiple forms of analyticity and with multiple ways for those forms to do theoretical work, we can see the contingent a priori and necessary a posteriori as perfectly consistent with a denial of the synthetic a priori and intuitionism. ATA says that all a priori truths are analytic and, hence, cases of the contingent a priori would be cases of the contingent analytic a priori. ATN3 says that the sentence that "p is necessary" is analytic for some necessary a posteriori proposition, p and not that p is analytic. I believe that this could be achieved with a compromise between Boghossian's own views and those from Gillian Russell in the most well-worked out piece on A/S, Russell (2008). Unfortunately, such a discussion is outside of the scope of this work.[13]

§5.6 CONCLUSIONS AND QUESTIONS MOVING FORWARD

The advanced state of this particular discourse allows me to state my conclusions here very succinctly. Uebel has gotten something right with LVC-POL. Richardson has gotten something right with the constraints she has put on it. Wuest has clarified this debate by focusing on social/political philosophies of science. Bright and Dutilh Novaes have shown that LVC work engaging deeply with FEPS and critical race theory can be productive. This is all made more plausible by the fact that Susan Stebbing, Izydora Da̦mbska, Karl Popper, and others during Stage 3 had social/political philosophies of the scientific worldview. Furthermore, there are other areas in LVC, FEPS, and critical race theory intersections, which could be places of fruitful engagement. As we saw, a new, LVC-inspired theory of analyticity could serve critical race theoretic alternative epistemologies and the feminist fight against assumed objectivity. Finally, I hope to see others continue the work of Bright, Dutilh Novaes, Haslanger, Mills, and Yap to find more such examples.

NOTES

1. Though these are the groups that were most dominant or written about the most, it is important to recognize that there were centers outside of these that made significant contributions to Stage 3 (e.g., Hans Reichenbach, Richard von Mises, and Hilda Geiringer in Istanbul or Feng Youlan and Tscha Hung in China or Juan David García Bacca, Antonio Caso, Nicolás Molina Flores, and Eduardo García Maynez in Mexico). In future work, I hope to dedicate time to arguing that one of the biggest issues keeping critical analytic projects from happening more is a rampant Eurocentrism in analytic philosophy.

2. To be clear, I hold that such a trend cannot be traced back to the logical empiricists—not that it does not exist.

3. It may also be that Richardson is building off of Uebel's distinction between more radical (Neurath, Frank) and more neutral (Carnap, Hahn) members of the LVC (Uebel 2005, 760). In that case, there is more structure built into it, but the argument is still inductive at that step—saying an argument about a sample of the members gives us good reason to hold something of the whole target group.

4. A particularly apt quote that Wuest includes is "Scientists and scientifically minded people have often been inclined to say that these "nonscientific" influences upon the acceptance of scientific theories are something which "should not" happen; but since they do happen, it is necessary to understand their status within a logical analysis of science. We have learned by a great many examples that the general principles of science are not unambiguously determined by the observed facts. If we add requirements of simplicity and agreement with common sense, the determination becomes narrower, but it does not become unique. We can still require their fitness to support desirable moral and political doctrines. All of these requirements together enter into the determination of a scientific theory (Frank 1957, 355)."

5. Again, to make clear that there is more agreement than disagreement between Richardson and myself, I would agree that Carnap can be accused of overemphasizing the logic of science to the detriment of the pragmatics of science.

6. Importantly, while there are analytic philosophers who show that there are problems with the Rawlsian myth, the greatest problems with the Rawlsian myth are from those in oppositional and marginalized traditions.

7. For an interesting discussion of Popper's philosophy of science in relation to political matters and Rawls' work, in particular, see pp. 286–90 of Schwartz (2012).

8. See especially Kripke's Preface to the 1980 edition. One cannot go even a couple pages without seeing comments on the immense importance of intuitions.

9. Note that, in endorsing epistemic egalitarianism—the view that nobody is an inherently better knower than any other—I am not denying that there is such a thing as expertise or that there are contingently better-knowers. That is, the word "inherently" is very important here. Expertise is not something one is born with. It is something that somebody acquires by going through processes which are, in principle, available to anyone. Thus, the source of this expertise would be something public, rather than a better faculty of private intuition. I take all of this to be a part of standpoint epistemology.

10. See especially chapters 1, 3, 6, and 11 of Cappelen (2012), as well as the Introduction and chapters 1, 5, 6, and 7 from Williamson (2007) for evidence of the influence of intuitionism on the epistemology of modality and philosophy, generally.

11. For other examples of work attentive to alternate epistemologies or epistemologies that pay attention to alternate perspectives consider Fricker (2007), Alcoff (2006), Medina (2012), Landemore (2012), and Bohman (2012).

12. In fact, Ted Sider has given a sketch of a very interesting version of this view in Sider (2003).

13. Since this section, like all of my thoughts on analyticity, builds off of my dissertation, see LaVine (2016a) for further discussion.

Chapter 6

Black Lives Matter and the Logic of Conversation

§6.0 OVERVIEW OF THE CHAPTER

In this chapter, I will argue for the claim that trying to replace, or even respond to, someone's saying "Black lives matter" with someone's saying "all lives matter" is mistaken and misdirected. Furthermore, I will show how we can utilize Paul Grice's logic of conversation—one of the primary contributions of the fourth stage of early analytic philosophy—to build a strong case for this thesis. Finally, along the way, I will try to gesture at reasons I believe that work along these lines is both practically useful and at the very heart of the philosophical enterprise. Put rather broadly, I believe that the Black Lives Matter movement is one of the more important forces in American society today and philosophers should hope to support real-world movements for rationality and morality like Black Lives Matter.

§6.1 HISTORICAL INTRODUCTION TO STAGE 4

The fourth stage of early analytic philosophy—that which I will call the period of ordinary language philosophy—differs markedly from the first three. Moore, Russell, and others explicitly saw themselves as breaking free from absolute idealism and other fashionable trends in similar ways to start the first stage. Exemplifying what I identified as the second stage, Russell and Wittgenstein recognized an affinity and influence between their works, while "logical atomism" was a term that Russell came up with for their own ideas. Throughout the third stage, Carnap, Frank, Hahn, Neurath, Stebbing, and others saw logical empiricism as part of a larger international movement unified by a core commitment to the scientific worldview. Ordinary language philosophy was not this way, though. The main players associated with it, philosophers like J. L. Austin, Paul Grice, Gilbert Ryle, and Ludwig Wittgenstein, did not call themselves "ordinary language philosophers," did not see themselves as unified or as part of a larger movement, and did not even have much in the way of similar positive, substantive, philosophical commitments.

Rather, what these thinkers had in common and what makes grouping them together worthwhile was a worry that too much faith in, and attention to, ideal languages in formal, logical, and scientific contexts can be, and had been, taken problematically far. Austin worried that this would make us forget that we do much more with language than describe and report. Wittgenstein worried that this would make us overestimate the finality, precision, and systematicity of language. Grice, on the other hand, worried that we would underestimate the amount and type of information conveyed by an utterance if we only had its formal, logical implications in mind.

Because of this lack of historical unity among the most important thinkers for ordinary language philosophy, this chapter will focus much less on how the fourth stage itself was *actually* concerned with social and political matters.[1] Instead, we will look more directly at how those with contemporary concerns *could* use ordinary language philosophy to help their causes. Furthermore, because this has already been done with Austin's work in chapter 1 and because Wittgenstein's later work does not allow for brief synopsis, we will focus on the work of Paul Grice. In particular, we shall look at how Grice's work on the philosophy of language (n.b. his logic of conversation) can be used to clarify the message of, and support, the Black Lives Matter movement (n.b. in relation to the debate over saying "Black lives matter" and "all lives matter").

Before we apply the logic of conversation to the debate over "Black lives matter" and "all lives matter," one further point must be made. Because I would argue that analytic philosophy is very naturally connected to public advocacy of movements like Black Lives Matter, it is important in discussing Grice's logic of conversation to recognize just how central his work has been to the development of analytic philosophy at-large. Put in this context, Grice's work on the logic of conversation can be seen to be of major transitional importance. Not only did this thinking grow out of many of the concerns of ordinary language philosophers, insofar as it showed that there are many more factors than the direct and literal meaning of a sentence, which determine when it is appropriate to use it, Grice also helped bring an end to the period dominated by ordinary language philosophy. Furthermore, since this latter process formed a large part of the transition out of the early phase of analytic philosophy (roughly 1898–1970), Grice's work can reasonably be claimed to be a classic and paradigm of the entire analytic tradition in philosophy. Again, that it naturally provides defenses of the Black Lives Matter movement should not be taken lightly. Rather, it should continue to make us think that analytic philosophy has lost its way with such a prevalent self-conception of it being politically neutral.

§6.2 THE ARGUMENT'S PRELIMINARIES

Black Lives Matter is arguably the most well-known political movement in America today. So entrenched is this movement that even its detractors have taken a page from their playbook. As *Daily Show* and *Saturday Night Live* veteran Michael Che has hilariously chronicled the dialectic, these critics

> don't tell you Black lives don't matter. That's not what they say—that's not the argument. They hit you with that slick shit—"well, *all* lives matter." Really, semantics? That'd be like if your wife came up to you and was like "do you love me" and you were like "baby, I love everybody, what are you talking about? I love all God's creatures. What are you saying? You're no different." (Che 2016)

Given that I am trained as a philosopher and mathematician, many are surprised when I start a talk or a piece of writing with comedic insights like this. That said, I think such surprise misunderstands both comedy and philosophy—they have much to give each other.[2] After all, comedy and philosophy at their best both seem to be about holding up a mirror to ourselves to critically reflect upon something we were missing, despite its being so close.

Following Che, I will argue here for the claim that trying to replace, or even respond to, someone's saying "Black lives matter" with someone's saying "all lives matter" is mistaken and misdirected.[3] Furthermore, I will show how, in addition to comedy, we can utilize Paul Grice's logic of conversation to build a strong case for this thesis. Finally, along the way, I will try to gesture at reasons I believe that work along these lines is both practically useful and at the very heart of the philosophical enterprise. Put rather broadly, I believe that the Black Lives Matter movement is one of the more important forces in American society today and that, by the very nature of philosophy, philosophers should be turning their methods toward issues of public concern such as this.[4] After all, one is simply not paying attention to the world around us if they think rationality and morality are anything but sorely needed in our public discourses. If philosophers understand these concepts as well as we claim to, we should hope to support real-world movements for rationality and morality like Black Lives Matter.

With all of that said, I have three main goals in this chapter. First, I wish to defend "Black lives matter" as a slogan against "all lives matter" by claiming that the latter violates the maxims of quantity and relevance from Grice's logic of conversation. Second, I wish to show that the Gricean analysis, in particular, provides a practically useful response to two standard objections given by critics of the Black Lives Matter movement. Third, I wish to briefly touch on why the first two goals represent significant findings going forward for both the public and the academic philosophy. In what follows, we will work toward these goals in order by progressing through the following sections:

(1) on the goals and purposes of the Black Lives Matter movement
(2) a snappy, nontechnical defense of "Black lives matter" over "all lives matter"
(3) a general introduction to Grice's logic of conversation
(4) the logic of conversation as applied to "Black lives matter" and "all lives matter"
(5) using the Gricean framework to respond to critics of "Black lives matter"
(6) "all lives matter," color-blindness, and oppressive (contractual) ignorance
(7) a discussion of the preceding in relation to related slogans of kindred movements
(8) the importance of slogans in the Civil Rights-Black Power movement.

§6.3 BACKGROUND ON THE BLACK LIVES MATTER MOVEMENT

As I will be arguing that Grice's Cooperative Principle from the logic of conversation gives us reasons to support and endorse the Black Lives Matter slogan and because conversational contexts are essential to the logic of conversation, I think it is important to provide a brief context for asserting "Black lives matter." This seems especially necessary given the discouraging extent to which critics of saying "Black lives matter" have remained ignorant of, or have purposefully distorted, the goals and purposes of the Black Lives Matter movement entirely.[5] Because of this, I would like to briefly present some of these stated goals and purposes that are so crucial to understanding the goals and purposes of an utterance of "Black lives matter."

Here, I stick to the explicitly stated goals and purposes of the movement's creators, Alicia Garza, Opal Tometi, and Patrisse Cullors, so as to make my purpose in writing this chapter very clear. This is not an attempt to rationally reconstruct the movement, or to say that it is in need of a defense, or to co-opt it in some other way. Rather, this is an attempt to support the movement, as is, with yet another way of explaining why we should all want to say "Black lives matter" rather than "all lives matter." To have such widespread appeal, it is best to have many different strategies for gaining allies. I think that Grice's logic of conversation and analytic philosophy, generally, can motivate one such strategy.

From her story initially published on the official Black Lives Matter website, Alicia Garza reports that the movement began as

> a response to the anti-Black racism that permeates our society and also, unfortunately, our movements. Black Lives Matter is an ideological and political intervention in a world where Black lives are systematically and intentionally targeted for demise. It is an affirmation of Black folks' contributions to this society, our humanity, and our resilience in the face of deadly oppression. (Garza 2014)

What is particularly important for our purposes is that this means that the relevant conversational context of an utterance of "Black lives matter" is doubly Black-centered. First, it is part of a discussion of systematic oppression of black people in the United States and around the world. Second, it is a response to the need to acknowledge and affirm black peoples' contributions to the civilizations that have subjugated them and their own cultures.

It is, unfortunately, outside of the scope of this or any one chapter to summarize any of the myriad contributions to civilizations from black folks that the Black Lives Matter movement aims to affirm.[6] Thankfully, though, Garza has nicely summarized in her story some of the current oppression that the Black Lives Matter movement aims to dismantle (of course, this is to not even mention anything about the previous 500 years of oppression).[7] In particular, we must recognize, understand, and address the systems which lead to rampant poverty in black communities. As of 2018, 22 percent of black Americans lived in poverty and 24 percent of Indigenous Americans, compared to 9 percent of white Americans (Kaiser Family Foundation 2020). We must recognize, understand, and address the variety of unjust systems which have led to roughly 1 million black people incarcerated in the United States. Racial profiling, sentencing disparities, differential access to legal counsel, differential police presence, and so on have created a situation where "African Americans are incarcerated at more than 5 times the rate of whites" (NAACP 2020). We must recognize, understand, and address the myriad ways in which institutions around the United States have relentlessly assaulted black women. For instance, as of 2017, black women earn just 60.8 percent of the annual earnings of white men (Hegewisch 2018).

This just scratches the surface, though, as black children are exposed to much greater danger as well, being five times as likely to have lead poisoning than white children (Smiley 2016, 202). Increased danger falls on black queer people and black people with disabilities as well. In a 2019 report, it was found that

> it is clear that fatal violence disproportionately affects transgender women of color, and that the intersections of racism, sexism, homophobia, biphobia, transphobia, and unchecked access to guns conspire to deprive them of employment, housing, healthcare and other necessities, barriers that make them vulnerable. (Human Rights Campaign 2019)

Furthermore, "Persistent race-sex inequality in severe [disability life expectancy] over age and time indicates the nature of disability may be far worse for women, especially black women" (Soneji 2006).

While this is a useful summary of some of the goals and purposes of the Black Lives Matter movement—most importantly for our purposes, as starters of a conversation focused on differential and disproportionate treatment and devaluing of black folks in this society—I would encourage readers to look at the piece from which these passages came and all of the guiding principles from the Black Lives Matter website.[8]

§6.4 A PRELIMINARY DEFENSE OF "BLACK LIVES MATTER" OVER "ALL LIVES MATTER"

In addition to these preliminaries on the Black Lives Matter movement, I think it is important to give a preliminary version of this chapter's basic argument. This will serve two general purposes. First, it will allow us to see the extent to which conversations from ordinary, public life blend into conversations from academic philosophy. There is far too much elitism in the academy today, which actively tries to hide and distort this fact. Second, it will allow us to see what can be gained by explicitly bringing these conversations together. This is something I hope to see more of in the coming years of the discipline and as the Black Lives Matter movement and the public philosophy movement grow in their reach.

Interestingly enough, the gist of my entire chapter has been put to me before by a friend and colleague in an insightful one-sentence analogy not dissimilar to that from Michael Che.[9] He said that saying "all lives matter" in response to "Black lives matter" is like saying "why aren't we talking about lupus?" when we are at a breast cancer rally. In other words, just because we specify a concern for one particular thing, this doesn't mean we aren't concerned with any other things or even other things of that very same genus. There are simply reasons to have dedicated conversations sometimes. Our deciding to not talk about lupus in such a situation is not a sign that we do not care about lupus. That is simply not relevant to the purposes of a breast cancer rally. Also, just as somebody saying "why aren't we talking about lupus?" at a breast cancer rally could easily be taken to be implicating[10] that they do not think we need to bother dedicating time to breast cancer, somebody saying "all lives matter" in response to "Black lives matter" can easily be taken to be implicating that they do not think we need to bother dedicating time to black lives.

I have also heard this same basic idea put in other equally clever and insightful ways. In the Macklemore, Ryan Lewis, and Jamila Woods song, "White Privilege II," this thought has been expressed by Jonathan Cunningham with the following:

> Black Lives Matter, to use an analogy, is like if there was a subdivision and a house was on fire. The fire department wouldn't show up and start putting water on all the houses because all houses matter. They would show up and they would turn their water on the house that is burning, because that's the house that needs the help the most.[11]

I have also had a student of mine put this to me in the following way—saying "all lives matter" in response to "Black lives matter" is to mistake "Black lives matter" for meaning *only* Black lives matter, as opposed to the more appropriate Black lives matter *too* or Black lives matter *also*.[12] We turn now to showing how we can use Paul Grice's work on the logic of conversation to give yet one further way to express this root defense of the Black Lives Matter slogan. In doing so, I hope to provide a new way to respond to critics of the "Black lives matter" slogan and movement and to provide an example of the kind of public analytic philosophy I have been advocating in previously published work.[13]

§6.5 GRICE'S LOGIC OF CONVERSATION, COOPERATIVE PRINCIPLE, AND CONVERSATIONAL MAXIMS

For our purposes, the crucial phenomenon behind Grice's logic of conversation is that we often communicate a lot more with our utterances than the direct and literal meaning of the words occurring in the sentence(s) uttered. For instance, if my mother is at my house and she says to me "Jeez, do you even know how to turn on your heat?" it would be very odd if I simply responded "yes" and ended the conversation there. My mother is not simply expressing the question, which is the semantic content of this interrogative and looking for its answer. In ordinary circumstances, she would be taken to be asserting that she is cold and requesting that I turn the heat on to help with that. Notice, though, that no lexical item from this sentence directly and literally means anything having to do with being cold. Again, my mother was able to communicate a great deal more than the literal meaning of the words she used.

Grice's brilliance from the logic of conversation lectures involved recognizing that this extra-semantic communication and our understanding of it do not happen in haphazard fashions. Rather, Grice held that there is a structured logical system, which we implicitly learn when learning a language and which we invoke to efficiently communicate in these kinds of cases. That is, there are principles that we assume speakers and audiences know and, which we use to infer what a speaker has intended to communicate from the direct and literal meaning of that which was uttered. The primary principle of this system was dubbed the "Cooperative Principle" and reads:

> Make your conversational contribution such as it is required, at the stage at which it occurs, by the accepted purpose or direction of the talk exchange in which you are engaged. (Grice 1989, 26)

That is to say, a conversation does not consist of random utterances one after the other. Rather, we have coordinated conversations for particular purposes, those purposes connect one utterance to the next, and those purposes help dictate what is communicated by a particular utterance above and beyond its semantic content.

While it is difficult to get much mileage out of the cooperative principle on its own, much more work is done when we add the maxims of conversation Grice formulated to fill out this principle. In particular, Grice argued that, at the very least, satisfying the cooperative principle is to abide by the following maxims of quality, quantity, relevance, and manner.

Maxims of Quantity
[M1] Make your conversational contribution as informative as is required.
[M2] Do not make your conversational contribution more informative than is required.
Maxims of Quality
[M3] Do not say what you believe to be false.
[M4] Do not say that for which you lack adequate evidence.
Maxim of Relevance[14]
[M5] Make your conversational contribution relevant to the purposes of the conversation.
Maxims of Manner
[M6] Avoid obscurity of expression.

[M7] Avoid ambiguity.
[M8] Be brief.
[M9] Be orderly.

Grice holds that we assume speakers will be employing these maxims when they utter something in conversation. Furthermore, as speakers, we assume audiences will be assuming that we are employing them. So, for instance, if I tell someone that I have four tattoos, they will infer that I have *exactly* four tattoos. They will do so because it is assumed that I have been obeying the maxims of quantity and quality. If I have fewer than four tattoos, I will have said something false. If I have more than four tattoos, I will have not given enough information. Examples like these can easily be generated for all of the maxims.

§6.6 "ALL LIVES MATTER" AND THE MAXIMS OF QUANTITY AND RELEVANCE

What I want to do now is apply some of these lessons from the logic of conversation back to our discussion of "Black lives matter" and "all lives matter." My primary thought here is going to be that saying "all lives matter" in response to "Black lives matter" is to violate the maxims of quantity and relevance from the logic of conversation. Remember, the maxims of quantity tell us that we are only supposed to give as much information as is required for the purposes of that conversation we are engaged in. In particular, this means that we should not give more information than is required. One way that this particular maxim often works out is that we should not say things in a conversation that we take to be completely obvious and our conversation partners take to be completely obvious. So, for instance, if I had made some assertions in this chapter such as "you are awake" or "you know how to read," you would think I had made some very bizarre assertions. You would not think that because they are not true, though. Rather, it is because they are so obviously true that you would have a hard time figuring out what the purpose of my asserting them was.

I think that an utterance of "all lives matter" puts us in the exact same situation. It seems to me that the fact that all lives matter is completely and totally obvious to (almost) everybody. Because of this, the maxim of quantity would tell us that it is too much information to say "all lives matter." It is completely obvious (and, importantly, obvious that it is obvious), so we do not need to bring it up. Because it communicates almost nothing to say that all lives matter, there seems to be no purpose to it. Rather, the only thing achieved seems to be signaling one's unwillingness to say "Black lives matter." That said, since black lives mattering is a logical consequence of all lives mattering, why one would be willing to assert that all lives matter and unwilling to assert that black lives matter is left a complete mystery. This is one of the main reasons I argue for this chapter's primary thesis.

That said, I also think that responding to Black Lives Matter proponents by saying "all lives matter" violates the maxim of relevance from the logic of conversation. When somebody says that black lives matter, there is a reason that they have specified a particular racial group. As we discussed earlier in relation to the quotation from Garza, this is supposed to be communicating that there is differential treatment of white people and people of color in our society, which is in dire need of being discussed. So, the relevant purposes of the conversation when somebody says "Black lives matter" is to start a conversation about differential treatment of different racial groups. Because of this, to come back with a response of "all lives matter," where we are no longer differentiating between racial groups, is to completely and totally miss the relevant purposes of this conversation.

This is the sense in which "all lives matter" violates the maxim of relevance. The primary purpose of a conversation started with "Black lives matter" is to talk about unjust, differential treatment of people of color. To respond with "all lives matter" is to ignore these purposes. Even if one disagrees that there is unjust, differential treatment of black people in the United States and around the world—a position that I believe no person can hold while being reasonable—saying "all lives matter" does not communicate that. It simply co-opts the conversation and disrespectfully ignores what the creators and proponents of the Black Lives Matter movement wanted to have a conversation about.

§6.7 "BLACK LIVES MATTER" AND THE MAXIMS OF QUALITY AND QUANTITY

So far, I do not think I have said much different than what was said in earlier sections. You might wonder then, why in the world do we need to bring in this technical machinery from the philosophy of language to make this point that we can already make in ordinary ways of talking about things? I think the answer to this perfectly reasonable question becomes clear when we move from pointing out which maxims "all lives matter" violates to pointing out which maxims we have *not* said that "all lives matter" violates. In particular, we have not claimed that saying "all lives matter" violates the maxims of *quality*. To see precisely how this is important, we must first lay out one of the criticisms of the Black Lives Matter slogan that I believe the logic of conversation can help us respond to.

When I have tried to have conversations like this with people before and tell them that they should not say "all lives matter," I have often gotten a response along the lines of "well, does that mean you don't *believe* that all lives matter? Do you think it's *not true* that all lives matter?." So, it seems that the basic criticism can roughly be represented in the following simple argument:

P1: Many Black Lives Matter supporters think you should not say "all lives matter."
P2: If one thinks you should not say "all lives matter," then they must not believe that all lives matter.
CONCLUSION: Many Black Lives Matter supporters do not believe that all lives matter.

Notice that this is not at all what we have said, though. Again, we have not said that the maxims of quality have been violated. And, importantly, it is the maxims of quality that talk about truth and falsity, quality of evidence, and so on. This means we have not said that it is *untrue* that all lives matter. What we have said is that it is missing the point of the conversation and to not take your conversation partner seriously and respectfully to say "all lives matter." So, the logic of conversation gives us a clear way to respond to the criticism that preferring "Black lives matter" over "all lives matter" means one must not believe that all lives matter. That is, Grice's work gives us a clear way to show how P2 can be false. So, contra the critics, this shows that we can perfectly well believe that all lives matter and still think it is completely inappropriate to say "all lives matter," especially in response to someone's saying "Black lives matter."

One further and somewhat-related criticism of the Black Lives Matter movement is that it is not inclusive enough—it says that *only* black lives matter. Again, though, it certainly does not do so directly. What Black Lives Matter proponents say directly is that black lives matter. To only say that black lives matter is importantly different from saying that only black lives matter (that is, "only" plays very different roles in these phrases depending on its scope).[15] So, the critics must claim that saying "Black lives matter" conversationally implicates that *only* black lives matter. Thus, we are again in a position to use Grice's logic of conversation to help figure out and evaluate the dialectic.

So, does any part of Grice's logic of conversation give us reason to think that uttering "Black lives matter" further communicates that only black lives matter? As I mentioned earlier, I think it does not—instead involving the implicature that black lives matter *too*. I am not alone in this, either. In fact, every single proponent of the Black Lives Matter movement I have ever had this conversation with has said the same thing. This is not something idiosyncratic to my circle of friends and allies, though. People with an international audience have claimed the same (Bee 2016; Roose 2015). The creators of the movement have even weighed in on this question explicitly. Rather than an attempt at narrowing the conversation to only black lives, Garza explains that the movement is intended to be a "broadening [of] the conversation to include Black life." In another memorable passage, Garza explains the thought process thusly:

> Given the disproportionate impact state violence has on Black lives, we understand that when Black people in this country get free, the benefits will be wide reaching and transformative for society as a whole. . . . We remain in active solidarity with all oppressed people who are fighting for their liberation and we know that our destinies are intertwined. (Garza 2014)

Impressively, Garza shows here that even if one cannot get on board with Black Lives Matter due to concerns of justice, which I think we obviously should, there are purely prudential reasons for anyone to support this broadening of the conversation to include black lives. As many associated with the Black Lives Matter movement have argued "once all Black people are free, all people will be free" and the benefits come to each and every member of the more-free society (Ransby 2018, 3).

That so many Black Lives Matter proponents would have rejected the claim that only Black lives matter is quite significant in trying to determine whether this is an implicature of saying "Black lives matter." This is because, as Grice famously noted, conversational implicatures, unlike logical implications, are *cancelable*. That is, one can say things and invoke mechanisms to block an implicature that would normally go along with the utterance. So, while it makes no sense to say that "he's married and he's a bachelor," it makes perfect sense to say "do you know how to turn the heat on? I don't want you to turn it on. I've just never actually seen you turn it on and am genuinely curious given how bad you are with technology." This shows that *he's not a bachelor* is a logical implication of *he's married*, whereas *I want you to turn the heat on* is only an implicature of *do you even know how to turn the heat on?* So, even if it were reasonable for critics to originally hear "Black lives matter" as implicating that only Black lives matter, any ounce of conversation with a black lives matter supporter would cancel this implicature immediately. That critics have not noticed this is yet another sign that they have very rarely taken the time to even begin trying to understand the Black Lives Matter movement.

Of course, there is the further question of whether or not it is reasonable to think that saying black lives matter would implicate that only black lives matter in the first place. I think that this is clearly not reasonable and that Grice's maxims suggest the "too" rather than the "only" reading in any number of similar cases. For instance, when one holds up a sign that says "Equal rights for LGTBQ+ people" at a Gay Pride Parade, it is clear that they desire equal rights for LGBTQ+ people *too*. After all, it would not make much sense to discuss *equal* rights if there was *only* a desire for them to apply to one proper subgroup of the society. Furthermore, if somebody were looking at a standard logic syllabus one tends to find in American philosophy classrooms today and said "you know, women have studied and written on logic," the implicature would be that women have studied and written on logic *too*, not only or exclusively women. Generally, when there is a background belief that a property tends to go along with a certain group, to specify that the property holds among some proper subset of the group is to implicate that the property applies to the subgroup *as well*, not exclusively. So, to say that "Black lives matter" when there is a background belief that lives tend to matter, is to implicate that black lives matter too.

Finally, to sum up, saying "Black lives matter" does not logically commit one to thinking that only black lives matter, it does not conversationally implicate that only black lives matter, and, even if it did, that implicature would have been canceled many times over by now.

§6.8 "ALL LIVES MATTER," "I DON'T SEE COLOR," AND HALF-ASSED ATTEMPTS AT RACIAL EQUITY

Now, I can imagine someone wanting to respond to the preceding section by saying that even if Grice's work shows how one *could* be unwilling to say "all lives matter" despite believing that all lives matter, why would one *actually* want to avoid it? I think that there are quite a number of reasons one could give in response to this question, but I will stick to a few of my own. To begin with, I am a supporter of the Black Lives Matter movement and I believe that saying "all lives matter" is to distance one's self from this movement. I do not want to do that. So, even if I felt inclined to express my belief that all lives matter, I would not be inclined to do so via the string "all lives matter." I would want to express this proposition via something that pointed to the relevance of culturally competent discussions that utilize racial categories and distinctions and I would say something more like "Black lives and Asian lives and Latinx lives and Indigenous lives and white lives and so on matter." This is because I would want to communicate that I think white folks need to think about race more than they do. Color-blindness (read "racial-illiteracy") has, for the most part, become nothing more than the *en vogue* way to try to show that one is not a racist without actually having to do anything. Oddly enough, though, color-blindness is sometimes backed up with mistaken readings of famous civil rights leaders and critical race theorists. For instance, I have experienced people saying things like "I don't see color" or "any movement which distinguishes people based on race is, by definition, a racist movement" and then defending it with quotes like the following: "I have a dream that my four little children will one day live in a nation where they will not be judged by the color of their skin, but by the content of their character" (King, Jr. 1963).

To think that Martin Luther King, Jr. is advocating color-blindness here is absurd. To not judge someone by their race is not to fail to see their race. One can distinguish between races without evaluating any of them positively or negatively. Furthermore, failure to ever make such distinctions allows white people to be ignorant of the mechanisms of racial construction and racialization—eventually leading to a failure to see institutional, structural, or implicit racism. As Eduardo Bonilla-Silva has famously argued, this leads to "racism without racists"—where racial optimism abounds, but the situation for black folks and other people of color does not improve at anywhere near the same rate (Bonilla-Silva 2003). Or, to use Charles Mills' framework, so long as people do not think or talk about race, they can pretend that the racial contract they agreed to is actually a full-blown social contract—that our society has been set up by all for the benefit of all, rather than set up by some racially privileged folks primarily for the benefit of themselves (Mills 1997). In fact, in the post-Civil Rights era of de facto white supremacy, this pattern of systemic ignorance has become one of the primary tools of perpetuating and reinforcing racist structures.[16] To put things simply, in order to recognize and combat racism, we must be willing to think in racial terms—we cannot be color-blind and we cannot pretend to be postracial.

For those unfamiliar with these works, perhaps another way to put this is that it is important to recognize that there are numerous different *types* of problems created by trying to respond to or replace "Black Lives Matter" with "all lives matter." Doing so invalidates the self-expression on the part of the original utterer, ignores their intentions behind making the utterance, and causes harm in at least one further important way. Unlike the former of these ways, which encourage a kind of individualized racism, the latter is more related to structural racism. In particular, in discouraging people from making utterances using racial distinctions, it discourages people from having any thoughts framed in terms of racial distinctions, and contributes to the historical, institutional, and systematic ignorance, which allows white supremacy to be perpetuated in a post-Jim Crow America. As Mills points out very early in his work, the racial contract, whereby only a racially privileged subset of the population benefits from the bringing together of individuals into a society, is political, moral, and *epistemological*. Furthermore, it is this epistemological dimension that traditional social contract theorists have missed. They have not recognized how, or that, there is a set of conventions "about what counts as a correct, objective interpretation of the world, and for agreeing to this view, one is ("contractually") granted full cognitive standing in the polity, the official epistemic community" (Mills 1997, 17–18). Here, it seems that a tacit agreement to hold discussions concerning race to a minimum (e.g., by trying to replace "Black lives matter" with "all lives matter") constitutes one of those conventions.

To summarize, the unspoken consensus behind the white supremacist racial contract of modernity has been that a pattern of racial ignorance will be imposed for white people. "All lives matter" replacing "Black Lives Matter" continues this discouraging of cognition and knowledge with racial concepts involved—it encourages white ignorance. As Mills points out, this makes it so white people can end up being "unable to understand the world they themselves have made" (Mills 1997, 2017). Contributing to this systematic lack of understanding has very problematic consequences for social justice efforts. Following the downfall of Jim Crow laws, white people are much more inclined to need to fail to see or think very much about racial injustices to be okay with a world that contains so many such injustices. This is part of why we should not be surprised that the New Jim Crow is the prison-industrial complex—a set of practices that literally removes many people of color from sight for white people.[17] For these same reasons, then, other deviations of the "Black Lives Matter" slogan such as "blue lives matter"—which seem to suggest there is just as much reason to talk about any other groupings of people beside races—are equally problematic as "all lives matter." Just leave the "Black Lives Matter" slogan alone. It is quite brilliant in its brevity.

§6.9 RELATIONSHIP TO OTHER CURRENT LIBERATION MOVEMENTS AND SLOGANS

Given what I have just argued here, it is perhaps important to investigate what such a view would have to say about a use of the related slogan, "Native lives matter." This has been employed in notable protests at least since 2014. It has also induced a decent bit of debate as to the appropriateness of such a usage. Because of this, one way we can put my view to the test is by seeing what its consequences would be on the question of whether or not it is appropriate to use "Native lives matter" as a slogan. Here, I will argue that, under many circumstances, the utterance of "Native lives matter" is both appropriate and important to the Black Lives Matter movement and liberation movements generally.

To see why this is, remember that I argued that we should not respond with "all lives matter" to "Black lives matter" due to violations of the maxims of relevance and quantity from the logic of conversation. "Black lives matter" attempts to have a race-conscious discussion about differential treatment in order to advocate for a humanity that is denied by all-too-regular actions on the part of the state and individuals. Folks who say "all lives matter" are being completely irrelevant to these purposes. With these principles in mind, it should be clear that "Native lives matter" is not going to fall prey to the same problems as "all lives matter." To say "Native lives matter" is keeping the conversation in the realm of differential treatment along racial lines. Furthermore, the point about the maxims of quantity and being treated as obvious do not apply to "Native lives matter." It has been painfully clear throughout the history of European and Indigenous contacts that many people of European descent do not believe that Native lives matter.

In fact, it is important to note that the histories of white supremacist systems and individuals rejecting the humanity of black and Indigenous peoples have been intimately intertwined in America. As Nikkita Oliver argues in her piece showing that utterances of "Native lives matter" need not be co-optings of utterances of "Black lives matter," "[i]t's not something Americans like to talk about, but the inception of the U.S. was largely incumbent upon two forces—the genocide of Native peoples and the enslavement of Black peoples from Africa" (Oliver 2018). Furthermore, this intertwining of oppressions faced by black peoples and Native peoples is not just a distant historical fact. "The United States was built upon genocide, stolen land, and stolen peoples—and this difficult, unconfronted truth continues to inflict harm on both Native and Black peoples today, through state-sanctioned violence, police terrorism, and mass incarceration" (Oliver 2018). For this reason, "Native lives matter" should not be seen as a problematic slogan and, in fact, should be seen as part of a movement greatly in line with the Black Lives Matter movement. As Oliver puts it, "[w]e often say that when Black people get free, we all get free. Likewise, I believe that when the sovereignty of Native nations is recognized, the sovereignty of all beings impacted by U.S. imperialism will be recognized" (Oliver 2018).

With this connection in mind, it might also be worthwhile to look into relationships that our discussion has to slogans of other contemporary liberation movements. Given the attention I paid to the fact that "Black lives matter" implicates that black lives matter *too*, one natural place to look is the #MeToo movement. What can we learn from the fact that, while both of these slogans intend to communicate something *too*, something also, one of them does so via implicature and the other does do via explicit semantic content? To answer this, first remember that I argued that an utterance of

"Black lives matter" is able to implicate that black lives matter too because of a background belief that lives generally tend to matter. That is, when there is a background belief that a property tends to go along with a certain group, to specify that the property holds among some proper subset of the group is to implicate that the property applies to the subgroup *as well*, not exclusively. So, when people use the phrase "#MeToo" to signal that they have suffered sexual assault, violence, or harassment, this seems to signal that there is not a background belief that women and people with marginalized gender identities tend to suffer such oppression.

Furthermore, this seems to be instrumental to the important work done by the #MeToo slogan. As explained on the movement's website, "#MeToo" has helped to "de-stigmatize the act of surviving by highlighting the breadth and impact of a sexual violence worldwide" (#MeToo 2018). That is, there is an unfortunate fact that societies around the world have somehow worked on the assumption that sexual violence does not happen or that, when it does, it is infrequent and the result of individual "bad apples." The #MeToo hashtag allowed for a unified way to draw attention to just how prevalent sexual violence actually is—illustrated by the fact that you will see "you are not alone" on the Me Too movement's home page. This is useful for the fight to end sexual violence in allowing a means for survivors to band together, but also to help change the background beliefs on the prevalence of sexual violence. Unfortunately, roughly one out of six women has been raped or has survived an attempted rape.[18] This is a systematic issue, not one of isolated, problematic individuals. This is part of what seems to be implicated by the simple use of "Me" in "#MeToo." This slogan will show up so often that one need not even directly mention that the topic is sexual violence.

Thus, the use I have made of Grice's logic of conversation not only allows us a way to support and defend the Black Lives Matter movement, but also the Native Lives Matter and #MeToo movements. This generalized connection between ordinary language philosophy and liberation movements should again help us to see that these connections between social justice and the history of analytic philosophy are not aberrations. Such a fact means that analytic philosophers not engaging with such movements in the latter parts of the twentieth century and the early parts of the twenty-first century should be seen as a failure on the part of analytic philosophy. Furthermore, I think social justice activists should see this generalized connection as reason to expect there to be more analytic work, which could be helpful to our activism. Theories that can unify liberation movements while still being sensitive to individual context and intersectional factors are difficult to come by. If Grice's logic of conversation allows for this, we should bring it in to the fight.

All of that said, I do want to make it clear that Grice's logic of conversation certainly has some pitfalls here as well. As Luvell Anderson rightly argues, Grice's resources are too narrowly focused—centering only on the interlocutors in a discussion and *understanding* in the sense of one interlocutor recognizing the intentions of the other (Anderson 2017, 9–10). Presumably systems and institutions above and beyond the interlocutors as well as those interlocutors' practical understanding of how to navigate them are relevant to the situation here. So, while I think that using this Gricean framework has some practical advantages—given its accessibility to those without philosophical training—it certainly does not tell the whole story. On top of that, it does not illuminate features of the scenario that lend itself to generalization and remediation. For that, we again turn to the work of Anderson.

Anderson addresses breakdowns in communicative exchanges like the one we have been discussing in a paper on what he calls "hermeneutical impasses." Here, he recognizes that the "Black lives matter" vs. "all lives matter" exchange shares important features with the way some detractors have taken Colin Kaepernick's protest of systemic racism and with the way some rural white audiences respond to *Atlanta*. What these cases all have in common is that they involve "agents engaged in communicative exchanges [who] are unable to achieve understanding due to a gap in shared hermeneutical resources" (Anderson 2017, 3).

Once we have this general definition of "hermeneutical impasse," we can start to taxonomize them by sources of this gap in shared hermeneutical resources. Was it willful or unwilful? If willful, was this on the part of the speaker or the hearer (Anderson 2017, 6)? Either way, was the relevant source of that gap in shared hermeneutical resources linguistic or otherwise? If it was linguistic, was it about lacking a shared language or about some particular unit from that utterance? If it wasn't linguistic, was this a result of cultural distance and unfamiliarity or outright prejudice? These questions matter because different responses require different remedies and strategies for solution. Recognizing what some of these are is also useful for a further recognition that "structures of our environment make hermeneutical impasses difficult to avoid, if not inevitable" (Anderson 2017, 2). In particular, "the way institutions and power relations affect the production of interpretive schemas . . . [show] how hermeneutical impasses become entrenched" (Anderson 2017, 17). So, while I do not think that Grice's logic of conversation can do much to understand the functioning of these general structures (though Anderson's work still shows how analytic tools can be helpful here), I do think it can be a useful and important piece of the fight against them.

§6.10 "WE SHALL OVERCOME," "FREEDOM NOW," "BLACK POWER," BLACK LIVES MATTER

I want to end by making it clear why I go through all of these—what some have called, "fuss."[19] Why spend 9,000 words defending one three-word slogan over another, especially when they only differ in one word and one is a logical consequence of the other? To answer this, we must think about the importance of slogans for social movements, generally, and for black rights and liberation movements, in particular. Slogans have been extremely important for organizing and rallying social movements, as well as for creating and expanding a common ground among their supporters. The Civil Rights and Black Power movements were no different here, either. This fact is particularly important given that the Black Lives Matter movement has been explicitly created as an attempt to rebuild these earlier movements in evermore inclusive, expansive ways. As historian Barbara Ransby points out, the movement has been "distinct in its inclusivity" with "Black women hav[ing] been prominent in leadership" and "address[ing] the racism and violence experienced by the LGBTQAI communities" (Ransby 2018, 2–4).

More specifically, these earlier movements rallied around slogans such as "we shall overcome," "freedom now," "Black power," "power to the people," and so on. What is particularly relevant for our purposes is the significance that was attached to *changes* from one of these slogans to another for the Black Lives Matter precursors. Those familiar with these movements will know that much has been made of the switch from "we shall overcome" and "freedom now" to "Black power" among SNCC members and supporters in 1966. As Richard Benson put it in his book on Malcolm X and the radicalization of the black student movement:

> The opportunity for Carmichael to use the new agreed upon "Black Power" slogan occurred at the same time the adopted "Meredith March Against Fear" came to an apex on June 16th, 1966. . . . The Meredith march had escalated into more than just a march against fear. The march became the symbol of the restless behavior of a generation of young activists who began as advocates for nonviolent participation against the vestiges of Jim Crow. The march marked the beginning of an era that characterized the sentiment of Black Nationalism revitalized for a generation who felt that the leadership of the Civil Rights Movement was no more than glorified spokesmen who had been appropriated by the white American media. This new generation of young activists from SNCC represented a new aggressive activist style that was not attached to a religious dogma as its predecessor, the Nation of Islam. In the tradition of Malcolm X, SNCC sought to provide a level of consciousness coupled with rhetoric for

the masses of Black people who were tired of marches and sit-ins. "We shall overcome" was replaced by "Black Power," and the Black American climate would never be the same. (Benson III, 65)

So, the message is clear—a change in slogan is seen as a change in the movement.[20] If people are going to advocate for a change from "Black lives matter" as a slogan to "all lives matter" as a slogan, then they'd better make it clear what it is about the Black Lives Matter movement that needs changing. Until I see reason to believe this movement needs fundamental change, I stand in solidarity with it and leave you with the words of one of its creators explaining why:

when Black people cry out in defense of our lives, which are uniquely, systematically, and savagely targeted by the state, we are asking you, our family, to stand with us in affirming Black lives. Not just all lives. Black lives. Please do not change the conversation by talking about how your life matters, too. It does, but we need less watered down unity and more active solidarities with us, Black people, unwaveringly, in defense of our humanity. Our collective futures depend on it. (Garza 2014)

NOTES

1. Of course, this is not to say that there was no such concern, but simply that I will not be focusing on it as I have in previous chapters. Austin, for instance, is remembered by Stuart Hampshire in the obituary he wrote for Austin in the following manner: "In Austin's generation, the social and political implications of the teaching of philosophy, and of the forming of habits of thought in a ruling class, were certainly not unnoticed, and he was acutely conscious of them. He seriously wanted to 'make people sensible' and clear-headed, and immune to ill-founded and doctrinaire enthusiasms" (Hampshire 1960, x).

2. For an interesting take on the relationship between comedy and philosophy, see the conversation with comedians and philosophers, Kenny and Keith Lucas at https://www.pastemagazine.com/articles/2017/04/the-hard-work-of-being-chill-a-conversation-with-t.html.

3. As it should become clear, the string "Black lives matter" will show up in multiple different ways in this chapter. Sometimes, I will be directly discussing these words as a slogan. Other times, I will be discussing the movement that has grown around those words. When I am focused on the slogan, I will contain the words in quotes. When I am focused on the movement, the words will not show up in quotes and the first letter of each word will be capitalized, signaling that I am using a proper name for the movement.

4. This should not be taken to give the implicature that Black Lives Matter is solely an American movement. See Angela Davis', *Freedom is a Constant Struggle: Ferguson, Palestine, and the Foundations of a Movement* for reason to believe otherwise.

5. For evidence of this and a comedic take on it, see the "Most Lives Matter" segment from Samantha Bee's July 25, 2016, episode of her show.

6. Some great places for readers in academia to begin this process include Chancellor Williams' *The Destruction of Black Civilization,* Kessler et al., *Distinguished African-American Scientists of the Twentieth Century,* Lewis Gordon's *An Introduction to Africana Philosophy,* and Scott Williams' "Mathematicians of the African Diaspora" at http://www.math.buffalo.edu/mad/.

7. Another impressive and concise summary of the destructive and oppressive forces of white supremacy occurs in Charles Mills, *The Racial Contract,* 98–101. For an overview of how this history interacted with the history of philosophy, see Lewis Gordon, *An Introduction to Africana Philosophy.*

8. The passages that have been quoted come from Garza's Black Lives Matter herstory, but again, I encourage readers to peruse all of http://blacklivesmatter.com/.

9. Many thanks to Dr. John Youngblood for this analogy.

10. For the purposes of this chapter, one implies an implication and implicates an implicature. Implication is a semantic issue, whereas implicature is a pragmatic concern.

11. Many thanks to Jonathan Cunningham, co-founder of The Residency, a youth development through hip-hop social justice program based in Seattle, WA, for allowing me to use his words.

12. Many thanks to Zaneta Bailey for this way of putting things.

13. See Chick and LaVine (2014) and LaVine (2016b), in particular.

14. This phrasing is adopted from Soames (2003b, 201).

15. This is not a unique phenomenon, either. It is true that I have only stated finitely many arithmetic truths in my life. That does not mean that I have stated there are only finitely many arithmetic truths.

16. Notably, Bonilla-Silva and Mills are not at all unique in identifying white ignorance as a great source of racist injustices. For instance, Lewis Gordon says of Bernard Boxill's work that he "argues against colorblind notions of social justice since that would require ignoring the existence of an identifiable group who has suffered historic and present racial discrimination" (see Gordon, *An Introduction to Africana Philosophy,* 112). Sally Haslanger, in *Resisting Reality,* suggests that similar phenomena account for the utility of ideology critique in thinking about social justice. Furthermore, philosophers are far from the only thinkers who have noted this phenomenon. Ta-Nehisi Coates also talks about the role of systematic myths and ignorance in creating a dream-like state in many white Americans, one which allows for perpetuation of white supremacy—n.b. Coates, *Between the World and Me,* 8–12. Trevor Noah, *Born a Crime,* also gives insightful and entertaining takes on the ways in which ignorance of the existence of mixed families was essential to apartheid South Africa. Finally, an extremely useful anthology on the epistemology of ignorance, edited by Shannon Sullivan and Nancy Tuana, was published in 2007.

17. For discussion of these terms, "prison-industrial complex" and "New Jim Crow," and the theses behind their use, see Alexander, *The New Jim Crow*, and Davis, *Freedom is a Constant Struggle*.

18. This was gotten from the Rape, Abuse, and Incest National Network, citing the National Institute of Justice & Centers for Disease Control & Prevention, Prevalence, Incidence and Consequences of Violence Against Women Survey (1998).

19. For a humorous and insightful take on why it is so important to not let people get away with not saying "Black lives matter," see Michael Che's recent stand-up special, *Michael Che Matters* (Che 2016).

20. For further discussions of the immense importance placed on the introduction of the "Black power" slogan, see Collier-Thomas *Sisters in the Struggle*, Greenberg *Remembering SNCC*, and the famous 1987–1990 PBS documentary, *Eyes on the Prize*.

Chapter 7

Quinean Naturalized, Socialized Epistemology for Critical Theory

§7.0 OVERVIEW OF THE CHAPTER

As ordinary language philosophy and the last remnants of logical empiricism faded away, they were not clearly replaced by any one movement, trend, doctrine, method, or topic. Anscombe, Foot, and others led a distinctively analytic revival of more traditional ethical theorizing. Marcus, Carnap, Prior, Kripke, and Montague led a similar revival of interest in modality and intensionality. At the same time, Willard Van Orman Quine led a charge in the exact opposite direction—extensionalism and distrust of modal distinctions playing large roles in his overall pragmatic naturalism. Since the first trend can obviously be connected to public and practical concerns and the second has been dealt with in earlier chapters, this chapter will focus on how we can connect Quine's highest-level commitments of holism, naturalism, and pragmatism to philosophical work on social justice. In particular, I will discuss applications of Quinean methodology to issues of race and gender by Charles Mills and Sally Haslanger, as well as how we can see these as more Quinean than Quine sometimes was. I will end with some suggestions that this completes the rough sketch of a meta-philosophical view, which most centrally combines ideas from Bright, Dutilh Novaes, Haslanger, and Mills with the logical empiricists.

§7.1 THE FALL OF ORDINARY LANGUAGE PHILOSOPHY AND A MULTITUDE OF NEW DIRECTIONS

Given the lack of a unified theory, movement, or school being denoted by "ordinary language philosophy," it is very difficult to say clearly when it ended and, thus, what followed it. Because of this, it will be helpful to the demarcation of Stage 5 to say that we are interested in the period between the heyday of ordinary language philosophy and Saul Kripke's *Naming and Necessity* lectures. This last stage of early analytic philosophy, before Kripke and Rawls ushered in new directions for the analytic movement, is most naturally connected with the 1960s. The 1940s were dominated by Wittgenstein and the Oxford trio of J. L. Austin, Gilbert Ryle, and P. F. Strawson. As Schwartz says, "during and just after World War II the center of gravity of British analytic philosophy shifted from Cambridge University to Oxford" (Schwartz 2012, 119).

While Wittgenstein died in 1951, the 1950s were also a time of significant work in ordinary language philosophy. G. E. M. Anscombe edited and published Wittgenstein's *Philosophical Investigations* in 1953, only to put out her own groundbreaking book in 1957, *Intention*. Austin's lectures, which would become *How to Do Things with Words,* were given in 1955, his philosophical papers came out in 1956–1957, and his *Sense and Sensibilia* lectures were completed in 1959 shortly before his untimely death in early 1960. So, even though we still have work to do in nailing down what to focus on in our post-ordinary language philosophy and pre-Kripke/Rawls stage, we know that we will primarily be focused on the 1960s.

Again, unlike the earlier stages of the early analytic period, there is less of a consensus on what and whose story to tell for this fifth stage that is centered around the 1960s. Volume 2 of Soames' *Philosophical Analysis in the Twentieth Century,* breaks the time between 1950 and 1970 down into seven parts—four focused on the rise and fall of ordinary language philosophy, one on the naturalism of W. V. O. Quine, one on Donald Davidson's semantics, and one on Saul Kripke's semantics and metaphysics (Soames 2003b). Glock speaks of this time period as part of the collapse of logical positivism that was begun by Quine's criticisms and completed by the three-pronged rehabilitation of metaphysics coming from Quine's naturalistic ontology, Strawson's descriptive metaphysics, and Kripke's modal metaphysics (Glock 2008). Finally, Schwartz also says that no single movement or school dominated analytic philosophy starting in the 1960s. Rather, Quine, Kuhn, and others brought a pragmatist strain of thought to the forefront of the analytic scene at the same time that Ruth Barcan Marcus, Rudolf Carnap, Arthur Prior, Saul Kripke, and Richard Montague led a revival of interest in modality that helped the aforementioned rehabilitation of metaphysics. Perhaps most obviously relevant to a book on social justice, Schwartz also focuses on the fact that during this time Anscombe and Philippa Foot led a revival of analytic philosophers focusing on traditional ethical theorizing that would eventually bring to life applied ethics in an analytic vein through thinkers like Judith Jarvis Thomson, Peter Singer, and James Rachels (Schwartz 2012).

Despite this fracturing of the stories written about the development of early analytic philosophy during the 1960s from some of the major historians of the period, there is a strand that they all focus on. In particular, Soames, Glock, and Schwartz all make a special place for Quinean holism and naturalism during this time. Such a fact is undoubtedly appropriate given the depth and longevity of Quine's contributions. One simply could not write a serious book about the early analytic period without significant discussion of Quine's work. Looking into his career a bit more, the 1960s is a quite natural decade to choose as a focal point. If one looks at the dozen most important and most-cited works of Quine's career, they stretch from his 1936 paper, "Truth by Convention," to his 1990 book, *The Pursuit of Truth*. This leaves the midpoint of Quine's principal contributions as 1963, the mean of these publication dates in 1964, and a median publication date of 1967. Furthermore, the decade started with his most-cited work, *Word and Object*, and ended with the other of his most mature and original systematic works, *Ontological Relativity and Other Essays*.

Because of all of this, the focus of our chapter on the last stage of early analytic philosophy will be Quine's work from the 1960s, which brings his earlier individual contributions to logic, the philosophy of language, and the philosophy of science into an overarching system. This will also be another good test for my primary theses. For as little work as there has been on the other protagonists of this story in relation to social and political matters, even less has been written on Quine's work in relation to these matters.[1] And, for as little as these other protagonists wrote on social, political, and ethical matters in traditional ways, they wrote much more than Quine did (which was almost nothing). In the few such instances that Quine did write about social and political matters, it became clear that he had quite different political persuasions than the generally leftist tendencies I have been encouraging and which we find in some of his predecessors.[2] Hence, it will be particularly significant if we can show even Quine's work to have significant potential for critical work on social justice. Again, so as to avoid the criticism that we are cherry-picking or grasping at straws, we will focus on undoubtedly central themes of Quine's work—holism and naturalism. We will look at ways in which these could contribute to theorizing about race and gender with a focus on the works of Sally Haslanger, Charles Mills, Lynn Hankinson Nelson, and Claude Steele.

§7.2 QUINEAN HOLISM AND NATURALISM

The first prominent piece of Quine's systematic philosophy was a friendly critique of the logical empiricists' program and the role that the analytic/synthetic distinction (henceforth, A/S) played in it—a critique that ultimately led to his adoption of holism.[3] This forms an appropriate starting point for our discussion given that Haslanger says "although it took me years to recognize its influence, V. W. O [sic] Quine's essay 'Two Dogmas of Empiricism' (1951) was at the core of my philosophical training" (Haslanger 2012, 13). While he is most famous for the arguments given in this 1951, "Two Dogmas," Quine first took aim at the logical empiricists' doctrines in his 1936, "Truth by Convention." This work questioned the feasibility of the group's explanation of their favorite subclass of analytic truths, the logical truths (or, as some liked to call them following Wittgenstein,[4] "tautologies"). Taking their inspiration from Wittgenstein's account of the logical constants in the *Tractatus*, the Vienna Circle held that, because statements of logic seemed immutable and knowable in ways that no other substantive statements were, there had to be something peculiar about their truth. Empiricists at heart, they claimed that the explanation was that logical truths were analytic and made true by our semantic conventions surrounding the logical constants.

Here is where one of Quine's most famous arguments comes in, one which had "as its very specific but significant target the view that the primitive logical constants get their meanings through implicit definition" (Russell 2008, 163). This is Quine's regress argument, which is supposed to arise after we realize that the infinite nature of the set of logical truths means that we must use *generalized* stipulations, if stipulations are somehow supposed to account for logical truth (Quine 1936, 107–14). As I see it, Quine's basic charge here is that drawing out consequences of general stipulations (i.e., implicit definitions) uses logic and, thus, cannot be the story about how we come to know logic in the first place. Basically, if we are using logic to draw out such consequences, we must already know logic prior to these stipulations.

While this seems compelling at first glance, I believe this argument equivocates on "knowledge" in a problematic way. That is because the method of justification associated with implicit definitions assumes that we *know how to use* logical principles to get to *explicit, propositional knowledge* about logic. So, we do not here have propositional knowledge about logic justifying the same propositional knowledge about logic as the "regress" tag would suggest. Rather, implicit definition of logical constants shows how knowledge-that concerning logical properties can be reduced to knowledge-how concerning the use of logical rules. One might say that this just pushes the question back to how we can learn to apply the introduction and elimination rules, which are meant to implicitly define the logical constants in the first place. This is exactly what the connection between implicit definitions and conventional rules is supposed to explain, though. Presumably there is nothing particularly mysterious about how we learn to follow rules about identifying and connecting forms of sentences.

So, if Quine's work on A/S and logical empiricism is going to be of use for contemporary feminist and antiracist work, it must come later than Quine (1936). After this, Quine's criticisms of the logical empiricists' program got much more intense. In his address at the December 1950 APA meeting in Toronto, which became "Two Dogmas," Quine not only tried to undermine *their explanation* of precisely how A/S was important for philosophy, he also tried to make the positive argument that A/S is philosophically *insignificant*. This is because Quine claimed either that there are no analytic truths at all or, even worse, that there is no such thing as a coherent A/S. This was done with two different arguments—the circularity argument and the argument from holism.

Importantly, I think that Glock may ultimately be right that the former amounts to nothing more than

> the rather odd complaint that "analytic" can be explained only via notions with which it is synonymous, and not via notions with which it is not synonymous. . . . The idea that legitimate concepts must be translatable into a purely extensional language presupposes that intensional notions have been discredited, which is what the circularity-charge set out to do. (Glock 2003, 75)

That said, much worse for Quine is the fact that, post-Kripkean theories of analyticity break out of this Quinean circle in that, at the very least, they do not have "analyticity" being inter-definable with, for example, "necessity" and "synonymy." Paul Boghossian, for instance, defends an updated version of the Wittgensteinian and Carnapian view that analyticity is to be spelled out in terms of implicit definitions (Boghossian 1996). Implicit definitions will only provide synonyms in the rare cases where the logical form of the implicit definition is that of an identity statement or a universally quantified biconditional, though. So, Quine's circularity argument, even if successful, would only cause problems for implicit definitions, which had the form of identity statements or universally quantified biconditionals. Boghossian's most important cases of implicit definitions—the introduction and elimination rules for logical constants—which do not have these forms, would be left untouched.[5]

This means that, even if Quine were making a criticism, which is reasonable against a certain type of view, contemporary theories of A/S are not tokens of such types. Because of this, if there is something of importance for contemporary critical work in Quine (1951), it will have to be his confirmational holism argument. Quine begins this argument by asking "What . . . is the nature of the relationship between a statement and the experiences which contribute to or detract from its confirmation?" (Quine 1951, 35–36). Against the verificationism, which seems to allow that all individual statements taken in isolation admit of unique classes of experiences which would confirm or infirm them, Quine says "My countersuggestion, issuing essentially from Carnap's doctrine of the physical world in the *Aufbau*, is that our statements about the external world face the tribunal of sense experience not individually but only as a corporate body" (Quine 1951, 38).

The upshot of this second argument seems to be that, because testing by an observation statement can only happen for a multi-membered class of general hypotheses, inference rules, rules of measurement, and auxiliary hypotheses (i.e., holism), no failed experiment ever dictates a particular solution. The decision to drop any one of these—a general hypothesis, an inference rule, which led from it to a prediction, an assumption that a measuring device was in working order, or even an observation statement—will put us back in good standing with respect to logic and empirical adequacy. Hence, no belief is immune from revision (i.e., universal fallibilism), and, we can revise all of our beliefs.

Quine thinks this final move, from holism to universal fallibilism, defeats A/S for the following reasons:

P1: If there is an A/S, then there are some statements that are always and everywhere immune from revision (namely, the analytic truths).
P2: No statement is immune from revision in this way. (Confirmational Holism and Under-determination of Theory choice arguments)[6]
CONCLUSION: There is no A/S. (P1, P2, Modus Tollens)

And, once we have this criticism of A/S, this short argument gets us to Quine's naturalism quite quickly. As Quine put it in *Theories and Things*, his naturalism consists of "the recognition that it is within science itself, and not in some prior philosophy, that reality is to be identified and described" (Quine 1981, 21). That is, along with this acceptance of holism and the dropping of an A/S, comes a dropping of a distinction between philosophy and science. We see this by the last page of "Two Dogmas," when Quine says "ontological questions, under this view, are on a par with questions of natural science" (Quine 1951, 43).

Despite this early focus on a naturalized ontology/metaphysics (which would continue throughout his career), it is Quine's application of naturalism to *epistemology,* which has been most influential. Furthermore, this would seem appropriate to Quine, given that he thought "Where naturalistic renunciation shows itself most clearly and significantly is in naturalistic epistemology" (Quine 1995, 252). Starting in the same place that his confirmational holism argument started almost twenty years earlier, Quine's investigation into a naturalized epistemology can be seen as starting with the thought that "If we are out simply to understand the link between observation and science, we are well advised to use any available information, including that provided by the very science whose link with observation we are seeking to understand" (Quine 1969, 76). When we do this, "Epistemology, or something like it, simply falls into place as a chapter of psychology and hence of natural science. It studies a natural phenomenon, viz., a physical human subject" (Quine 1969, 82).

To try to tease this out a bit more, we can use Hilary Kornblith's formulation, which holds that naturalized epistemology can be defined in terms of the following two questions:

(Q1) "How ought we to arrive at our beliefs?"
(Q2) "How do we arrive at our beliefs?" (Kornblith 1994, 1)

In particular, one is engaged in a naturalistic epistemology iff they believe that they cannot answer Q1 without engaging with answers to Q2. Importantly, this leaves open multiple possibilities about the precise relationship between Q1 and Q2. One could be a radical naturalist in holding that Q1 should simply be replaced by Q2. Or, one could be a conservative naturalist, leaving room for a distinction between them, but simply holding that some of the work on Q1 is achieved by answers to Q2. Quine, himself, seems to waffle between these readings—sometimes saying radical sounding things like "Epistemology in its new setting, conversely, is contained in natural science, as a chapter of psychology" and sometimes saying conservative sounding things like "epistemology merges with psychology, as well as with linguistics" or "we can now make free use of empirical psychology" (Quine 1969). We will return to this in the subsequent sections. For now, all we need to understand is that Quine's systematic philosophy started from holism and naturalism, as well as that his naturalized epistemology was most central to this work.

§7.3 THE POLITICALLY REVISIONARY AND NATURALIZED PHILOSOPHY OF HASLANGER AND MILLS

As was mentioned, though Quine himself seemed to keep his work as far away from politics as possible, the last three decades have begun to see a significant amount of impressive work on this front. Beginning around Nelson (1990), and greatly buoyed by Antony (1993), Mills (1997, 1998), Clough (2003), and Nelson and Nelson (2003), quite a few feminists, antiracists, and Marxists have illustrated the emancipatory potential of many different aspects of Quine's work. That said, when it comes to systematic development of a Quinean critical theory with holist and naturalistic tendencies playing center stage, I think we can do no better than the works of Sally Haslanger and Charles Mills.

In what follows, I will sketch some of the fundamental ways that Haslanger and Mills extend Quine's work to emancipatory ends. This will be done for the sake of moving toward the next section, which is intended to show that, in doing so, Haslanger and Mills are actually more faithful to Quine's insights than Quine was. Finally, so as to connect this to the aspirations of the larger book project, we will begin this discussion with extensions of Quine's naturalized epistemology—arguably the most lastingly influential piece of Quine's work from the 1960s.

In his earliest contributions to naturalized epistemology, Mills builds off of Kornblith's characterization of it in terms of Q1 and Q2 from §7.2 (Mills 1998, 33). Distinguishing between a radical naturalized epistemology—which merely replaces Q1 with Q2—and a conservative naturalized epistemology—which recognizes that answers to Q1 must be built off of answers to Q2—Mills opts for the latter. After all, one standard goal of much antiracist and feminist work of different persuasions has been undermining prevalent hegemonic ideologies—a task that does not fit easily with the radical route. The point in calling something a hegemonic ideology is to criticize its relations to power and to say we should head in an objectively better direction. Invoking objective normativity and holding that belief-forming processes associated with these ideologies should be undermined combine much more naturally with the conservative route. Hence, Mills combines a methodological conservatism with a political radicalism.[7]

Mills is concerned with such a naturalizing of epistemology in critical philosophy of race, gender, and class, among others, for a number of different reasons. First and foremost, by thinking about how we *ought* to form beliefs through an inquiry into how we *actually* form beliefs, we will be led to see that knowledge and belief are social to their very core. That is, the individualist, bordering on solipsist, approach to knowledge, which has been prevalent throughout modern Western epistemology since Descartes' *Meditations,* will be seen to be problematic in the extreme if we look to our actual belief-forming processes. We do not gain beliefs in isolation like Descartes' meditator. Rather, what beliefs we have or do not have is greatly conditioned by our relationships, both positive and negative, to other people. Since our relationships to other people are greatly dependent upon social identities, what beliefs we have or do not have is then greatly conditioned by our social identities.

While Quine did not take things in this direction himself, his work should greatly invite such recognitions. As Mills put it in one of his more recent contributions,

> But though mainstream philosophy and analytic epistemology continued to develop in splendid isolation for many decades, W. V. O. Quine's naturalizing of epistemology would initiate a sequence of events with unsuspectedly subversive long-term theoretical repercussions for the field. . . . For it then meant that the cognitive agent needed to be located in her specificity—as a member of certain social groups, within a given social milieu, in a society at a particular time period. (Mills 2017, 50)

This naturalized and *socialized* epistemology would be important, for example, in the understanding and critique of racism given that, "In particular, the analysis of the implications for social cognition of the legacy of white supremacy has barely been initiated" (Mills 2017, 51). Chapter 3 was an attempt to contribute to this initiation by showing how empirical results on implicit racial bias, white ignorance, and racial stereotyping could illustrate the social nature of our actual belief-forming processes in ways relevant to philosophical methodology.

Importantly, not only would this naturalized, socialized epistemology provide a route for analytic epistemologists to contribute to our understandings of race and racism, it would also provide a site for the merging of analytic epistemology with established traditions in black liberation thinking. This is because sociological work and literary work foundational to writings on and from the African-American experience echo these themes:

> For what people of color quickly come to see—in a sense the primary epistemic principle of the racialized social epistemology of which they are the object—is that they are not seen at all. Correspondingly, the "central metaphor" of W. E. B. Du Bois' *The Souls of Black Folk* is the image of the "veil,". . . . Similarly, Ralph Ellison's classic *Invisible Man* . . . Recounts . . . the protagonist's quest to determine what norms of belief are the right ones in a crazy looking-glass world where he is an invisible man. (Mills 2017, 53–54)

That is to say, taking a Quinean, rather than Cartesian, approach to epistemology will allow us to see that ignorance is often not a passive absence of knowledge, but an actively instilled false belief with protections built into it—a fact that has been recognized in African-American literature for more than at least a century and a half. Such a recognition would have, and in epistemology of ignorance circles has already begun to have, great impact on the norms for going from ignorance to knowledge that get discussed in epistemology journals, conferences, and seminars. At the very least, such a recognition shows they will need a new (set of) step(s) dedicated to systematically clearing away false beliefs before being able to see the light.

Furthermore, as alluded to in this and previous chapters, one of the common themes running through Haslanger's work is naturalized, socialized epistemology for the sake of social critique and ideology critique. Going beyond Quine, throughout many chapters of Haslanger (2012) the case is made that "Much can be gained . . . by including *both social science and moral theory*—broadly construed—in the web of belief that has a bearing on our inquiry" (Haslanger 2012, 15, original emphasis). That is, once we are holists in the epistemological realm, we should see that epistemological inquiry is going to require socially grounded and socially relevant knowledge as well.

Furthermore, this ought to be expected with a naturalism in line with other contemporary analytic staples—for example, semantic externalism and scientific essentialism. A combination of these will make us realize that it is not unusual for us to talk about objects, kinds, and systems in the world without a complete grasp of those things we are discussing (Haslanger 2012, 14). Sometimes this merely partial grasp happens because we are deferring to genuine expertise. Other times, though, this happens because problematic institutions have pulled the proverbial wool over our eyes. In understanding which cases are which and how the differences occur, we will see that gendered and racialized ideologies play a significant role here. Thus, feminist values could greatly improve our work in normative epistemology given that for decades feminists have shown there are many ways in which our actual attributions of knowledge are not tracking knowledge but rather explicitly sexist or implicitly androcentric assumptions (Haslanger 2012, 345). So, to do naturalized, socialized epistemology well, we will need to bring in a moral critique of sexism and androcentrism.

On top of that, this naturalized and socialized epistemology will have significant consequences for ontology as well, since "in the social realm, knowledge, or what purports to be knowledge, is entangled with the reality it represents" (Haslanger 2012, 406). That is to say, Haslanger and Mills also show us that Quinean naturalistic tendencies help for an antiracist, feminist ontology as well. Thus, just as Quine would have us see that our ontological commitments should be based on our best scientific theories, Haslanger and Mills look to empirical social science in their ontologies of race and gender. When doing so, they are largely led to *social construction* as the primary process necessary for understanding social ontology.

Very usefully summing this thought process up in the realm of gender, Haslanger says that we should see that genders are constructed by treating different groups of people differently—specifically through evaluation via different norms and ideals—femininity for woman and masculinity for men. In particular,

> The ideal of Woman is an externalization of men's desire . . . this ideal is projected onto individual females and is regarded as intrinsic and essential to them. Accepting these attributions of Womanhood, individual women then internalize the norms appropriate to the ideal and aim to conform their behavior to them. (Haslanger 2012, 93)

This social nature of the creation of gender roles and norms is important for our action in the world by making us recognize the radical contingency of the existence of these particular roles and norms. If these hierarchical roles were created by us acting and organizing in certain ways, we could undermine this hierarchy with different collective action.

Similarly, Mills holds that we will do much better theoretical and activist work if our social ontology is guided by the actual sociological facts. For instance, our focus should not be the "official ontology of the ideal Enlightenment, where abstract raceless and colorless individuals are treated as persons equally deserving of respect." An honest look at history and sociology will show that we are much too far from that ideal for it to be useful. Rather, we should direct our attention to the "naturalized social ontology, the ontology of the divided enlightenment" where individuals are divided into person and subperson classes based on whether they are racialized as white or as people of color. Along with this division of social ontological categories, a naturalized social ontology will recognize a division of relations standing as norms for these different groups—with white persons treating nonwhite subpersons with disrespect and subpersons treating persons with deference added to the initial picture of all persons treating each other with respect (Mills 1998, 71). Again, this would make much current work in moral philosophy, philosophical anthropology, and the like moot. We must first understand disrespect, deference, subpersonhood, and the divisions they track before we can hope to understand and encourage respect among all persons.

Finally, this utility of naturalism for critical theories of race and gender does not end with epistemology and metaphysics, either. Throughout his work, Mills can be seen as instituting a naturalistic outlook, bringing together philosophy and empirical science, in all areas of philosophy. In chapter 1 of Mills (1998), where Ralph Ellison's sum of first-person and third-person perspectives is compared to Descartes' sum of body and mind, we see a naturalized and holist philosophy of the self and personhood built off of demographics of the field of philosophy, patterns in syllabi and citation practices, patterns in conceptual evasion, documents from abolitionist, antiimperialist, feminist, and Marxist political actors, phenomenologies of oppression, literary expressions, and more. In chapter 7, a naturalized ethics is developed out of social and moral psychological thinking which shows that "communities systematically privileged by an unjust social order will as a rule be less attentive to its inequities" (Mills 1998, 141–42).

Of course, arguably Mills' greatest contributions have come from his naturalizing tendencies in social and political philosophy. In this realm, Mills' naturalized theory is most clearly contrasted with Rawlsian ideal contract theory. As was discussed in chapter 6, when we look to the actual historical facts, we will see that we are so far from an ideal state that the most promising avenue for social and political norms is not trying to figure out the ideal form of government and trying to attain it—it is too far outside of our collective zone of proximal development. Rather, we should start with the actual state of affairs to come up with concrete norms for moving in a better direction. When doing so, we will see that, more fruitful than imagining an ideal social contract, is understanding the nonideal (i.e., actual, naturalized) racial contract, which has been something of a global political system in the modern world. This project has allowed for more than two decades of prescient insights from Mills. Hence, we should see that there is nothing accidental about the ability of some theorists to connect naturalizing tendencies in philosophy to emancipatory ends. There are very systematic reasons that they fit together in important ways.

§7.4 HASLANGER AND MILLS AS MORE QUINEAN THAN QUINE

Thus, throughout Haslanger's and Mills' work on epistemology, metaphysics, phenomenology, ethics, and social and political philosophy, we see a holist, naturalist, critical perspective. The connections between theirs and Quine's holisms and naturalisms are not at all superficial, either. Direct reference to Quine (1951) and Quine (1969), as well as to confirmational holism and naturalized philosophy are easy to find in their writings. So, it is not at all a stretch to call Haslanger and Mills Quinean thinkers. I want to argue in this section that they are, in fact, better Quineans than Quine himself was. That is to say, they more consistently apply Quinean principles than Quine himself did. In particular, they have more coherent views than Quine with respect to both the role of social science within a naturalistic worldview and the role of normativity in epistemological and philosophical projects.

To start my case for this, we should make clear that Quine's naturalistic impulses to blur the boundaries between disciplines, especially between philosophy and science, did not lead to him using inputs from all different fields. When Quine discusses or uses the results from empirical science, they are almost always inputs from the natural sciences. At times, this is actually explicit, with "Two Dogmas" encouraging "a blurring of the supposed boundary between speculative metaphysics and *natural* science" (Quine 1951, 20, my emphasis). Other times this is implicit in his far greater reliance on particular natural sciences than particular social sciences. In the anthology of his in which Quine first included "Two Dogmas" (Quine 1953), he discusses physics on thirteen pages and biology on another, with just one discussion of history and three for psychology. In the book that started his systematic contributions of the 1960s, *Word and Object*, physical particles are discussed on nine pages, relativity theory on three, neutrinos on two, and chemistry on one, with sociology appearing once and psychology four times. This is actually quite more lopsided toward the natural sciences than it seems once we recognize how Quine understands psychology. As he says in his systematic work on the other end of the 1960s, "Epistemology, or something like it, simply falls into place as a chapter of psychology and hence of *natural* science. It studies a *natural* phenomenon, viz., a *physical* human subject" (Quine 1969, 82, my emphases).

Despite this paltry engagement with, and discussion of, social science, Quine's own views would seem to encourage such engagement with social science just as they encourage engagement with natural science. By the end of his career, Quine seems to have recognized this as well since "Quine certainly takes the natural sciences, especially physics, as paradigmatic. As he says himself, however, he uses the word 'science' broadly; he explicitly includes psychology, economics, sociology, and history" (Hylton & Kemp 2019). Of course, in doing so, he refers to social sciences as "softer sciences" and says that is the rule that their relationship to empirical checkpoints is negligible (Quine 1995, 49). He does not allow for a distinction between analytic and synthetic statements based on empirical significance. Thus, he does not allow for a distinction between pure ontological and natural scientific investigation into what there is because "The unit of empirical significance is the whole of science" (Quine 1951, 39). Social science is part of the whole of science and this previous statement seems to hold of social science as well. So, holism and a generalized naturalism would also seem to encourage a socialized naturalism.

Furthermore, there are more specific naturalistic projects Quine is concerned with which should have pushed him in the direction of social scientific findings. For starters, remember that Quine's primary epistemic metaphor is Neurath's boat:

> I see philosophy and science as in the same boat—a boat which, to revert to Neurath's figure as I so often do, we can rebuild only at sea while staying afloat in it. . . . All scientific findings, all scientific conjectures that are at present

plausible, are therefore in my view as welcome for use in philosophy as elsewhere. (Quine 1969, 126–27)

It should be more significant for Quine that *we* are at sea and *we* need to fix the boat *we are* on. This recognizes that belief-formation and testing are sociological phenomena as much as they are psychological and physical phenomena. Presumably, this would make sociology extremely useful for a naturalized epistemology.

This Neurath's boat analogy of us working together to form our beliefs is borne out by the sociological findings as well. For instance, demographic characteristics of research teams have been found to have significant epistemic effects—"Diversity has been shown to create a cognitive and social environment that is a positive indicator for innovation and a negative indicator for routine tasks" (Nelson 2014, 88). Furthermore, the common ground shared among the educational environment can have significant epistemic effects. Building off of Jane Elliott's "angry eye" experiment, which suggested that "the environment, and [one's] status in it, seemed to be an actual component of their ability" (Steele 2010, 28), Claude Steele went on to show that for example, "women tended to underperform in advanced math classes, where evidence suggests they feel the collar of gender stigma, but not in advanced English classes, where evidence suggests the collar is less felt" (Steele 2010, 31–32).

This phenomenon of stereotype threat, where learning and knowledge are significantly connected to social facts, showed up in cases connected to race as well.

> Black students performed dramatically worse than equally skilled white students when the test was presented as an ability test, when they were at risk of confirming the negative ability stereotype about their group; but they performed just as well as equally skilled whites when the test was presented as nondiagnostic of intellectual ability, when they were at no risk of confirming the ability stereotype. (Steele 2010, 56)

Furthermore, literature on implicit bias that we have already mentioned shows that social identity has a nonnegligible impact on perception, the very foundation of empiricist epistemology (e.g., "[r]ace can bias people to see harmless objects as weapons when they are in the hands of black men" (Payne et al. 2018)). This should be especially significant to philosophers given that traditional fallacies such as hasty generalization and confirmation bias are other standard manifestations of implicit bias.[8]

What these findings also show is that we can significantly distinguish different inquiries with respect to how good they are. That is to say, diverse research teams and teams where stereotype threat is mitigated by "giving people facing identity threat information that enables a more accurate and hopeful personal narrative about their setting" (Steele 2010, 169) satisfy Quine's own criteria for theories better than those without these characteristics. As Quine says, "As an empiricist I continue to think of the conceptual scheme of science as a tool, ultimately, for predicting future experience in the light of past experience" (Quine 1951, 41). Precisely what much social psychological and sociological research of the past few decades has shown is that different social frameworks for inquiry serve as better and worse tools for this.

This would seem to suggest we need to distinguish a merely causal relationship that can obtain between evidence and belief from a robustly justificatory relationship between them. Furthermore, the standard narrative in Quine scholarship until recently has been that "'Epistemology Naturalized' (1969) is usually read as abandoning the 'normative' project of traditional epistemology in favor of a psychological description of the causal processes involved in belief acquisition" (Sinclair 2014, 350). That is to say, our naturalism needs to allow for Mills' conservative distinction between Q1 and Q2 and allow for radical, normative, evaluative work. As Haslanger puts it, "Much can be gained . . . by including *both social science and moral theory*—broadly construed—in the web of belief that has a bearing on our inquiry" (Haslanger 2012, 15, original emphasis). Without these in his web of belief, Quine seems to be misunderstanding the conclusions of his own views.

§7.5 EXTENDING HASLANGER AND MILLS WITH VIENNESE THOUGHT

While we have seen reasons to value Quinean holism and naturalism for our critical work, there is also reason to not necessarily follow Quine down all paths. Haslanger and Mills have given two ways to do this by not undervaluing what social science and moral theory can bring to our holistic, interdisciplinary inquiry. I would like to end with yet another way to do so and reach similar conclusions to these two, despite rejecting some of what is common to all of Quine, Haslanger, and Mills.[9] In particular, so as to see that there are ways to combine some of the critical insights gleaned from the logical empiricists as well as from Quinean holism and naturalism, this will build off of the neological empiricist suggestions I made in chapter 5. In particular, we will show how a theory with A/S at center can be made perfectly consistent with Quine's holism and the socialized naturalism we found in Haslanger and Mills.

A/S Can be Consistent with Confirmational Holism

Given that Quine's confirmational holism argument was put forth directly for the sake of challenging A/S, this may seem surprising. In order to see that it is possible, though, remember the formulation we gave of this argument earlier:

P1: If there is an A/S, then there are some statements, which are always and everywhere immune from revision (namely, the analytic truths).
P2: No statement is immune from revision in this way. (Confirmational Holism and Under-determination of Theory choice arguments)
CONCLUSION: There is no A/S. (P1, P2, Modus Tollens)

While Quine's argument is not far off track, I think that he has really shown that the logical empiricists' particular explanation of the mechanisms behind analyticity are wrong. Despite this, I think that there are reasons to hold on to a different, but extremely similar account of A/S.

What is most important to point out in response to this argument is how old-fashioned a definition of "analyticity" P1 involves. Of course, this is not a complaint that ought to be lodged primarily at Quine. He was only following (some of) the empiricists' lead in this matter. One need not have these views while holding on to the existence of an A/S, though. So, it seems to me that Quine really has P1* at his disposal, rather than P1.

P1*: If the logical empiricists' explanation of A/S is correct, then there are some statements that are always and everywhere immune from revision.

With this new premise, only the empiricists' take on A/S needs to be threatened. Obviously, this invites us to come up with a new theory of A/S—one that does not fall prey to Quine's criticism here. I plan to sketch just such a theory before completing this chapter.

Importantly, others have already done this before me. For instance, Paul Boghossian's theory of analyticity is not at all in conflict with Quine's holistic fallibilism. Boghossian says "my own view is that the minimal notion [of a priority] forms the core of the idea of a priority" and that this minimal notion is distinguished from others insofar as it denies the claim that analytic and a priori justification are indefeasible by any future empirical evidence (Boghossian 1996, 62). Besides being consistent with it, Gillian Russell's views on A/S actually *embrace* Quinean holism. In Russell (2014), she states that even logical truths are "analytic, and the analyticity explains [their] distinctive modal status. But the epistemology of logic is holist [and] rather Quinean." So, in this way, we see that Quine can be thought of as pushing the discussion on A/S in more promising directions, rather than putting an end to it.

One further way we can see how Quinean holism could be consistent with holding that there is an A/S is by getting clearer on which objects are supposed to be analytic and synthetic. It is a notorious fact that, for all the talk of clarity, rigor, and precision it engendered, many thinkers were frustratingly slippery with their talk of analyticity. While something like "true in virtue of meaning" always played center stage, many formulations talked of "definitions," "synonyms," "logical constants," "conventions," "deductions," "variations," and various other philosophically loaded terms which are not obviously analytically connected to one another. Even the domain of objects it was supposed to be that could be true in virtue of meaning was not exactly clear. For some, it was statements. For others, propositions. And, some even held that it was *remarks* that were analytic or otherwise. It is small wonder the noncommittal usage of "analytic *truth*" became so popular.

For these reasons, it is quite useful that Nathan Salmon's and Russell's work on analyticity (Salmon 1986; Russell 2008) gave us clear arguments for the view that it is *sentences* that are either analytic or synthetic. The easiest way to see this is by building off Kripke's work, which clearly distinguished the notions of necessity, a priority, and analyticity as metaphysical, epistemic, and semantic in nature, respectively. Semantics, being linguistic in nature, is concerned with linguistic objects like morphemes, words, discourses, and *sentences*. Furthermore, as Russell (2008) has succinctly argued—since analytic truths are true *in virtue of* their meanings—whatever the objects of analyticity are must be things that *have* meanings. Things like propositions do not fill this role. They do not *have* meanings, they *are* meanings. And what are they meanings of? Sentences.

Of course, we have not actually fully answered our question yet. This is because there are multiple ways we can count, identify, and distinguish sentences from one another. In one sense of the word "sentence," there are two sentences displayed after this one:

"I am here now."   "I am here now."

In another sense of the word "sentence," there is just one sentence here. Put in the language of Peirce's famous distinction, we have here one single sentence type, of which I have displayed two different tokens (Peirce 1931–58, sec. 4.537).

Thus, the question for Salmon and Russell is whether or not we take sentence tokens or sentence types to be the primary bearers of "analytic" and "synthetic." This is a particularly important question if one is to have their theory of A/S be in line with the many advances in philosophical semantics of the Marcus-Kripke-Kaplan-Putnam-Burge tradition. Much of this tradition's work on indexicality and contextual factors has shown that the semantic properties of a sentence token are not necessarily the same as those of the type it instantiates. Furthermore, given that we will be concerned with the relationship between analyticity, necessity, and a priority, that the objects of necessity and a priority seem to be propositions, and that it is only individual sentence tokens that express propositions, the answer to this question is not trivial.

What is most relevant for our purposes is simply the potential this possibility opens up for the dialectic. If "analytic" and "synthetic" were primarily predicated of sentence tokens, then the holism argument would no longer be worrisome for A/S. Since it would not be sentence types that would be analytic or synthetic, that any sentence type could be assented to at one time, but rejected later would not be a threat to A/S. The proponent of A/S could simply say that one token of the type was analytic, but that the second token (representative of the theory revision) of that same type was no longer analytic (i.e., that, while P1* is true, P1 is false). Furthermore, this is not just a bare logical possibility, it is actually the view of a number of neo-Wittgensteinian thinkers such as Hans-Johann Glock (1996), PMS Hacker (1996), and Severin Schroeder (2009). The precise details of their views are unimportant for our purposes. Rather, it is just important to recognize that Quinean holism can be made perfectly consistent with holding on to A/S and explore one such set of views.

A Positive Account of A/S with Haslangerian and Millsian Naturalism in Mind

Remember, I argued in chapter 5 that the logical empiricists' views on A/S were driven by the belief that we must not allow intuition or pure reason as a source of knowledge or justified belief because of how it would disrupt public methods of dispute resolution, an important component of public reason. A doctrine of analyticity was central to this project because the synthetic (necessary) a priori was the traditional source of Kant's claiming we had knowledge from pure intuition. Hence, an epistemology free of intuition seemed to require an account free of only the synthetic a priori. Unfortunately, the most influential logical empiricist strategy for achieving this identified the extensions of 'analytic," "necessary," and "a priori" on the one hand, and "synthetic," "contingent," and "a posteriori" on the other. This left their account of A/S vulnerable to Kripke's discovery of the necessary a posteriori and contingent a priori. Here, we will try to extend the views on A/S put forth in chapter 5, which allowed us to reject epistemic hierarchy and the epistemic neutrality principle that formed a part of the problematically gendered Assumed Objectivity.

Extending and building on the work of Descartes, Russell, Kaplan, Kripke, and Kant, Campbell (2017) argues for a view on the relationship between analyticity, a priority, and necessity that he calls "octopropositionalism." This term is chosen because there are *eight* different possible categories of the form "x y z," where x is "analytic" or "synthetic," y is "necessary" or "contingent," and z is "a priori" or "a posteriori"—all of which Campbell (2017) argues have nonempty sets of propositions satisfying them.[10] Given that Gillian Russell—who has published more sophisticated work on analyticity in the contemporary literature than anyone else by a good amount—has argued that the debate on the analytic/synthetic distinction is greatly improved by recognizing there are many more than analytic necessary a priori and synthetic contingent a posteriori truths, it could easily be assumed that octopropositionalism is the natural direction that contemporary thinking on A/S should be going. While I tend to agree with much more of octopropositionalism than most throughout the history of thought on A/S would, I am only a hexapropositionalist—believing it very important to deny that there are any synthetic a priori truths (necessary or contingent).

This particular denial of octopropositionalism is important because it represents a maximal position that one can take, which both accepts the contributions of Kripke, Kaplan, and Russell, yet still denies octopropositionalism. It is, in a certain sense, the only middle ground between the Direct Reference, realist, externalist semantics of the Kripke–Kaplan–Russell tradition and octopropositionalism. This is because Campbell (2017) has very usefully shown that there are different subsets of the set of all these categories, which can act as a basis for a complete vector space of propositions satisfying all eight categories. That is, if there are atomic sentences of only (certain collections of) three of these categories, truth-functions of them will yield sentences belonging to all eight categories. In particular, two three-membered sets could serve as such a basis:

[B1] {analytic necessary a posteriori, synthetic necessary a priori, analytic contingent a priori}
[B2] {synthetic necessary a posteriori, synthetic contingent a priori, analytic contingent a posteriori}

If the conditions for either B1 or B2 were met, then octopropositionalism would follow. Since B1 requires synthetic necessary a priori and B2 synthetic contingent a priori truths, to accept Kripke, Kaplan, and Russell, and to deny octopropositionalism, one must rule out the synthetic a priori altogether. Interestingly, this middle ground view of hexapropositionalism, with a denial of both categories involving the synthetic a priori, starts to look a lot like something we could call a contemporary descendant of logical empiricism.

Remember, their account of A/S was always intended primarily to rule out the synthetic a priori. The logical empiricists understood the analytic a priori just fine—analytic truths come from our meaning conventions, some of our meaning conventions can be accessed a priori, and so, some of our knowledge of analytic truths will be a priori.

The question then is, why do we want an account of A/S, which rules out the synthetic a priori but accepts post-Kripkean advances? As was discussed in chapter 5, I believe that various accounts of the synthetic a priori and necessary a posteriori and the role of intuition of essences in our knowing such types of facts seem to lend themselves to epistemic hierarchy—a belief that some are inherently better knowers than others. Again, the essentially private and contested nature of armchair intuitions hinders the public dispute resolution, which is integral for an epistemic egalitarianism free of epistemic hierarchy. There is no method of public dispute resolution when one's intuition-delivered judgments conflict with another's. This, I believe, is simply unacceptable.

That said, this is surely not the only evidence we can find for the claim that, not only can verificationism be taken as a way of promoting public reason, it was at least partly intended to make contributions to public dispute resolution. The very first sentence of Ayer's own magnum opus, *Language, Truth, and Logic*, says "The traditional disputes of philosophers are, for the most part, as unwarranted as they are unfruitful.." (Ayer 1936, 33). Furthermore, as Carnap often made clear, "The scientific character makes possible the cooperation of different people" (Carnap 1964, 135) and "so we believe that in philosophy too progress is made by making cooperation possible" (Carnap 1964, 136). Much as doctrines of public reason are aimed at promoting group cohesion while respecting the autonomy of individuals, Carnap associated logical empiricism with "movements which strive for meaningful forms of personal and collective life, of education, and of external organization in general.... It is an orientation which acknowledges the bonds that tie men together, but at the same time strives for free development of the individual" (Carnap 1967, xvii–xviii). Importantly, as we saw in chapter 5, Carnap was not unique among members of the Vienna Circle on this front, either.

When we left off in chapter 5, we had just considered the suggestion that a neological empiricist might argue that rather than saying the proposition's necessary *truth* is explained by linguistic conventions, we should say it is the proposition's *necessity* that is explained by linguistic conventions. This would be achieved by claiming that sentences attributing modalities that *are* linguistic conventions. Something like this view has been proposed by Ted Sider when he wrote:

> I take it that logical, analytic and mathematical truths do not owe their truth to convention, except in the uninteresting sense in which every true sentence partly

owes its truth to the conventions that give that sentence its meaning. It might still be a convention to call logical, analytic, and mathematical truths necessary. It would be analytic to "necessary" that logical, analytic and mathematical truths are necessary. "Necessary" would be a word used for truths of certain kinds. (Sider 2003, 203–4)

A view such as this would be an advance over earlier versions of conventionalism because it does not involve conventionalism about propositions, but conventionalism about sentences instead. It also does not require saying that there is anything different or conventional about the *truth* of necessary vs. contingent truths, just about their modal statuses. As Sider explains,

So, provided "2+2=4" is a mathematical truth, the following sentence will be true: Necessarily, 2+2=4. Convention can do this much. It need not play any role in making it true that 2+2=4, or in making this be a mathematical truth. (Sider 2003, 204)

Again, on such a view, convention does not make it *true* that 2+2=4. Convention makes it *necessary* that 2+2=4.

Being more explicit about this, we get such a version of conventionalism by precisifying the third version of the analytic theory of necessity from chapter 5 (ATN3):

(ATN3) Any true sentence token of the form "x is y," where "x" is replaced by something that refers to a proposition and "y" is replaced by "necessary," "possible," "impossible," etc. is metaphysically analytic.

An obvious question to ask here is, why in the world would anyone adopt this version—ATN3? That is, what makes this anything other than an ad hoc move? Answering this question requires giving an upshot for the difference between adopting a convention that "x is contingent" vs. adopting a convention that "x is necessary." Giving a full answer to this question requires work outside of the scope of this chapter, but I think we can point to a potentially plausible answer by returning to our earlier thoughts on A/S. In particular, the picture of A/S adopted by myself—and built out of some historically prominent defenders of ATN—had reference occurring as a result of adopting conventions that certain sentences only be given an interpretation, which makes them true. This is how the reference relation is initially instantiated for the implicit definition theorist. That said, such stipulations are consistent with a number of different interpretations going forward. As Quine's inscrutability of reference argument shows, we need to do more to keep the reference relation fixed on a particular relatum.

This is what the conventions specified in ATN3 are for. They give us details about the persistence conditions of the reference relation. If, for example, we have a simple sentence attributing a property expressed by "f" to an object expressed by "x" and we adopt the implicit definition "f(x) is necessary," then anything that ceases to be f, also ceases to be x. If instead we adopt the implicit definition that "f(x) is contingent," then we will not rule out an object having "x" properly apply to it simply because "f" ceases to be true of it.

Returning to the political potential of such a view, this would allow us to give an account of precisely why we should deny epistemic neutrality and, thus, Assumed Objectivity. Given the potential for the belief in natures/ essences to contribute to sexism and racism, this should be invited. Therefore, in particular, since necessity and, thus, essence are the result of conventions about the persistence conditions of the reference relation, we need not think that essences are fully mind-independent. When somebody tries to discuss essences of genders, races, or classes as built into the fabric of the universe and which need to be abided, we have every reason to deny them out of hand.

§7.6 ANOTHER EXAMPLE OF POLITICALLY REVISIONARY NATURALIZED EPISTEMOLOGY AND ONTOLOGY

Another place we can find utility for this neological empiricist view, which takes significant input from Quine, Mills, and Haslanger, is with respect to mental illness. One of the most prominent features of each of these thinkers with respect to epistemology is an anti-foundationalist fallibilism, which holds that certainty is an unnecessary criterion for knowledge. That is, following Quine, much contemporary metaphysical work has rejected "the thought that we might have or *need* certainty, or direct access to reality, in order to make legitimate ontological claims" (Haslanger 2012, 145). This is important, since a significant number of people with mental illnesses manifest their symptoms in relation to certainty and doubt. As a result, this move away from a Cartesian, individualist, internalist search for foundational certainty has a chance to undermine some of the worries that Moorean epistemology was ableist, which were brought up in chapter 3.[11]

Remember, we said there that promoting conservative Moorean common sense and appeals to intuition has an exclusionary impact with respect to those with Obsessive Compulsive Disorder. Those with OCD are encouraged to detach from automatic and immediate cognitions and conceptions as even inherently meaningful, let alone true. If we were to require MCS, people with OCD would then be essentially bad philosophers. This strikes me as unlikely, given that there are features of many people with OCD that make them more inclined to do philosophy than others. As Hershfield and Nicely point out, those with OCD are often expert noticers—those with mental obsessions often being experts at noticing mere possibilities and potentialities (Hershfield & Nicely 2017, 12–14). The importance to philosophy of modalities, which are related to possibility and potentiality, make this a nice feature for doing philosophy.

When people with OCD get in trouble is when they obsess about the possibility of some state of affairs, s, more than the fact that the actuality is most likely to make ~s true. S seems bad and "you don't like feeling bad. So you set out to get some certainty that your obsessive thought is harmless or inaccurate, or at least that it will go away" (Hershfield & Nicely 2017, 3). This certainty/reassurance seeking then creates a negative reinforcement loop always needing more and more certainty. When we recognize that anything depending on experiential input from the world could possibly have been otherwise, we will recognize that uncertainty is a function of all a posteriori and contingent matters.

For this reason, folks with OCD are significantly helped by learning to yield to uncertainty (Hershfield & Nicely 2017, 115–18). Hence, a naturalist, fallibilist epistemology, which encourages us to do just that, will have the potential to quite literally help the recovery of such folks with OCD. If knowledge does not require certainty, the search for certainty will be seen to be unnecessary and recognizing this will encourage the person with OCD to be more accepting of making decisions in the face of uncertainty. As the Director of The OCD and Anxiety Center of Greater Baltimore says, "Improving your ability to open up to, accept, or even embrace uncertainty in the face of OCD is essential to getting mastery of the disorder" (Hershfield 2017).

Notice that this also provides us with another example of how knowing some empirical facts about how our brains work can be useful for epistemology. Knowing something about how many people with OCD's brains function, it is sometimes a very important norm of investigation for those with OCD that they should not always be out for absolute certainty. This is also a way in which the work of the logical empiricists can be uniquely helpful for those with OCD. The only certainties to be found in our theoretical structures on such a view are those we decide to conventionally impose—the analytic truths. Every matter of empirical fact admits of uncertainty. This means that *almost* all of our significant beliefs are such that it will be nonsense to expect certainty of them.

Such a recognition of the possibility for certainty, but the fleeting nature of it, can also be very useful for those with OCD. Someone with OCD could notice that there is a type of certainty attached to logical truths like the law of identity or mathematical truths like those of arithmetic. Having such a hard-wired desire for certainty, they may come to want and expect this from as many of their beliefs as possible, which could then be a trigger for significant spikes. Hence, recognizing that there can be a form of certainty in some truths, which cannot be applied to all beliefs and, in fact, mostly will not occur, is useful for yielding to uncertainty.

This is not an isolated instance, either. Understanding mathematical concepts like that of *asymptotic behavior* can aid in OCD folks' understanding of their progress in treatment. This is because "What sets OCD apart from other so-called 'chronic' conditions is that you can expect to get better and better as time goes on . . . but as you get better and better, this progress slows and never really gets down to zero" (Hershfield & Nicely 2017, 9–10). Thinking about OCD in these ways also points to the utility we can find in blurring disciplinary boundaries and taking a holist, multicultural, pluralist, pragmatist perspective. One of the very best paths to OCD remission is vipassana meditation (Twohig, Hayes, & Masuda 2006; Wahl 2013; Krygiera et al. 2013). The dual focus on concentration and mindfulness involved allows one to become aware of, and break free from, the negative reinforcement loops referenced earlier. In further work, I hope to build off of these ideas to systematically develop a number of ways in which analytic and Buddhist traditions can come together in helping to understand and live with OCD. For now, it is important to simply recognize that some such connections exist.

§7.7 CONCLUSIONS AND QUESTIONS MOVING FORWARD

There are many different strands of thought we could have talked about with respect to Stage 5. For topics, we could have discussed Anscombe and Foot reviving interest in traditional normative ethics or Marcus, Carnap, Prior, Kripke, and Montague doing similarly with respect to modal logics. For doctrinal differences, we could have discussed the demise of the belief that ordinary languages are best understood with informal, piecemeal, and atheoretical approaches to language and the rise of truth-conditional semantics. With respect to the larger historical context for Stage 5, we could have discussed the consequences of McCarthyism on analytic institutions. Given the particular dialectical space of my primary theses, though, it made most sense for us to discuss the potential of Quine's system-building work from the 1960s to contribute to critical theories of race and gender.

In doing so, we focused primarily on Quine's confirmational holism and subsequent philosophical naturalism. Quine's view that it is only holistic bodies of hypotheses, inference rules, auxiliary assumptions, and measuring rules, which are confirmed or infirmed led to an alternative picture than one holding there is a sharp distinction between philosophical disciplines and empirical sciences. Since this was most influential for his naturalized epistemology, which held that questions about how we ought to form beliefs are based on questions about how we actually do form beliefs, we were concerned here with showing its critical potential.

In particular, we saw that Sally Haslanger and Charles Mills have shown that naturalized epistemology is necessary for seeing the extent to which knowledge is a social phenomenon and the role that epistemology needs to play in undermining the perpetuation of hegemonic racialized and gendered ideologies if we wish to undermine the perpetuation of racist and sexist systems. We also saw that this can be generalized into a systematic critical naturalism involving ontology, phenomenology, ethics, social and political philosophy, and more. Perhaps most interestingly, in relying on social science and moral theory, Haslanger and Mills respected a holistic, naturalized system relying on as many traditionally distinguished disciplines as possible, and, in doing so, were being more Quinean than Quine. To see that this naturalistic, interdisciplinary perspective is one of the most important parts of Quine's legacy for critical work, I showed how very similar conclusions could be drawn while varying views on the analytic/synthetic distinction and scientific essentialism. By adopting ATN3, the view that the existence of essences is socially constructed, but individual essences are determined a posteriori, we were able to do so. Finally, I gestured at some further work that such views could do for philosophers interested in social justice by considering an example of how such views can help in understanding and processing of OCD.

NOTES

1. There are, of course, notable exceptions to this, which will be discussed throughout the chapter. Given my particular concerns and space constraints, Louise Antony's work on this front will be unfortunately absent. That said, I greatly encourage readers to study Antony (1993).

2. For instance, Quine once felt the need to clarify, "I was never drawn to socialism and communism as [Bertrand Russell] was." Of course, this was also in the midst of discussing how Nazi racism made him feel that doing the philosophy of logic was not important enough. He needed to enlist in the navy to fight this racism (Borradori 1994). On the other hand, one of the very few matters of politics discussed in his autobiography also has Quine showing his disdain for all of the progressive political activity happening at Harvard in the 1960s and being quite comfortable with casual racism (Quine 1985). That said, it is worth noting that Lynn Hankinson Nelson provides some interesting biographical notes about Quine, for example, that after "Lynn published her first book *Who Knows: From Quine to a Feminist Empiricism* (Temple,

1990) . . . Quintessentially Quine . . . wrote 'You have me dead to rights'. . . 'But . . . the idea of a feminist epistemology still has an aura of unreality to me. I must read on.'" in a hand-written note she received from him about the book (Clough 2003, 63). Many thanks to Rick Creath for helping me recognize the difficulty in understanding the messy relationship between Quine's life/thought and traditional conservatism.

3. As with all of my thoughts on analyticity, this draws heavily from my dissertation (LaVine 2016a).

4. Section 4.46 of Wittgenstein, Ludwig (1921). *Tractatus Logico-Philosophicus*, in *Annalen der Naturphilosophie* 14. English translation by C. K. Ogden (1922).

5. For a contemporary theory of A/S, which clearly does not allow for "analyticity" and "necessity" to be interdefinable, see Russell (2008). On this view, necessary truths are propositions true at all circumstances of evaluation, while analytic truths are sentences true at all contexts of introduction (because true in virtue of reference determiners, rather than propositional content). This allows for contingent analytic truths and necessary synthetic truths.

6. In case it is not clear how we get to this, a sub-argument for it might look something like the following:

> P1: If we want to test theoretical statements, then we must obtain predictions in the form of singular observation statements from them.
>
> P2: If we must obtain predictions in the form of singular observation statements from theoretical statements, then we need to use inference rules, auxiliary hypotheses, and measurement rules.
>
> P3: If we need to use inference rules, auxiliary hypotheses, and measurement rules to obtain testable predictions from theoretical statements, then all that is ever subjected to testing is a collective body of theoretical statements, inference rules, auxiliary hypotheses, and measurement rules.
>
> P4: If all that is ever tested are such collective bodies, then no statement is immune from revision and any general theory can be shielded from refutation.
>
> C: If we want to test theoretical statements by observations, then no statement is immune from revision and any general theory can be shielded from refutation.

7. Given that this is a point Mills regularly references, it would be interesting to try to weigh in on a dialectic involving Mills and Alice Crary, who has recently argued that, along with bell hooks' claim that to be truly feminist, a movement must be politically radical, we must add a claim that, "In order to qualify as truly 'feminist', a movement also has to be methodologically radical" (Crary 2018).

8. Some further thoughts of Quine's that seem to strongly suggest he should be more concerned with social science include "Total science, mathematical and natural and human, is similarly but more extremely underdetermined by experience." And "The totality of our so-called knowledge or beliefs, from the most casual matters of geography and history to the profoundest laws of atomic physics or even of pure mathematics and logic, is a man-made fabric which impinges on experience only along the edges."

9. Properly speaking, what is common to them all is lack of a utilization of A/S. Mills does not address his views on A/S. Quine obviously denies that there is a distinction between analytic and synthetic truths. Finally, Haslanger occasionally suggests that she would also deny this—saying that her philosophical outlook was tutored by Quine's legacy, which called such a sharp divide into question (Haslanger 2012, 13). More recently, she has put analytic truths in scare quotes and implicated there are dangers of A/S—"On my view, a cultural technē is a set of social meanings—including concepts, scripts, background assumptions ("analytic" truths), inferential patterns, salient metaphors, metonyms, conceptual oppositions, and (broadly speaking) grammar —that provides tools for interpreting and responding to each other and the world around us" (Haslanger forthcoming, 3) and "Putnam (1962/1975) provides an important early discussion of the importance of amelioration in science and the dangers of maintaining the analytic/synthetic distinctions" (Haslanger forthcoming, 12).

10. Campbell (2017) uses the term "empirical," rather than "a posteriori."

11. Chapter 4 also brings up some significant sites of engagement with naturalistic philosophy. In particular, the inability of the voluntary racial eliminativist to tell us how to take concrete steps toward a better state of affairs than the current one where racial causation is so prevalent should make us recognize that:

> communications experts tell us that when facts do not fit with the available frames, people have a difficult time incorporating new facts into their way of thinking about a problem. [Names of black women killed by police] have slipped through our consciousness because there are no frames for us to see them, no frames for us to remember them, no frames for us to hold them. As a consequence, reporters don't lead with them, policymakers don't think about them, and politicians aren't encouraged or demanded that they speak to them. (Crenshaw 2016)

This means that there are social scientific results, which will need to be brought together into a naturalistic ideology critique.

Part 4

Conclusion

§8.0 OVERVIEW OF CONCLUSION

In this conclusion, I try to bring together the disparate claims of a book which may otherwise seem somewhat scattered. I summarize the main conclusions of the previous chapters and show how they serve as sub-conclusions in arguments for the primary theses mentioned in the introduction. I briefly mention several major trends in analytic philosophy I see to be of importance since 1970. I preview answers to some questions I believe will be of importance to ask in order to help get the discipline moving toward a more just future and that are most naturally connected to my primary theses. Finally, I end by reminding readers where I think it will be important to consider potential failures of my work.

§8.1 SUMMARY OF CONCLUSIONS

For the last eight chapters, I have been arguing for the basic theses that

(1) there is much to be gained by bringing together inquiry into critical theories of race and gender, on the one hand, and analytic philosophy, on the other
(2) there is much more precedent for this type of work in the history of early analytic philosophy than is traditionally recognized.

Furthermore, I intended that these theses be adopted on both the *method* disambiguation of "analytic philosophy" and the *movement* disambiguation of "analytic philosophy." On the former reading, where "analytic philosophy" refers to a method of doing philosophy that places logical and linguistic analysis at its foundation, I argued in parts 1 and 2 that

P1: Analytic philosophy has philosophy of language and logic at its core. (Definition 1 from Introduction)
P2: There are productive engagements between feminist and antiracist inquiry and the history of the philosophy of language. (chapter 1)
P3: There are productive engagements between feminist and antiracist inquiry and the history of logic. (chapter 2)
CONCLUSION: There are productive engagements between feminist and antiracist inquiry and all of the history of analytic philosophy, the method.

In part 3, I argued with respect to the latter reading, where "analytic philosophy" refers to a movement within the history of philosophy, that

P1: Stage 1 through Stage 5 are all of the stages of early analytic philosophy. (Definition 2 from Introduction)
P2: There are productive engagements between feminist and antiracist inquiry and Stage 1 of the history of early analytic philosophy. (chapter 3)
P3: There are productive engagements between feminist and antiracist inquiry and Stage 2 of the history of early analytic philosophy. (chapter 4)
P4: There are productive engagements between feminist and antiracist inquiry and Stage 3 of the history of early analytic philosophy. (chapter 5)
P5: There are productive engagements between feminist and antiracist inquiry and Stage 4 of the history of early analytic philosophy. (chapter 6)
P6: There are productive engagements between feminist and antiracist inquiry and Stage 5 of the history of early analytic philosophy. (chapter 7)
CONCLUSION: There are productive engagements between feminist and antiracist inquiry and all of early analytic philosophy, the movement within the history of philosophy.

Despite all of the hope that these two primary conclusions might suggest, I also tend to believe that the time since 1970, when analytic philosophy completed its turn from revolutionary movement to entrenched hegemon, has involved a significant slide back on this front.[1] That is what has made the book something I believe to be worth adding to the literature on the history of analytic philosophy. Of course, this is just the view I hold with respect to *some* general trends in the history of analytic philosophy. Importantly, I think there are also a number of promising developments in the most recent history of analytic philosophy. Because there is so much room for improvement, it is to these that we will turn in this chapter as a way of laying out where I think some promising avenues of research exist.

Before I do that, I must add one very important caveat. I do not want my focusing on the positive potential of early analytic philosophy to be mistaken for praising the institution of analytic philosophy. If anything, this is meant as a significant criticism of the field. The extent to which it has become disengaged, purely academic, and obtuse is disturbing to say the least. My point in focusing on the fact that a promotion of social justice was central to early analytic philosophy was to point out the fact that this change is not only disturbing but it actually misunderstands its own genesis as well. The proper inheritors of the tradition of Russell, Moore, Carnap, Neurath, Stebbing, Austin, and Marcus are folks like Liam Kofi Bright, Catarina Dutilh Novaes, Sally Haslanger, Rebecca Kukla, Charles Mills, Audrey Yap, Naomi Zack, and the like.

Unsurprisingly, then, my discussion of promising avenues for future research can largely be summed up—there is lots more awesome philosophy like theirs to be done! This is more than just because I most closely identify with their work (though this is true as well). Rather, it is because the picture of analytic philosophy that I have argued we should adopt would have these thinkers as the culmination, as the protagonists. As Dutilh Novaes and Geerdink show, and I echoed in chapter 3, the first stage of early analytic philosophy is best understood not only as a rejection of British idealism in favor of commonsense realist pluralism led by Moore and Russell, but is also the start of one of the most prominent dialectics throughout analytic philosophy—the question of whether we should take a conservative approach or a revisionary, transformative approach to commonsense analysis (Dutilh Novaes & Geerdink 2017, 70–71). Just as Dutilh Novaes (2018) argued that Carnap and Haslanger share a politically revisionary approach, I said we could understand some of why we should adopt a politically revisionary take on analysis by looking at Stebbing's and Mills' work.

Also, in chapter 4, we saw additional reason to think Dutilh Novaes was right in pointing out ideology critique as the primary point of difference between Carnapian explication and Haslangerian ameliorative analysis (Dutilh Novaes 2018, 17–18). In particular, we saw that the metaphysics as disguised ethics view—which was exemplified by Bright's (2017) analysis of Carnap's (and logical empiricist, generally) voluntary racial eliminativism—suffered from overidealization in failing to engage in racial ideology critique on our way to a society which is antiracist. Hence, we adopted a politically revisionary *critical* analysis as the way to best integrate the views of Bright, Dutilh Novaes, Haslanger, and Mills.

Given the importance of Stebbing and Carnap to my evaluation of this story of the first two stages, chapter 5's discussion of Stage 3 (where logical empiricism, Cambridge analysis, and the Lvov-Warsaw school of logic and mathematics led) was a natural point for a major challenge. We found this in the work of Sarah Richardson (2009a, 2009b)—which challenged both the historical and normative aspects of the Left Vienna Circle thesis that Carnap and like-minded thinkers had a political philosophy of science. Despite the importance of Richardson's work, I ultimately doubled down, saying there were political philosophies of science throughout Stage 3—within the logical empiricists, critical rationalists, Cambridge analysts, and the Lvov-Warsaw school. Instead, Richardson's work simply set some significant restraints on productive LVC engagements with FEPS, critical theories of race, queer theory, etc. Because of how important these constraints are, we will come back to them at the end of this chapter.

Given the significant controversy over treating ordinary language philosophy as a unified, coherent group, I did not want to attribute much more of a commonality between them than an interest in not centering philosophical work around formal, abstract, ideal language. Hence, chapter 6 on Stage 4 focused on a very concrete contribution to a concrete matter of justice—as a sign of what we get when we do not focus on abstract, ideal situations. In particular, Paul Grice's logic of conversation was used along with Charles Mills' work on the racial contract to argue that some of the most standard objections to the Black Lives Matter movement are straightforwardly racist.

Finally, continuing this trend of focusing on the real world, chapter 7's discussion of Stage 5 focused on Quine's work from the 1960s coming up with a holist, naturalistic system of thought. Here, we saw how Haslanger and Mills show that a thoroughly naturalistic and interdisciplinary outlook would include significant contributions from social science and moral theory, both of which were paid insufficient time and energy by the logical empiricists and Quine. Therefore, this whole book can be seen as an attempt to start sketching a politically revisionary, nonideal, naturalistic, critical analysis built off of the work of Bright, Dutilh Novaes, Haslanger, and Mills.

§8.2 MOVING THIS FORWARD INTO A RESEARCH AND ACTIVISM PROGRAM, PART I

As is alluded to with this talk of "a politically revisionary, non-ideal, naturalistic, critical analysis" built off of the work of Bright, Dutilh Novaes, Haslanger, and Mills, I aspire to bring portions of this into a semi-cohesive research program. One of the primary ways I want to take these theses, suggestions, and methods forward into a larger program is by combining insights from the different stages into sustained discussions of particular issues. The lack of this in the preceding chapters follows largely from the idiosyncratic aims I had there. Because establishing the mere existence of fruitful intertwining of such inquiries throughout all stages was my goal, I proceeded largely by individual case studies from the history of early analytic philosophy and connected them to a wide variety of concerns surrounding critical theories of race and gender. This leaves me open to the criticism that these individual cases, which have not been systematically connected to each other much beyond the previous section, are not telling of anything *central* to philosophizing in the analytic tradition that lends itself to *systematic* critical theory. I hope to have my future work directly address such a criticism and, in the rest of this section, will sketch one such case in the hopes of readers not taking this as a damning criticism.

Given some of the issues discussed in these various chapters, the most natural place to start is with work in the metaphysics of race. I will attempt to respond to the aforesaid criticism by connecting the methods, tools, and theses discussed in the previous eight chapters and applying them together in one sustained contribution to the foundational problems in the metaphysics of race. As discussed earlier, the metaphysics of race focuses on questions concerning existence and essence. What, if anything, are the essences of races like—what *kind* of thing is a race?—and do those kinds of things exist in the actual world?

Again, there are often thought to be three standard types of positions in the metaphysics of race distinguished by their answers to these two questions (Haslanger 2012, 299–302). Race naturalists hold that races do exist and that their essences are best studied by the natural sciences. Race eliminativists hold that races would be naturalistic if they existed, but all of our best genetics shows that such naturalistic divisions between racial groups do not actually exist. Finally, social constructionists agree with the naturalist in holding that races exist and agree with the eliminativist that our best science shows they cannot be naturalistic. Rather, since they are brought into existence by social processes, constructionists believe that races are best studied by the social sciences.

I think we can use the history of early analytic philosophy to provide a case for a social constructionist account of race by engaging some of the foundational principles suggested in previous chapters with contemporary positions from Alcoff, Appiah, Glasgow and Woodward, Hardimon, Haslanger, McPherson, and Mills. Illustrating the fact that there are a number of ways to utilize theses I have defended and suggestions I have considered with these interlocutors in mind, the methods for navigating between them will be logical, semantic, empirical, social, and political. In particular, it will be argued that, for all of the value we can get out of his impressively clear conceptual framework, Hardimon's deflationary realist views suffer from an inferential problem at a very crucial step. McPherson's deflationary pluralism and Appiah's particular brand of eliminativism will be criticized on political and semantic grounds. Most broadly, I believe that that they make achieving racial justice more difficult than necessary and involve making unnecessary changes to the standard meanings of "race" and "racism." Finally, Glasgow and Woodward's basic racial realism will be rejected on empirical grounds, saying it cannot sufficiently account for how essential to social science racial terminology is currently. This will lead to a social constructionist account of race combining Alcoff, Haslanger, and Mills. A preview of the details follows.

While I believe the last several decades of the literature speaks largely toward social constructionism being the most plausible framework among the Big Three—even for those forms of naturalism consistent with Lewontin (1972) and Rosenberg et al. (2002), such as Andreasen (2004), Hardimon (2012), Kitcher (2007)—there have recently been several prominent works that grant this fact and still are not versions of social constructionism. One of these, Glasgow and Woodward (2015) does so by holding that, even if social constructionism is preferable to naturalism and eliminativism, we still should not adopt constructionism. This is because all three suffer from a common false assumption.

In particular, all three suffer from "the elitist premise"—the view "that to be real, race must be scientifically relevant" (Glasgow & Woodward 2015, 453). For instance, eliminativism gained prominence when it began to look like the best empirical evidence showed that race is not central to work in genetics or biology more generally—something that naturalists had bet the reality of races on. Furthermore, social constructionists hold that the reality of race is tied up with and dependent upon the fact that race is directly relevant to the social sciences. Glasgow and Woodward aim to build a metaphysic of race, which denies this elitist premise and, thus, falls outside of the Big Three.

Bringing even further possibilities to the dialectic, Michael Hardimon's 2017 book, *Rethinking Race: The Case for Deflationary Realism*, shows that a Big Four would not be enough either. Unlike Glasgow and Woodward, rather than denying a common basis of eliminativism, naturalism, and constructionism, Hardimon's deflationary realism *combines* them all together. It says that there is a certain sense in which all of these views express something true. The key to the metaphysics of race, then, is coming up with a framework that shows how such a view can be consistently held.

Starting with Glasgow and Woodward, their *basic racial realism* is built off of a definition of "basic kind" where anything meeting it must not only exist mind-independently, but also fail to be directly relevant to science. Otherwise, it would not be a basic kind, but rather a natural kind or social kind (depending on whether it was directly relevant to natural science or social science). Given that they take races to be basic kinds, this means they hold that race is not directly relevant to either natural or social science. Thus, we get their basic racial realism—the view that races are basic kinds.

That said, one simply cannot do large-scale social science of Western society without involving race. For example, consider the history and sociology of housing patterns within the United States since 1900. If one is looking into such matters, one of the most striking features that will come out is the phenomenon of racialized residential segregation. That is, throughout the twentieth and twenty-first centuries, a variety of different levels of social institutions have created and enforced the physical separation of the neighborhoods of different racial communities. This has made it so these social institutions have supported and harmed them to very different extents. Furthermore, these facts have been shown to be crucial to explaining access to educational opportunities, employment opportunities, recreational opportunities, environmental burdens, environmental benefits, and health outcomes (Williams & Collins 2001; Chang 2003; LaDuke & Cruz 2012; Bell 2013; Rothstein 2017). We must understand and incorporate these results from the social sciences if we are to do metaphysics equipped to help fight environmental injustice, health injustice, etc. In other words, social science needs the concept of race and, thus, races cannot be basic kinds.

With this example of how naturalistic and political considerations can help in the metaphysics of race, we turn to semantic and logical considerations in relation to Hardimon's deflationary realism. Given the immense amount of talking past one another that regularly happens when people talk about race, Hardimon's (2017) contributions to the literature on race undoubtedly begin with his disambiguations between, and clear definitions of, four different race concepts. These are the racialist, minimalist, populationist, and social race concepts. If he had written nothing else about race, this fourfold distinction and clarification would have been a welcome contribution. Sketching this work rather broadly, the *racialist race* concept was the one first used in the modern discussion of race—famously by philosophers such as Locke and Kant, but also by theorists such as Blumenbach, Gobineau, and Meiners. Someone who believes there are racialist races holds that different races have distinct biological essences, which are signaled by outward physical differences, but are also telling of normatively relevant and hierarchical moral, intellectual, and aesthetic differences. Given this, commitment to the existence of racialist races obviously lends itself to heinous projects.

That said, the racialist race concept is to be distinguished from a much more bare-bones version of a race concept. This *minimalist race* concept is one where all normative and deeper differences are stripped away. The only differences that remain as racial are patterns of a small handful of inheritable, visible physical features, which trace to particular geographic regions. Furthermore, this concept can be refined even more into a more directly biologically minded concept—the populationist race concept—"a nonracialist (nonessentialist, nonhierarchical) candidate scientific concept that characterizes races as groups of populations belonging to biological lines of descent" (Hardimon 2017, 3). Of course, this is not the race concept that most who have thought they could study race via the natural sciences were using—they were using the racialist race concept. Because of that, such folks thinking that there have been racialist races have caused them to unjustly treat groups as racialist races. These groups mistakenly treated as racialist races then give us the referents of the social race concept.

With this disambiguation of "race" out of the way, we have the conceptual tools necessary to state Hardimon's deflationary realism. The deflationary realist will hold that

(1) Lewontin (1972) and Rosenberg et al. (2002) show there are no racialist races.
(2) That said, they leave open the possibility that minimalist races exist and, in fact, upon further reflection, we will see that they do exist.
(3) Populationist races, the scientific correlate of minimalist races, probably exist.
(4) The fact that groups have been treated as racialist races despite them not existing has created social race groups.

Given that (1) corresponds to the eliminativist position, (3) to the naturalist position, and (4) to the constructionist position, (2) is the most distinctive aspect of Hardimon's deflationary realism. For this reason, I will eventually need to spend the most time on the justification behind (2) and the belief in the existence of minimalist races.

Most broadly, justification for (2) relies at a crucial point on reasoning that if one has stripped away the empirical falsehoods and moral heinousness from historically prominent accounts of race, one will end up with the "logical core" of the concept—"a hidden but already existing meaning for 'race'" (Hardimon 2017, 28) with the "essential features of the ordinary concept of race" (Hardimon 2017, 57). I argue that one simply cannot infer the latter from the former. Sometimes stripping away the empirical falsehoods and moral heinousness behind a concept leaves one with nothing essential or ordinary at all—what we might call the logical *shell* of the concept, rather than the core.

In place of these, I would argue for a social constructionist view, which combines aspects of Alcoff's, Haslanger's, and Mills' views. This will partly involve accepting at face value something said by Glasgow and Woodward, who argue of Haslanger that, although she "lays out the linguistic framework for her view, she gives no argument for moving from the more modest proposal of basic racial realism to the harder-to-defend interpretation of racial discourse that leads to constructionism" (Glasgow & Woodward 2015, 455). That said, once one adopts the views on reference magnetism that Haslanger lays out—that kind terms refer to the most objectively unified kind that the paradigm instances of the term belong to (Haslanger 2012, 305)—the more unified social kind will be seen as the referent. Hence, since social constructionism better accounts for the fact that race is relevant to social science, if one adopts standard views in the philosophy of language, social constructionism has a better claim to accounting for the referent of "race" than Glasgow and Woodward's basic racial realism.

So, to recount, I claim we can get an argument for a social constructionist analysis of race by combining work from the previous chapters into a politically revisionary critical and naturalistic form of analysis. Empirical studies will be used to prefer a social constructionist view over basic racial realism. Logical grounds will be used to prefer social constructionism over deflationary realism. Semantic and political considerations will be used to prefer constructionism over eliminativism. Again, at this stage, none of this is meant to be persuasive in the direction of a social constructionist analysis of race. It is merely meant to show that there is room for the disparate conclusions of the previous chapters to be brought together systematically.

§8.3 MOVING THIS FORWARD INTO A RESEARCH AND ACTIVISM PROGRAM, PART II

If it has not become clear, my goal is to start at the place I see large swaths of analytic philosophy now and move little by little toward where I think we ought to be. This strategy comes from thinking that we are simply much too far from an ideal situation in the discipline. To try to start from just how much more radical and critical I think analytic philosophy needs to be would simply be too far outside of our collective zone of proximal development. From my own experience in the field, something like Soames' characterization saying that "philosophy done in the analytic tradition aims at truth and knowledge, as opposed to moral and spiritual improvement" is the most influential (Soames 2003a, xiv). The work in the first eight chapters of this book was intended to start showing the existence of trends within analytic philosophy, which challenge and complicate this narrative.

The previous section outlined one project, which would begin to move farther away from Soames' narrative by showing that these trends come together in something systematic, which can be applied in a number of particular cases. Another plan for moving this program forward and further away from Soames' narrative is to show that there is something about the nature of logic and the philosophy of language that make these trends unsurprising. That is to say, not only do I want to systematize the five chapters from part 3, I want to systematize the work from parts 2 and 3 together.

Therefore, in addition to building the individual pieces from various chapters into a method that would be systematically applied in particular cases, I would also like to build a larger research program by heading in the other direction. In particular, I would like to take some of the specific examples from chapters 1 and 2 and generalize them into an account connected to the nature of linguistic and logical analysis. This is because I do not think there should be anything idiosyncratic about either the historical or contemporary figures I have discussed here engaging in critical linguistic and critical logical analysis. Rather, it is something about the nature of inquiry into language and logic that make them particularly well suited for such projects.

While I do not have the space to get into any detail in this venue, a preview of this work will again be instructive for understanding why I think the criticism mentioned in the first paragraph of §8.2 is not damning. With respect to logic, I began to sketch the view that logic is, by its very nature, connected to political goals of equality and justice in chapter 2. This is because I view logic, reason, and rationality much in the way that John Mohawk has portrayed the Great Peacemaker's views on these matters. Again, Mohawk says that, in founding the Haudenosaunee Confederacy between the Mohawk, Oneida, Onondaga, Cayuga, and Seneca nations, the Peacemaker was driven to "rais[e] the idea of rational thinking to the status of a political principle" (Mohawk 1986, xvii). This is because the Peacemaker's goal was to replace violence, war, and revenge with diplomatic reasoning as the means for navigating and settling disagreements and competing claims. In this way, I hope to show that Peacemaker's vision has much to teach us on how to view, study, and promote logic—namely, as a means to peace and recognition of equal humanity.

Similarly, I want to argue for a view of the philosophy of language where it ought to be primarily concerned with bettering relationships between people and, in particular, large groups of people who create, perpetuate, or suffer injustice. The basic idea here will be that language is primarily a vehicle by which people interact with one another. In fact, especially in a modern, globalized world, it is *the primary* way that people interact with one another. Sharing a physical space, where other means of interpersonal interaction become possible, is becoming a smaller and smaller percentage of the instances in which we connect with other people. Rather, we do so by using language to share information across vast distances. Furthermore, language is partly how we constitute groups of people, with communities requiring an ability to communicate, requiring rules that are communicable, and so on. Because of all of this, we are engaging in a systematic evasion if we do not think of the philosophy of language as essentially value-laden and socially and politically oriented. While some early analytic philosophers recognized this at times, a broader recognition of this in analytic philosophy of language today will require a gestalt shift—one I hope to encourage for years to come.

§8.4 CONSTRAINTS ON SUCH A RESEARCH PROGRAM

Before ending, I want to return to Richardson's constraints placed on what is needed for a productive engagement between analytic philosophy and FEPS. Here, I believe the most important imperative provided was *do not further marginalize the oppressed*! This is particularly important in the context of work on the history of early analytic philosophy since the tradition has always been extremely Eurocentric and androcentric. This is not just true in the sense of who was tacitly excluded and included, either. Active, even if unintentional, Eurocentrism was found in both the words and actions of a number of the tradition's giants (remember we have already discussed this with respect to Stebbing 1939 in chapter 3). Even though they were friends, all Moore would say in response to a paper by Surendra Nath Dasgupta on Vedanta epistemology was "I have nothing to offer myself. But I am sure that whatever Dasgupta says is absolutely false" (Dasgupta 1971, 74). This seems quite problematic given that Moore spent a good deal of time offering his thoughts on European views of which he was sure they were absolutely false. It has also been argued that Moore's editorial practices played a significant role in the disappearance of Indian philosophy from *Mind*.[2]

Russell, too—even when being guided by the very promising principle that philosophy should inculcate humility—regularly says things conditioned by white supremacist hubris.[3] For instance, we find the standard Eurocentric trope that "in philosophy, the Arabs were better as commentators than as original thinkers" and, thus, we should care about Arabic thought only because "if the Arabs had not preserved the tradition, the men of the Renaissance might not have suspected how much was to be gained by the revival of classical learning" (Russell 1945, 283). Partly in his defense, Russell also acknowledges that referring to any part of the Medieval period as a "Dark Age" "marks our undue concentration on Western Europe" due to the advances of China, Japan, and Islam during this time. In the very same breath, though, he takes "our [Western] superiority since the Renaissance" to be somehow uncontroversial (Russell 1945, 399).[4]

Furthermore, Russell parrots the view which Park (2013) has shown to be an integral part of the racist historiography of the late eighteenth and early nineteenth centuries that "the Greeks were fond of attributing the wisdom of their pioneers to travels in Egypt, but what had really been achieved before the Greeks was very little" (Russell 1945, 212).[5] He also uses problematic language, referring to Muslims as "Mohammedans," while recognizing some of the reasons this is problematic—"the Religion of the Prophet was a simple monotheism. . . . The Prophet made no claim to be divine, nor did his followers make such a claim on his behalf" (Russell 1945, 420). Thankfully, Russell also adds that he is "quite willing to suppose that my views, like other men's, are influenced by social environment" (Russell 1945, 827).

Because of this, one of the significant ways in which analytic philosophy, including my own, needs to move is toward a much more global and gender-inclusive canon. Thankfully, this is something we find among the protagonists of my history. Haslanger regularly engages with Linda Martin Alcoff, Michelle Alexander, Michel Foucault, Kwame Ture, Lewis Gordon, Rodney Roberts, Susan Wendell, George Yancy, bell hooks, Audre Lorde, Lucius Outlaw, Michael Omi & Howard Winant, Kimberle Crenshaw, Henry Louis Gates Jr., Sonia Shah, Simone de Beauvoir, Langston Hughes, and Chima Korieh. Mills regularly engages with these folks and Cornel West, Emmanuel Chukwudi Eze, Martin Delany, David Walker, James Baldwin, Ralph Ellison, W. E. B. Du Bois, Richard Wright, Frantz Fanon, Marcus Garvey, Frederick Douglass, Howard Brotz, Angela Davis, Patricia Hill Collins, Abiola Irele, Chandra Mohanty, Karl Marx, Kobena Mercer, Mudimbe Mbiti, Susan Moller Okin, George Fredrickson, David Roediger, and Derrick Bell. Very similar praise can be directed at Bright and Dutilh Novaes. We who hope to have an analytic philosophy, which contributes to social justice, will need to do the same.

So, as much as I see lots of emancipatory potential in early analytic philosophy, there is undoubtedly a very significant problem with Eurocentrism in the analytic canon. I think this is a significant problem of my own work even. Because of that, I think some of the most important work going on, and going forward, is, and will be, that on analytic comparative philosophy. Of course, those doing so will need to take Stephanie Rivera Berruz's advice on doing such comparative philosophy where one is comparing a hegemonic with a marginalized tradition. In particular, we need to be sure to not engage in "comparative philosophy [that is] oriented around the 'West' for its sense of what counts as appropriately philosophical" (Rivera Berruz and Kalmanson 2018, 6).

While trying to abide by their advice, I hope to write a number of papers of the form, "what analytic philosophers could stand to learn from tradition x." As the examples brought up in the endnotes for chapter 2 suggest, these will primarily focus around comparative history of logic, language, and science. Looking to ancient China, there are very interesting discussions to be had about similarities and differences between analytic philosophy and the Mohist School's logic, ethics, and science and the School of Names' paradoxes. Ancient and Medieval India around the Gupta Empire also produced exceptional thinking on logic, life, and mathematics, which can lead to extremely fruitful engagement with analytic philosophy. Similarly, the mathematics, religion, and astronomy of the Classic (Medieval) Maya creates very interesting sites of engagement with the analytic tradition. Finally, as was suggested throughout chapter 2, the Medieval and Modern Islamic Golden Age is chock full of impressive thinking, which analytic philosophers could greatly learn from.

As mentioned in chapter 5 several times, all of the matters discussed would ideally have involved the Lvov-Warsaw school as well. Part of the reason that Stage 3 was brought to an end, generally, was Nazism, Fascism, and imperialism bringing about World War II. Given this and the role of anti-Semitism and anti-Slavism therein, it is hard to imagine the Lvov-Warsaw school being anything other than the most impacted group within the analytic tradition. Thus, I want to investigate the role of anti-Semitism and anti-Slavism in their reception (or lack thereof). Furthermore, as Anna Brozek has been impressively chronicling, the Lvov-Warsaw school was much more receptive to and supportive of women than the discipline is today. This creates great potential for intersectional analysis.

§8.5 CONCLUSION

As the previous sections indicate, I believe there is much more to be done and that this book may have brought up more questions than it answered. My hope, though, is to have contributed to the philosophical literature by showing that there is lots of room for critical analytic projects, which build off of early analytic philosophy. While there are a great deal of problems that can arise if we are not willing to amend methods and canons appropriately, Bright, Dutilh Novaes, Mills, Haslanger, Richardson, Kukla, Anderson, Yap, and others have given us lessons and models for doing this. My final plea to readers is simply to make your work more focused on bettering the world. It is a scary and unjust place. Analytic philosophy has tools to help lessen that. Take the aforementioned thinkers' lead and do it. I apologize if I have not lived up to their example.

NOTES

1. This coincided with the United States becoming the center of analytic philosophy in the wake of Quine, Kripke, and Rawls. As Naomi Scheman (2015) has argued, this process of more conservative analytic philosophy in the United States was most greatly impacted by McCarthyism. It was also greatly spurred on by the horrible experience of Nazism in Europe.

2. This argument can be found in Katzav's January 25, 2017, blog post building off of Katzav and Vaesen 2017 at https://digressionsnimpressions.typepad.com/digressionsimpressions/2017/01/the-disappearance-of-modern-indian-philosophy-from-mind-and-the-philosophical-review.html.

3. Many thanks to Eric Shliesser's blog posts "On Russell's History of Western Philosophy" from January 2020 for bringing these issues to my attention https://digressionsnimpressions.typepad.com/digressionsimpressions/2020/01/on-russells-history-of-western-philosophy-i.html.

4. These two passages not only suffer on their own, they have problems when combined as well. In particular, together they seem to ignore the fact that Renaissance European thought was made possible by original thought of Arab thinkers like al-Kindi, Ibn al-Haytham, Ibn Rushd, and Ibn al-Shatir. This is not to mention the Persian, Turkic, Berber, and Syriac thinkers who wrote in Arabic. For more discussion of this, see Saliba (2011).

5. That said, Russell's earlier work seems to recognize some of the orientalist problems that Edward Said would go on to analyze and criticize over a half of a century later—"From a cultural as opposed to an economic and political point of view, nothing could be a greater mistake than to regard Asia as a unity. It is scarcely too much to say that India and China differ from each other more than either differs from Europe" (Russell 1923).

Bibliography

Abramowitz, Jonathan. 1996. "Variants of Exposure and Response Prevention in the Treatment of Obsessive-Compulsive Disorder: A Meta-Analysis." *Behavior Therapy* 27, no. 4 (Autumn): 583–600.
Adichie, Chimamanda. 2009. "The Danger of a Single Story." Ted Talk.
Adichie, Chimamanda Ngozi. 2015. *We Should All Be Feminists*. New York: Anchor Books.
Alcoff, Linda Martin. 2006. *Visible Identities: Race, Gender, and the Self*. Oxford: Oxford University Press.
Alexander, Michelle. 2010. *The New Jim Crow: Mass-Incarceration in the Age of Colorblindness*. New York: The New Press.
Ambrose, Alice. 1952. "Linguistic Approaches to Philosophical Problems." *The Journal of Philosophy* 49, no. 9: 289–301.
Ambrose, Alice. 1960. "Three Aspects of Moore's Philosophy." *The Journal of Philosophy* 57, no. 26: 816–824.
American Psychiatric Association. 2013. *Diagnostic and Statistical Manual of Mental Disorders*, 5th Edition. Washington, DC: American Psychiatric Publishing.
Anderson, Elizabeth. 2015. "Feminist Epistemology and Philosophy of Science." *The Stanford Encyclopedia of Philosophy* (Summer 2019 Edition), Edward N. Zalta (ed.). https://plato.stanford.edu/archives/sum2019/entries/feminism-epistemology.
Anderson, Luvell. 2017. "Hermeneutical Impasses." *Philosophical Topics* 45, no. 2: 1–20.
Andreasen, Robin. 2004. "The Cladistic Race Concept: A Defense." *Biology and Philosophy* 19, no. 3: 425–442.
Anscombe, G. E. M. 1957. *Intention*. Oxford: Blackwell.
Anscombe, G. E. M. 1963. *An Introduction to Wittgenstein's Tractatus*. New York: Harper & Row Publishers.
Antony, Louise. 1993. "Quine As Feminist: The Radical Import of Naturalized Epistemology." In *A Mind of One's Own: Feminist Essays on Reason and*

Objectivity, Louise Antony and Charlotte Witt (eds.). Boulder, CO: Westview Press: 185–226.

Appiah, Kwame Anthony. 1996. "Race, Culture, and Identity." In *Color Conscious*, Appiah and Gutmann (eds.). Princeton, NJ: Princeton University Press: 30–105.

Atherton, Margaret (ed.). 1994. *Women Philosophers of the Early Modern Period*. Indianapolis: Hackett Publishing Company.

Austin, J. L. 1939. "Are There A Priori Concepts?" *Proceedings of the Aristotelian Society, Supplementary Volumes* 18: 83–105.

Austin, J. L. 1962. *How to Do Things with Words*. Oxford: Clarendon Press.

Ayer, A. J. 1936. *Language, Truth, and Logic*. London: Victor Gollancz.

Ayer, A. J. 1982. *Philosophy in the Twentieth Century*. New York: Random House.

Baillie, James (ed.). 2003. *Contemporary Analytic Philosophy: Core Readings*. Hoboken, NJ: Pearson.

Barghouti, Mourid. 2003. *I Saw Ramallah*. Cairo: American University in Cairo Press.

Beaney, Michael. 2006. "Stebbing, Lizzie Susan (1885–1943)." *Continuum Encyclopedia of British Philosophy* 4: 3023–3028.

Beaney, Michael (ed.). 2013. *The Oxford Handbook of the History of Analytic Philosophy*. Oxford: Oxford University Press.

Bee, Samantha. 2016. "Most Lives Matter." Accessed September 1, 2019. https://www.youtube.com/watch?v=zQuFPxCb-_o&list=PLur87nTwD0BuyQGoqlo8iyrSeSoJos4y3.

Bell, Jeannine. 2013. *Hate Thy Neighbor: Move-In Violence and the Persistence of Racial Segregation in American Housing*. New York: New York University Press.

Benacerraf, P. and Putnam, H. 1964. *Philosophy of Mathematics*. Upper Saddle River, NJ: Prentice-Hall.

Benson III, Richard D. 2015. *Fighting for Our Place in the Sun: Malcolm X and the Radicalization of the Black Student Movement 1960–1973*. New York: Peter Lang.

Berges, Sandrine. 2015. "On the Outskirts of the Canon: The Myth of the Lone Female Philosopher, and What to Do About it." *Metaphilosophy* 46, no. 3: 380–397.

Bernal, Martin. 1987. *Black Athena: The Afroasiatic Roots of Classical Civilization*. New Brunswick, NJ: Rutgers University Press.

Berto, Francesco and Plebani, Matteo. 2015. *Ontology and Metaontology: A Contemporary Guide*. New York: Bloomsbury Academic.

Biletzki, Anat and Matar, Anat (eds.). 1998. *The Story of Analytic Philosophy: Plot and Heroes*. New York: Routledge.

Boghossian, Paul. 1996. "Analyticity Reconsidered." *Nous* 30: 361–387.

Bohman, James. 2012. "Domination, Epistemic Injustice, and Republican Epistemology." *Social Epistemology* 26: 175–187.

Bonilla-Silva, Eduardo. 2003. *Racism without Racists: Color-blind Racism and the Persistence of Racial Inequality in the United States*. Lanham, MD: Rowman & Littlefield.

Boole, George. 1847. *The Mathematical Analysis of Logic, Being an Essay Towards a Calculus of Deductive Reasoning*. Macmillan, Barclay, & Macmillan.

Boole, George. 1854. *An Investigation of the Laws of Thought on Which are Founded the Mathematical Theories of Logic and Probabilities*. Basingstoke, UK: Macmillan.

Borradori, Giovanna. 1994. *The American Philosopher*. Chicago: University of Chicago Press.
Bright, Liam Kofi. 2017. "Logical Empiricists on Race." *Studies in History and Philosophy of Biological and Biomedical Sciences* 65: 9–18.
Bright, Liam Kofi. 2018. "Empiricism is a Standpoint Epistemology." Accessed September 1, 2019. http://sootyempiric.blogspot.com/2018/06/empiricism-is-standpoint-epistemology.html.
Bright, Liam Kofi. 2019. "Carnap Did Nothing Wrong." Accessed September 1, 2019. http://sootyempiric.blogspot.com/2019/04/carnap-did-nothing-wrong.html.
Bright, Liam Kofi, Malinsky, Daniel, and Thompson, Morgan. 2016. "Causally Interpreting Intersectionality Theory." *Philosophy of Science* 83, no. 1: 60–81.
Brozek, Anna. 2017. "Maria Kokoszynska: Between the Lvov-Warsaw School and the Vienna Circle." *Journal for the History of Analytical Philosophy* 5, no. 2: 19–36.
Brozek, Anna and Jadacki, Jacek. 2018. "Izydora Dąmbska: The First Lady of the Twentieth-Century Polish Philosophy." In *The Lvov-Warsaw School: Past, and Present*, Ángel Garrido and Urszula Wybraniec-Skardowska (eds.). Basel: Birkhauser: 223–233.
Burgess, John. 1996. "Marcus, Kripke, and Names." *Philosophical Studies: An International Journal for Philosophy in the Analytic Tradition* 84, no. 1: 1–47.
Burgess, John. 1998. "How Not to Write History of Philosophy: A Case Study." In *The New Theory of Reference: Kripke, Marcus, and its Origins*, P. W. Humphreys and J. H. Fetzer (eds.). Dordrecht: Kluwer Academic: 125–136.
Burgess, John. 2009. *Philosophical Logic*. Princeton, NJ: Princeton University Press.
Butler, Judith. 1999. "A 'Bad Writer' Bites Back." *New York Times*, March 20, 1999. https://archive.nytimes.com/query.nytimes.com/gst/fullpage-950CE5D61531F933 A15750C0A9 6F958260.html.
Cahill, Kevin. 2004. "Ethics and the *Tractatus*: A Resolute Failure." *Philosophy* 79: 33–55.
Campbell, Douglas Ian. 2017. "The Eightfold Way: Why Analyticity, Apriority, and Necessity are Independent." *Philosophers' Imprint* 17, no. 25: 1–17.
Cappelen, Herman. 2012. *Philosophy without Intuitions*. Oxford: Oxford University Press.
Carnap, Rudolf. 1934. *Logische Syntax der Sprache* (English translation *The Logical Syntax of Language*). New York: Humanities, 1937.
Carnap, Rudolf. 1947. *Meaning and Necessity*. Chicago: University of Chicago Press.
Carnap, Rudolf. 1950. "Empiricism, Semantics, and Ontology." *Revue Internationale de Philosophie* 4: 40–50.
Carnap, Rudolf. 1963. "Intellectual Autobiography." In *The Philosophy of Rudolf Carnap*, P. A. Schilpp (ed.). Chicago: Open Court: 3–84.
Carnap, Rudolf. 1964. *Interview with Rudolf Carnap*. German TV.
Carnap, Rudolf, Hahn, Hans, and Neurath, Otto. 1929. "The Scientific Conception of the World." In *Empiricism and Sociology*, Marie Neurath and R. S. Cohen (eds.). Dordrecht: Reidel: 299–318.
Chalmers, David, Manley, David, and Wasserman, Ryan. 2009. *Metametaphysics: New Essays on the Foundations of Ontology*. Oxford: Oxford University Press.

Chang, Iris. 2003. *The Chinese In America: A Narrative History.* New York: Penguin Books.
Chapman, Siobhan. 2013. *Susan Stebbing and the Language of Common Sense.* New York: Palgrave Macmillan.
Che, Michael. 2016. *Michael Che Matters.* Netflix Originals.
Chick, Matt and LaVine, Matthew. 2014. "The Relevance of Analytic Philosophy to Personal, Public, and Democratic Life." *Essays in Philosophy* 15, no. 1: 138–155.
Clough, Sharyn. 2003. *Siblings Under the Skin: Feminism, Social Justice, and Analytic Philosophy.* Aurora, CO: Davies Group.
Coates, Ta-Nehisi. 2015. *Between the World and Me.* New York: Spiegel and Grau.
Coffa, J. Alberto. 1991. *The Semantic Tradition from Kant to Carnap: To the Vienna Station.* Cambridge: Cambridge University Press.
Collier-Thomas, Bettye and Franklin, Vincent (eds.). 2001. *Sisters in the Struggle: African American Women in the Civil Rights-Black Power Movement.* New York: New York University Press.
Copeland, B. J. 1996. *Logic and Reality: Essays on the Legacy of Arthur Prior.* Oxford: Clarendon Press.
Corcoran, John. 1989a. "Argumentations and Logic." *Argumentation* 3, no. 1: 17–43.
Corcoran, John. 1989b. "The Inseparability of Logic and Ethics." *Free Inquiry* 9: 37–40.
Crary, Alice. 2018. "The Methodological is Political." *Radical Philosophy* Issue 2.02, Series 2.
Crary, Alice and Read, Rupert. 2000. *The New Wittgenstein.* New York: Routledge.
Crary, Alice and Shieh, Sanford (ed.). 2006. *Reading Cavell.* New York: Routledge.
Creath, Richard. 2009. "The Gentle Strength of Tolerance: The Logical Syntax of Language and Carnap's Philosophical Programme." In *Carnap's Logical Syntax of Language*, P. Wagner (ed.). London: Palgrave Macmillan: 203–214.
Creath, Richard. 2017. "Logical Empiricism." *The Stanford Encyclopedia of Philosophy*, Edward N. Zalta (ed.). https://plato.stanford.edu/archives/fall2017/entries/logical-empiricism.
Crenshaw, Kimberle Williams. 1991. "Mapping the Margins: Intersectionality, Identity Politics, and Violence against Women of Color." *Stanford Law Review* 43, no. 6: 1241–1299.
Crenshaw, Kimberle Williams. 2016. "The Urgency of Intersectionality." Ted Talk.
Critchley, Simon. 2001. *Continental Philosophy: A Very Short Introduction.* Oxford: Oxford University Press.
Curry, Tommy. 2010. "Concerning the Underspecialization of Race Theory in American Philosophy: How the Exclusion of Black Sources Affects the Field." *The Pluralist* 5, no. 1: 44–64.
Curry, Tommy. 2011. "The Derelictical Crisis of African American Philosophy: How African American Philosophy Fails to Contribute to the Study of African-Descended People." *Journal of Black Studies* 42, no. 3 (April): 314–333.
Dasgupta, Surama. 1971. *An Ever-Expanding Quest of Life and Knowledge.* New Delhi: Longman Group Ltd.
Davis, Angela. 2016. *Freedom Is a Constant Struggle: Ferguson, Palestine, and the Foundations of a Movement.* Chicago: Haymarket Books.

De Morgan, Augustus. 1847. *Formal Logic*. Taylor and Walton.
De Morgan, Augustus. 1860. *Syllabus of a Proposed System of Logic*. Walton, Malbery.
Devitt, Michael. 2015. "Relying on Intuitions: Where Cappelen and Deutsch Go Wrong." *Inquiry* 58, no. 7–8: 669–699.
Diamond, Cora. 2000. "Ethics, Imagination and the Method of Wittgenstein's *Tractatus*." In *The New Wittgenstein*, A. Crary and R. Read (eds.). New York: Routledge: 149–173.
Dotson, Kristie. 2012. "A Cautionary Tale: On Limiting Epistemic Oppression." *Frontiers: A Journal of Women Studies* 33, no. 1: 24–47.
Douglas, Heather. 2003. "Hempelian Insights for Feminism." In *Siblings Under the Skin: Feminism, Social Justice, and Analytic Philosophy*, Sharyn Clough (ed.). Aurora, CO: Davies Group: 283–306.
Du Bois, W. E. B. 1897. "Strivings of the Negro People." *The Atlantic Monthly* August: 194–197.
Dummett, Michael. 1978. *Truth and Other Enigmas*. Cambridge, MA: Harvard University Press.
Dummett, Michael. 1993. *Origins of Analytical Philosophy*. London: Gerald Duckworth & Co.
Dutilh Novaes, Catarina. 2020. "Carnapian Explication and Ameliorative Analysis: A Systematic Comparison." *Synthese* 197: 1011–1034.
Dutilh Novaes, Catarina and Geerdink, Leon. 2017. "The Dissonant Origins of Analytic Philosophy: Common Sense in Philosophical Methodology." In *Innovations in the History of Analytic Philosophy*, S. Lapointe and C. Pincock (eds.). London: Palgrave Macmillan: 69–102.
Evans, Gareth. 1973. "A Causal Theory of Names." *Proceedings of the Aristotelian Society* (Supplementary Volume) 47: 187–208.
Fan, Y., Shepherd, L. J., Slavich, E., Waters, D., Stone, M., Abel, R., and Johnston, E. L. 2019. "Gender and Cultural Bias in Student Evaluations: Why Representation Matters." *PLoS ONE* 14, no. 2: e0209749.
Fitch, Frederic. 1949. "The Problem of the Morning Star and the Evening Star." *Philosophy of Science* 16: 137–141.
Fitch, Frederic. 1950. "Attribute and Class." In *Philosophic Thought in France and the United States*, M. Farber (ed.). Buffalo, NY: University of Buffalo Publications in Philosophy: 640–647.
Floyd, Juliet and Shieh, Sanford (eds.). 2001. *Future Pasts: The Analytic Tradition in Twentieth Century Philosophy*. Oxford: Oxford University Press.
Frank, Phillip. 1957. *Philosophy of Science: The Link Between Science and Philosophy*. Upper Saddle River, NJ: Prentice Hall.
Frege, Gottlob. 1879. *Begriffschrift*. Louis Nebert.
Frege, Gottlob. 1950. *The Foundations of Arithmetic*. Evanston, IL: Northwestern University Press.
Fricker, Miranda. 2007. *Epistemic Injustice*. Oxford: Oxford University Press.
Fricker, Miranda. 2013. "Epistemic Justice as a Condition of Political Freedom?" *Synthese* 190: 1317–1332.
Friedman, Michael. 1999. *Reconsidering Logical Positivism*. Cambridge: Cambridge University Press.

Fung, Yu-Lan. 1976. *A Short History of Chinese Philosophy*. New York: The Free Press.
Garza, Alicia. 2014. "A Herstory of the #BlackLivesMatter Movement." Accessed September 1, 2019. https://thefeministwire.com/2014/10/blacklivesmatter-2/.
Gellner, Ernest. 1959. *Words and Things: An Examination of, and an Attack On, Linguistic Philosophy*. London: Victor Gollancz.
Gettier, Edmund L. 1963. "Is Justified True Belief Knowledge?" *Analysis* 23: 121–123.
Gilliam, Walter S. et al. 2016. "Do Early Educators' Implicit Biases Regarding Sex and Race Relate to Behavior Expectations and Recommendations of Preschool Expulsions and Suspensions?" Yale Child Study Center.
Glasgow, Joshua and Woodward, Jonathan. 2015. "Basic Racial Realism." *Journal of the American Philosophical Association* 1, no. 3: 449–466.
Glock, Hans-Johann. 1996. "Necessity and Normativity." In *The Cambridge Companion to Wittgenstein*, Hans Sluga and David Stern (eds.). Cambridge: Cambridge University Press: 198–225.
Glock, Hans-Johann. 2003. *Quine and Davidson on Language, Thought, and Reality*. Cambridge: Cambridge University Press.
Glock, Hans-Johann. 2008. *What is Analytic Philosophy?* Cambridge: Cambridge University Press.
Godel, Kurt. 1930. "Die Vollständigkeit der Axiome des logischen Functionenkalküls." *Monatshefte für Mathematik und Physik* 37: 349–360.
Gordon, Lewis. 2008. *An Introduction to Africana Philosophy*. Cambridge: Cambridge University Press.
Gordon-Roth, Jessica and Kendrick, Nancy. 2015. "Including Early Modern Women Writers in Survey Courses: A Call to Action." *Metaphilosophy* 46, no. 3: 364–379.
Gorovitz, Samuel, Hintikka, Merrill, Provence, Donald, and Williams, Ron G. 1979. *Philosophical Analysis: An Introduction to Its Language and Techniques*. New York: Random House.
Greenberg, Cheryl Lynn. 1998. *Remembering SNCC: A Circle of Trust*. New Brunswick, NJ: Rutgers University Press.
Grice, H. P. 1989. *Studies in the Way of Words*. Cambridge, MA: University Press.
Hacker, P. M. S. 1996. *Wittgenstein's Place in Twentieth Century Analytic Philosophy*. Oxford: Blackwell Publishers.
Hacker, P. M. S. 2000. "Was He Trying to Whistle it?" In *The New Wittgenstein*, A. Crary and R. Read (eds.). New York: Routledge: 353–388.
Haller, Rudolf. 1988. *Questions on Wittgenstein*. New York: Routledge.
Hallett, Garth. 2008. *Linguistic Philosophy: The Central Story*. Albany, NY: SUNY Series in Philosophy.
Hampshire, Stuart. 1960. "J. L. Austin, 1911–1960." *Proceedings of the Aristotelian Society* 60: I–XIV.
Hardimon, Michael. 2012. "The Idea of a Scientific Concept of Race." *Journal of Philosophical Research* 37: 249–282.
Hardimon, Michael. 2017. *Rethinking Race: The Case for Deflationary Realism*. Cambridge, MA: Harvard University Press.

Harding, Sandra. 1986. *The Science Question in Feminism*. Ithaca, NY: Cornell University Press.
Haslanger, Sally. 2012. *Resisting Reality: Social Construction and Social Critique*. Oxford: Oxford University Press.
Haslanger, Sally. 2017. "Culture and Critique." *Aristotelian Society Supplementary Volume* 91, no. 1: 149–173.
Haslanger, Sally. Forthcoming. "Going On, Not in the Same Way." In *Conceptual Engineering and Conceptual Ethics*, Alexis Burgess, Herman Cappelen, and David Plunkett (eds.). Oxford: Oxford University Press: 230–260.
Hegewisch, Ariane. 2018. "The Gender Wage Gap: 2017; Earnings Differences by Gender, Race, and Ethnicity." *Institute for Women's Policy Research*.
Henkin, Leon. 1949. "The Completeness of the First-Order Functional Calculus." *Journal of Symbolic Logic* 14: 159–166.
Hershfield, Jon. 2017. "Mistaken Beliefs about Uncertainty Acceptance and OCD." Accessed September 1, 2019. https://www.intrusivethoughts.org/blog/mistaken-beliefs-uncertainty-acceptance-ocd/.
Hershfield, Jon and Nicely, Shala. 2017. *Everyday Mindfulness for OCD: Tips, Tricks, and Skills for Living Joyfully*. Oakland, CA: New Harbinger.
Holt, Jim. 1996 (January/February). "Whose Idea is it, Anyway?: A Philosophers' Feud." *Lingua Franca*: 29–39.
Holt, Jim. 2018. *When Einstein Walked With Godel: Excursions to the Edge of Thought*. New York: Farrar, Straus, and Giroux.
hooks, bell and West, Cornel. 1991. *Breaking Bread: Insurgent Black Intellectual Life*. Boston: South End Press.
Horkheimer, Max. 1937. "The Latest Attack on Metaphysics." In *Critical Theory: Selected Essays*. Seabury, 1972: 132–187.
Howard, Don. 2003. "Two Left Turns Make a Right: On the Curious Political Career of North American Philosophy of Science at Midcentury." In *Logical Empiricism in North America*, G. L. Hardcastle and A. W. Richardson (eds.). Minneapolis: University of Minnesota Press: 25–93.
Howard, Don. 2006. "Lost Wanderers in the Forest of Knowledge: Some Advice on How to Think About the Relation Between Discovery and Justification." In *Revisiting Discovery and Justification: Historical and Philosophical Perspectives on the Context Distinction*. Dordrecht: Springer: 3–22.
Hudson, W.D. 1972. *The Is/Ought Question*. London: Macmillan.
Human Rights Campaign. 2019. "Violence Against the Transgender Community in 2019." Accessed February 2, 2020. https://www.hrc.org/resources/violence-against-the-transgender-community-in-2019.
Humphreys, Paul and Fetzer, James (eds.). 1998. *The New Theory of Reference: Kripke, Marcus, and its Origins*. Dordrecht: Kluwer Academic.
Hylton, Peter and Kemp, Gary. 2019. "Willard Van Orman Quine." *The Stanford Encyclopedia of Philosophy* (Spring 2019 Edition), Edward N. Zalta (ed.). https://plato.stanfor d.edu/archives/spr2019/entries/quine/.
Kaiser Family Foundation. 2020. "Poverty Rate by Race/Ethnicity." Accessed February 2, 2020. https://www.kff.org/other/state-indicator/poverty-rate-by-raceethnicity/.

Katzav, J. and Vaesen, K. 2017. "Pluralism and Peer Review in Philosophy." *Philosophers' Imprint* 17, no. 19: 1–20.
Kessler, Kidd, Kidd, J. S., Kidd, Renée A., and Morin, Katherine A. 1996. *Distinguished African-American Scientists of the Twentieth Century*. Phoenix: The Oryx Press.
King Jr., Martin Luther. 1963. "I Have a Dream." Accessed September 1, 2019. https://www.naa cp.org/i-have-a-dream-speech-full-march-on-washington/.
Kitcher, Phillip. 2007. "Does 'Race' Have a Future?" *Philosophy and Public Affairs* 35, no. 4: 293–317.
Klement, Kevin. 2014. "Review of *The Oxford Handbook of the History of Analytic Philosophy* edited by Michael Beaney." *Notre Dame Philosophical Reviews* 2014.04.29.
Kneale, William and Kneale, Martha. 1962. *The Development of Logic*. Oxford: Oxford University Press.
Kobori, Osamu and Salkovskis, Paul. 2013. "Patterns of Reassurance Seeking and Reassurance-Related Behaviours in OCD and Anxiety Disorders." *Behavioural and Cognitive Psychotherapy* 41, no. 1: 1–23.
Kornblith, Hilary. 1994. *Naturalizing Epistemology*. Cambridge, MA: Massachusetts Institute of Technology Press.
Kripke, Saul. 1959. "A Completeness Theorem in Modal Logic." *Journal of SymbolicLogic* 24: 1–14.
Kripke, Saul. 1963. "Semantical Considerations on Modal Logic." *Acta Philosophica Fennica* 16: 83–94.
Kripke, Saul. 1980. *Naming and Necessity*. Oxford: Blackwell.
Krygier, J. R., Heathers, J. A., Shahrestani, S., Abbott, M., Gross, J. J., and Kemp, A. H. 2013. "Mindfulness Meditation, Well-being, and Heart Rate Variability: A Preliminary Investigation into the Impact of Intensive Vipassana Meditation." *International Journal of Psychophysiology* 89, no. 3: 305–313.
Kukla, Rebecca. 2014. "Performative Force, Convention, and Discursive Injustice." *Hypatia* 29, no. 2: 440–457.
LaDuke, Winona and Cruz, Sean Aaron. 2012. *The Militarization of Indian Country*. East Lansing: Michigan State University Press.
Landemore, Helene. 2012. *Democratic Reason*. Princeton, NJ: Princeton University Press.
Lapointe, Sandra. 2011. *Bolzano's Theoretical Philosophy: An Introduction*. New York: Palgrave Macmillan.
Lapointe, Sandra. 2014. "Bolzano and the Analytical Tradition." *Philosophy Compass* 2: 96–111.
LaVine, Matt. 2016a. *A Theory of Analyticity*. PhD Diss, University at Buffalo.
LaVine, Matt. 2016b. "Prior's Thank-Goodness Argument Reconsidered." *Synthese* 193, no. 11: 3591–3606.
LaVine, Matt and Tissaw, Michael. 2015. "Philosophical Anthropology." In *The Wiley Handbook of Theoretical and Philosophical Psychology*, J. Martin, J. Slaney, and K. Sugarman (eds.). Chichester, UK: Wiley Blackwell: 23–38.
Lewis, C. I. 1918. *A Survey of Symbolic Logic*. Berkeley: University of California Press.

Lewis, C. I. and Langford, C. H. 1932. *Symbolic Logic.* New York: Century Company.
Lewontin, Richard. 1972. "The Apportionment of Human Diversity." *Evolutionary Biology* 6: 381–398.
List, Christian. 2012. "The Theory of Judgment Aggregation: An Introductory Review." *Synthese* 187: 179–207.
MacDonald, Margaret. 1940. "The Language of Political Theory." *Proceedings of the Aristotelian Society*, New Series 41: 91–112.
MacKinnon, Catharine. 1987. *Feminism Unmodified: Discourses on Life and Law.* Cambridge, MA: Harvard University Press.
Malcolm, Norman and Von Wright, Georg Henrik. 2001. *Ludwig Wittgenstein: A Memoir.* Oxford: Oxford University Press.
Manzano, Maria. 2015. "The Roles Leon Henkin Played in Mathematics Education." *Proceedings of the Fourth International Conference on Tools for Teaching Logic*, 111–118.
Marcus, Ruth Barcan. 1946a. "A Functional Calculus of First Order Based on Strict Implication." *Journal of Symbolic Logic* 11: 1–16.
Marcus, Ruth Barcan. 1946b. "A Deduction Theorem in a Functional Calculus of First Order Based on Strict Implication." *Journal of Symbolic Logic* 11: 115–118.
Marcus, Ruth Barcan. 1947. "Identity of Individuals in a Strict Functional Calculus of Second Order." *Journal of Symbolic Logic* 12: 12–15.
Marcus, Ruth Barcan. 1961. "Modalities and Intensional Languages." *Synthese* 13, no. 4: 303–322.
Marcus, Ruth Barcan. 1967. "Essentialism in Modal Logic." *Noûs* 1, no. 1: 91–96.
Marcus, Ruth Barcan. 1980. "Moral Dilemmas and Consistency." *The Journal of Philosophy* 77, no. 3: 121–136.
Marcus, Ruth Barcan. 1993. *Modalities: Philosophical Essays.* Oxford: Oxford University Press.
Marcus, Ruth Barcan. 2010. "Proceedings and Addresses of the American Philosophical Association." *American Philosophical Association* 84, no. 2: 75–92.
Marcuse, Herbert. 1964. *One-Dimensional Man: Studies in the Ideology of Advanced Industrial Society.* Boston: Beacon Press.
Martinich, A. P. and Sosa, David (eds.). 2011. *Analytic Philosophy: An Anthology.* Oxford: Wiley-Blackwell.
Martinich, A. P. and Sosa, David (eds.). 2013. *The Philosophy of Language.* Oxford: Oxford University Press.
Masood, Ehsan. 2009. *Science and Islam: A History.* London: Icon Books.
McGuiness, B.F. 1971. *Prototractatus: An Early Version of Tractatus Logico-Philosophicus.* New York: Routledge.
Medina, Jose. 2012. *Epistemologies of Resistance.* Oxford: Oxford University Press.
Mercier, Hugo and Sperber, Dan. 2009. "Intuitive and Reflective Inferences." In *Two Minds: Dual Processes and Beyond*, J. St. B. T. Evans and K. Frankish (eds.). Oxford University Press: 149–170.
Mills, Charles. 1997. *The Racial Contract.* Ithaca, NY: Cornell University Press.
Mills, Charles. 1998. *Blackness Visible: Essays on Philosophy and Race.* Ithaca, NY: Cornell University Press.

Mills, Charles. 2015. "Decolonizing Western Political Philosophy." *New Political Science* 37, no. 1: 1–24.

Mills, Charles. 2017. *Black Rights/White Wrongs: The Critique of Racial Liberalism*. Oxford: Oxford University Press.

Mohawk, John. 1986. "Prologue." In *The White Roots of Peace*, Paul Wallace. The Chauncy Press.

Mohawk, John. 1989. "Origins of Iroquois Political Thought." In *New Voices from the Longhouse: An Anthology of Contemporary Iroquois Writing*, J. Bruchac (ed.). New York: Greenfield Review Press.

Moi, Toril. 2017. *Revolution of the Ordinary: Literary Studies after Wittgenstein, Austin, and Cavell*. Chicago: University of Chicago Press.

Monk, Ray. 1990. *Wittgenstein: The Duty of Genius*. Cape.

Moore, G. E. 1903a. "The Refutation of Idealism." *Mind* 12: 433–453.

Moore, G. E. 1903b. *Principia Ethica*. Cambridge: Cambridge University Press.

Moore, G. E. 1919. "External and Internal Relations." *Proceedings of the Aristotelian Society* 20: 40–62.

Moore, G. E. 1925. "A Defence of Common Sense." In *Contemporary British Philosophy*, J. H. Muirhead (ed.). London: George Allen & Unwin: 192–233.

Moore, G. E. 1939. "Proof of an External World." *Proceedings of the British Academy* 25: 273–300.

NAACP. 2020. "Criminal Justice Fact Sheet." Accessed February 2, 2020. https://www.naacp.org/criminal-justice-fact-sheet/.

Neale, Stephen. 2001. "No Plagiarism Here." *Times Literary Supplement* February 9, 2001: 12–13.

Nelson, Beryl. 2014. "The Data on Diversity." *Communications of the ACM* 57, no. 11: 86–95.

Nelson, Lynn Hankinson. 1990. *Who Knows: From Quine to a Feminist Empiricism*. Philadelphia: Temple University Press.

Nelson, Lynn Hankinson and Nelson, Jack (eds.). 2003. *Feminist Interpretations of W.V.O. Quine*. University Park: Pennsylvania State University Press.

Neurath, Otto. 1938. "Unified Science as Encyclopedic Integration." In *International Encyclopedia of Unified Science*, O. Neurath, R. Carnap, and C. W. Morris (eds.). Chicago: University of Chicago Press: 1–27.

Noah, Trevor. 2016. *Born a Crime: Stories from a South-African Childhood*. New York: Spiegel & Grau.

Nye, Andrea (ed.). 1998. *The Philosophy of Language: The Big Questions*. Oxford: Blackwell Publishers.

Oliver, Nikkita. 2018. "Black and Native Lives Need Each Other to Matter." Accessed September 1, 2019. https://medium.com/the-establishment/black-and-native-lives-need-each-other-to-matter-eba969fb5e43.

O'Neill, Eileen. 1998. "Disappearing Ink: Early Modern Women Philosophers and Their Fate in History." In *Philosophy in a Feminist Voice: Critiques and Reconstructions*, Janet Kourany (ed.). Princeton, NJ: Princeton University Press: 17–62.

O'Neill, Eileen. 2005. "Early Modern Women Philosophers and the History of Philosophy." *Hypatia* 20, no. 3: 185–197.

O'Neill, John. 2003. "Unified Science as Political Philosophy: Positivism, Pluralism, and Liberalism." *Studies in History and Philosophy of Science Part A* 34, no. 3: 575–596.

Park, Peter K. J. 2013. *Africa, Asia, and the History of Philosophy: Racism in the Formation of the Philosophical Canon, 1780–1830*. Albany, NY: SUNY Press.

Pateman, Carole. 1988. *The Sexual Contract*. Palo Alto, CA: Stanford University Press.

Patton, Lydia. 2018. "Laws of Thought and Laws of Logic after Kant." In *Logic from Kant to Russell*, Sandra Lapointe (ed.). New York: Routledge.

Payne, Keith, Niemi, Laura, and Doris, John. 2018. "How to Think About 'Implicit Bias'." Accessed September 1, 2019. https://www.scientificamerican.com/article/how-to-think-about-implicit-bias/.

Peano, Giuseppe. 1889. "The Principle of Arithmetic, Presented by a New Method." In *From Frege to Godel*, J. van Heijenoort (ed.). Cambridge, MA: Harvard University Press.

Peirce, C.S. 1958. *Collected Papers of Charles Sanders Peirce*. Cambridge, MA: Harvard University Press.

Pleitz, Martin. 2013. "Homophobia and the Limits of Scientific Philosophy." In *Richard Swinburne: Christian Philosophy in a Modern World*, N. Mossner, S. Schmoranzer, and C. Weidemann (eds.). Piscataway, NJ: Transaction Publishers: 169–188.

Post, Emil. 1921. "Introduction to the General Theory of Elementary Propositions." In *From Frege to Godel*, J. van Heijenoort (ed.). Cambridge, MA: Harvard University Press.

Prior, A. N. 1949. *Logic and the Basis of Ethics*. Oxford: Oxford University Press.

Prior, A. N. 1957. *Time and Modality*. Oxford: Oxford University Press.

Prior, A. N. 1959. "Thank Goodness That's Over." *Philosophy* 34: 12–17.

Prior, A. N. 1960. "The Autonomy of Ethics." *Australasian Journal of Philosophy* 38: 199–206.

Putnam, Hilary. 1985. "After Empiricism." In *Post-Analytic Philosophy*, J. Rajchman and C. West (eds.). New York: Columbia University Press.

Quine, W. V. O. 1936. "Truth by Convention." In *Philosophical Essays for A. N. Whitehead*, O. H. Lee (ed.). New York: Longmans: 90–124.

Quine, W. V. O. 1951. "Two Dogmas of Empiricism." *Philosophical Review* 60: 20–43.

Quine, W. V. O. 1953. *From a Logical Point of View*. Cambridge, MA: Harvard University Press.

Quine, W. V. O. 1960. *Word and Object*. Cambridge, MA: Massachusetts Institute of Technology Press.

Quine, W. V. O. 1969. *Ontological Relativity and Other Essays*. New York: Columbia University Press.

Quine, W. V. O. 1974. *Roots of Reference*. Chicago: Open Court.

Quine, W.V.O. 1985. *The Time of My Life: An Autobiography*. Cambridge, MA: Massachusetts Institute of Technology Press.

Quine, W.V.O. 1995. *From Stimulus to Science*. Cambridge, MA: Harvard University Press.

Rajchman, John and West, Cornel. 1985. *Post-Analytic Philosophy*. New York: Columbia University Press.
Ransby, Barbara. 2018. *Making All Black Lives Matter: Reimagining Freedom in the 21st Century*. Berkeley: University of California Press.
Rawls, John. 1971. *A Theory of Justice*. Cambridge, MA: Harvard University Press.
Rescher, Nicholas. 1963. *Studies in the History of Arabic Logic*. Pittsburgh: University of Pittsburgh Press.
Rini, Adriane. 2013. "Models and Values: Why Did New Zealand Stop Hiring Women Philosophers?" In *Women in Philosophy: What Needs to Change?* Katrina Hutchison and Fiona Jenkins (eds.). Oxford: Oxford University Press: 127–142.
Rivera Berruz, Stephanie and Kalmanson, Leah. 2018. *Comparative Studies in Asian and Latin American Philosophies Cross-Cultural Theories and Methodologies*. London: Bloomsbury Academic.
Romizi, Donata. 2012. "The Vienna Circle's 'Scientific World Conception': Philosophy of Science in the Political Arena." *HOPOS: The Journal of the International Society for the History of Philosophy of Science* 2, no. 2: 205–242.
Roose, Kevin. 2015. "The Next Time Someone Says 'All lives matter,' Show Them These 5 Paragraphs." Accessed September 1, 2019. https://splinternews.com/the-next-time-someone-says-all-lives-matter-show-them-1793849332.
Rorty, Richard. 1982. *Consequences of Pragmatism*. Minneapolis: University of Minnesota Press.
Rosenberg, Noah et al. 2002. "Genetic Structure of Human Populations." *Science* 298: 2381–2385.
Rothstein, Richard. 2017. *The Color of Law: A Forgotten History of How Our Government Segregated America*. New York: Liveright Publishing Corporation.
Russell, Bertrand. 1914. *Our Knowledge of the External World*. Chicago: The Open Court Publishing Company.
Russell, Bertrand. 1918. *Philosophy of Logical Atomism*. The Monist.
Russell, Bertrand. 1923. "Philosophy in India and China." *The Nation and the Athenaeum* 33, no. 15 (September): 748–749.
Russell, Bertrand. 1928. *Skeptical Essays*. London: George Allan and Unwin.
Russell, Bertrand. 1945. *A History of Western Philosophy*. New York: Simon & Schuster.
Russell, Bertrand. 1959. *My Philosophical Development*. London: George Allen and Unwin.
Russell, Bertrand and Kim, Hye-Kyung. 2004. *The Problems of Philosophy*. Barnes & Noble.
Russell, Gillian. 2008. *Truth in Virtue of Meaning: A Defence of the Analytic/Synthetic Distinction*. Oxford: Oxford University Press.
Russell, Gillian. 2010. "A New Problem for the Linguistic Doctrine of Necessary Truth." In *New Waves in Truth*, Cory Wright and Nikolaj Pedersen (eds.). New York: Palgrave Macmillan.
Russell, Gillian. 2014. "Metaphysical Analyticity and the Epistemology of Logic." *Philosophical Studies* 171, no. 1: 161–175.

Saliba, George. 2011. *Islamic Science and the Making of the European Renaissance.* Cambridge, MA: MIT Press.
Salmon, Nathan. 1986. *Frege's Puzzle.* Cambridge, MA: Massachusetts Institute of Technology Press.
Salmon, Nathan. 1993. "Analyticity and A Priority." In *Philosophical Perspectives 7: Logic and Language*, J. Tomberlin (ed.). Ridgeview: 125–133.
Sardar, Ziauddin. 2012. *Muhammad: All that Matters.* New York: McGraw-Hill Companies, Inc.
Sarkar, Sahotra. 1992. "Rudolf Carnap, 1891–1970: The Editor's Introduction." *Synthese* 93, no. 1/2: 1–14.
Saugstad, Andreas. 2001. "Saul Kripke, Genius Logician." Accessed September 1, 2019. https://bolesblogs.com/2001/02/25/saul-kripke-genius-logician/.
Scheman, Naomi. 2015. "Writers, Authors, and the Extraordinary Ordinary." In *The Future of Scholarly Writing: Critical Interventions*, A. Bammer and R.-E. Boetcher Joeres (eds.). New York: Palgrave Macmillan: 41–56.
Schroeder, Severin. 2006. *Wittgenstein: The Way Out of the Fly-Bottle.* Cambridge: Polity Press.
Schroeder, Severin. 2009. "Analytic Truths and Grammatical Propositions." In *Wittgenstein and Analytic Philosophy: Essays for P. M. S. Hacker*, P. M. S. Hacker, H.-J. Glock, and J. Hyman (eds.). Oxford: Oxford University Press: 83–108.
Schwartz, Stephen. 2012. *A Brief History of Analytic Philosophy from Russell to Rawls.* Oxford: Wiley-Blackwell.
Sebestik, Jan. 1997. "Bolzano, Exner, and the Origins of Analytical Philosophy." In *Bolzano and Analytic Philosophy*, W. Kunne, M. Siebel, and M. Textor (eds.). Grazer Philosophische Studien.
Sen, Amartya. 2011. *The Idea of Justice.* Cambridge, MA: Harvard University Press.
Serano, Julia. 2013. *Excluded: Making Feminist and Queer Movements More Inclusive.* Berkeley, CA: Seal Press.
Sesardic, Nevin. 2016. *When Reason Goes on Holiday: Philosophers in Politics.* New York: Encounter Books.
Sheffer, H. M. 1913. "A Set of Five Independent Postulates for Boolean Algebras, with Application to Logical Constants." *Transactions of the American Mathematical Society* 14: 481–488.
Sider, Theodore. 2003. "Reductive Theories of Modality." In *The Oxford Handbook of Metaphysics*, M. J. Loux and D. W. Zimmerman (eds.). Oxford: Oxford University Press: 180–206.
Sider, Theodore. 2010. *Logic for Philosophy.* Oxford University Press.
Sinclair, Robert. 2014. "Quine on Evidence." In *A Companion to W. V. O. Quine*, G. Harman and E. Lepore (eds.). Oxford: Wiley-Blackwell: 350–372.
Singer, Peter. 1972. "Moral Experts." *Analysis* 32: 115–117.
Smiley, Tavis (ed.). 2016. *The Covenant with Black America: Ten Years Later.* Carlsbad, CA: Hay House, Inc.
Smith, Barry. 1994. *Austrian Philosophy: The Legacy of Franz Brentano.* Chicago: The Open Court Publishing Company.

Smith, Quentin. 1995a. "Marcus, Kripke, and the Origin of the New Theory of Reference." *Synthese* 104, no. 2: 179–189.
Smith, Quentin. 1995b. "Marcus and the New Theory of Reference: A Reply to Scott Soames." *Synthese* 104, no. 2: 217–244.
Smullyan, Arthur. 1947. "Review of W. V. Quine, 'The Problem of Interpreting Modal Logic'." *The Journal of Symbolic Logic* 12: 139–141.
Smullyan, Arthur. 1948. "Modality and Description." *The Journal of Symbolic Logic* 13: 31–37.
Soames, Scott. 1995. "Revisionism about Reference: A Reply to Smith: Eastern Division Meetings of the APA Boston, December 1994." *Synthese* 104, no. 2: 191–216.
Soames, Scott. 2003a. *Philosophical Analysis in the Twentieth Century Volume 1: The Dawn of Analysis*. Princeton, NJ: Princeton University Press.
Soames, Scott. 2003b. *Philosophical Analysis in the Twentieth Century Volume 2: The Age of Meaning*. Princeton, NJ: Princeton University Press.
Soames, Scott. 2014. *The Analytic Tradition in Philosophy, Volume 1: The Founding Giants*. Princeton, NJ: Princeton University Press.
Sorenji, Samir. 2006. "Disparities in Disability Life Expectancy in US Birth Cohorts: The Influence of Sex and Race." *Social Biology* 53, nos. 3–4: 152–171.
Stainton, Robert (ed.). 2000. *Perspectives in the Philosophy of Language: A Concise Anthology*. Peterborough, Canada: Broadview Press.
Stebbing, L. Susan. 1914. *Pragmatism and French Voluntarism*. Cambridge: Cambridge University Press.
Stebbing, L. Susan. 1930. *A Modern Introduction to Logic*. London: Metheun.
Stebbing, L. Susan. 1932. "The Method of Analysis in Metaphysics." *Proceedings of the Aristotelian Society* 33: 65–94.
Stebbing, L. Susan. 1933. "Logical Positivism and Analysis." *Proceedings of the British Academy* 19: 53–87.
Stebbing, L. Susan. 1934. "Directional Analysis and Basic Facts." *Analysis* 2: 33–36.
Stebbing, L. Susan. 1935. "Review of Recent works by Rudolf Carnap." *Mind* 44: 499–511.
Stebbing, L. Susan. 1936. "Review of *Language, Truth, and Logic* by Alfred J. Ayer." *Mind* 45: 355–364.
Stebbing, L. Susan. 1938. "Review of *The Principles of Mathematics* by Bertrand Russell and *An Introduction to Symbolic Logic* by Susanne K. Langer." *Philosophy* 13: 481–483.
Stebbing, L. Susan. 1939. *Thinking to Some Purpose*. New York: Penguin Books.
Stebbing, L. Susan. 1941. *Ideals and Illusions*. Watts and Co.
Stebbing, L. Susan. 1942. "Moore's Influence." In *The Philosophy of G. E. Moore*, Paul Schilpp (ed.). La Salle, IL: Open Court: 517–532.
Steele, Claude. 2010. *Whistling Vivaldi: How Stereotypes Affect Us and What We Can Do*. New York: W. W. Norton and Company.
Strawson, P. F. 1992. *Analysis and Metaphysics*. Oxford: Oxford University Press.
Stroll, Avrum. 2000. *Twentieth-Century Analytic Philosophy*. New York: Columbia University Press.

Sullivan, Shannon and Tuana, Nancy. 2007. *Race and Epistemologies of Ignorance.* Albany, NY: SUNY Press.
Tang, Yi-Yuan, Holzel, Britta, and Posner, Michael. 2015. "The Neuroscience of Mindfulness Meditation." *Nature Reviews Neuroscience* 16: 213–225.
Tarski, Alfred. 1933. *Pojęcie prawdy w językach nauk dedukcyjnych.* Warsaw: Nakładem Towarzystwa Naukowego Warszawskiego.
Tarski, Alfred. 1944. "The Semantic Conception of Truth." *Philosophy and Phenomenological Research* 4: 341–376.
Tarski, Alfred. 1983. *Logic, Semantics, Metamathematics,* second edition, ed. J. Corcoran. Indianapolis: Hackett.
Tatum, Beverly Daniel. 2007. *Can We Talk About Race? And Other Conversations in an Era of School Resegregation.* Boston: Beacon Press.
Terzian, Giulia. 2017. "Boole." In *The History of Philosophical and Formal Logic,* Malpass and Marfori (eds.). London: Bllomsbury Academic: 143–164.
Twohig, M., Hayes, S., and Masuda, A. 2006. "Increasing Willingness to Experience Obsessions: Acceptance and Commitment Therapy as a Treatment for Obsessive-compulsive Disorder." *Behavior Therapy* 37, no. 1: 3–13.
Uebel, Thomas. 2004. "Carnap, the Left Vienna Circle and Neopositivist Antimetaphysics." In *Carnap Brought Home: The View from Jena,* S. Awodey and C. Klein (eds.). Chicago: Open Court: 247–278.
Uebel, Thomas. 2005. "Political Philosophy of Science in Logical Empiricism: The Left Vienna Circle." *Studies in History and Philosophy of Science* 36: 754–773.
Uebel, Thomas. 2010. "What's Right about Carnap, Neurath, and the Left Vienna Circle Thesis: A Refutation." *Studies in History and Philosophy of Science* 41: 214–221.
Uebel, Thomas. 2016. "Vienna Circle." *The Stanford Encyclopedia of Philosophy.* Zalta, Edward N. (ed.). https://plato.stanford.edu/entries/vienna-circle/.
Wahl, K. 2013. "Managing Obsessive Thoughts During Brief Exposure: An Experimental Study Comparing Mindfulness-Based Strategies and Distraction in Obsessive-Compulsive Disorder." *Cognitive Therapy & Research* 37, no. 4: 752–761.
Warren, Karen. 1990. "The Power and Promise of Ecological Feminism." *Environmental Ethics* 12, no. 2: 125–146.
Williams, Chancellor. 1987. *The Destruction of Black Civilization: Great Issues of a Race from 4500 B.C. to 2000 A.D.* Chicago: Third World Press.
Williams, David and Collins, Chiquita. 2001. "Racial Residential Segregation: A Fundamental Cause of Racial Disparities in Health." *Public Health Reports* 116: 404–416.
Williamson, Timothy. 2007. *The Philosophy of Philosophy.* Hoboken, NJ: Blackwell Publishing.
Wittgenstein, Ludwig. 1922. *Tractatus Logico-Philosophicus.* London: Routledge and Kegan.
Wittgenstein, Ludwig. 1953. *Philosophical Investigations.* Hoboken, NJ: Blackwell Publishing.
Wittgenstein, Ludwig. 1980. *Culture and Value.* Hoboken, NJ: Blackwell Publishing.

Wollstonecraft, Mary. 1792. *A Vindication of the Rights of Woman*. In the version by Jonathan Bennett presented at www.earlymoderntexts.com.
Wuest, Amy. 2015. *Philipp Frank: Philosophy of Science, Pragmatism, and Social Engagement*. PhD Diss, University of Western Ontario.
Yap, Audrey. 2010. "Feminism and Carnap's Principle of Tolerance." *Hypatia* 25, no. 2: 437–454.
Zack, Naomi. 2002. *Philosophy of Science and Race*. London: Routledge.
Žižek, Slavoj. 2009. *In Defense of Lost Causes*. New York: Verso Books.

Index

abduction, 18, 20, 48
Adichie, Chimamanda, 26n13 , 26n15, 62, 71, 82n2
Africa, 11, 24, 62, 132, 156, 161nn6–7, 161n15
algebra, 32–33, 37, 55n5
algorithm, 33, 55n5, 179
ambiguity, xxi, xxiv, 128, 149
analysis:analytic philosophy, xi–xiv, xvn2, xix–xxvi, xxx–xxxiv, 1–2, 13, 24, 29–30, 38, 50, 54, 67, 71, 74, 87, 93, 107n3, 111, 114, 124, 139n1, 142–43, 157, 193–95, 201, 203–5; analyticity, xxv, 25n3, 41, 129–31, 134–38, 166–68, 175, 177–83, 185, 187, 188n3, 188n5, 189n9; critical analysis, xx, 2, 79–81, 85, 99, 105, 113, 119, 139n1, 195–96, 205
Anderson, Luvell, xxxii, 158, 205
Anscombe, G. E. M., xxii, xxix, 3, 27n19, 42, 94–95, 98, 163–65, 186
APA, 2–4, 112, 167
Appiah, Kwame Anthony, 100, 197
Aristotle, 33, 55n2, 62
arithmetic, 56n5, 161n14, 185
Asia, 24, 62, 206n5
atomic, 86, 90–92, 181
Austin, J. L., xxii, xxix, xxxii, xxxvn2, 15, 142, 160n1, 164, 195

axiom, 21, 33–36, 56n5, 57n12
Ayer, A. J., xxii, xxvi–xxvii, 66, 112, 127, 182

Beaney, Michael, xxiii, 14, 127
Bee, Samantha, 161n5
Berlin Circle, 101, 110, 127, 129
bias, 57n14, 57n17, 117; implicit bias, xiv, xxxii, 23, 27n18, 31, 54, 61, 71–74, 76, 80–81, 108n12, 127, 171, 176
Black Lives Matter, x, xiii, xxxi–xxxii, xxxiv, Ch. 6 *passim*, 141–162, 196
Black Power movement, 144, 159–60, 162n19
Boghossian, Paul, 134–38, 167, 178
Bolzano, Bernard, xi–xxiii, 32, 55n4, 61, 63
Bonnilla-Silva, Eduardo, 104, 154, 161n15
Boole, George, 32–33
Bright, Liam Kofi, ix–x, xiii, xx, xxxii, xxxivn1, 82, 85, 88, 99–102, 110–11, 119–22, 129, 138, 163
British idealism, xxvi–xxvii, xxxi, 63–65, 74, 81, 88, 106, 141, 195
Burgess, John, 3–5, 7–13, 19, 22–23, 34, 36
Butler, Judith, xx, xxxivn2

Cambridge analysis, xxvi xxix, xxxi, 109, 111, 113, 127, 195–96
Carnap, Rudolf, xxi, xxv, xxvii, xxviii, xxix, 25n2, 33, 37–38, 40–41, 47, 55, 56nn11–12, 64, 74–75, 82, 83n10, 101–2, 105, 108n13, 110–12, 114–16, 120–25, 127, 129, 139n3, 139n5, 141, 163–64, 167–68, 182, 186, 195–96
causal theory of reference, 11
Chapman, Siobahn, xxviii, 61, 75–76, 87, 126
Che, Michael, 143, 146, 162n18
China, 55n2, 69, 89, 139n1, 203–4, 206n5
Civil Rights Movement, 101, 112, 144, 154, 159
classism, 31, 104–5
Coates, Ta-Nehisi, 161n15
Coffa, Alberto, xxv, xxvii, 63
colonialism, xxxvn4, 62, 76
common sense, xx, xxxii, xxxivn2, 61, 64–71, 73–82, 83n6, 106, 139n4, 184, 195
completeness, 21, 32, 34–35, 37, 48
Conant, James, 94–95
conservative, xx–xxi, xxxivn2, 64, 68, 70, 73–74, 77, 79, 81–82, 87, 93, 107n6, 169–70, 177, 184, 195, 205n1
consistency, 51, 61, 69–70, 80–81, 97, 116, 119, 137–38, 174, 177–80, 183, 198
contingent analytic, 25n3, 138, 188n5
contingent a priori, 41, 134–35, 138, 180–81
conversational maxims, 144, 147–51, 153, 156
cooperative principle, 144, 147–48
Corcoran, John, xxxi, 29–31, 47–48, 51, 54–55, 69
Crary, Alice, 93–94, 107n6, 111, 188n7
Crenshaw, Kimberle, 121, 189n11, 204
critical rationalism, 109, 111, 114, 128, 196

critical theory, xiv, xix–xxi, xxx–xxxiii, 61, 120, 129, 163, 170, 173, 186, 193, 196–97

The Daily Show, 143
Dambska, Izydora, 112, 126, 138
Davidson, Donald, xxiv, xxix, 3, 16, 164
Davis, Angela, 103, 161n4, 162n16, 204
deduction, 33–34, 38
De Morgan, Augustus, 32–33, 128
Descartes, Rene, 27n21, 170, 173, 181
descriptivism, 2–3, 5, 11, 41
difference principle, 128
direct reference, 8, 13, 174, 181
discursive injustice, xxx–xxxi, Ch. 1 *passim*, 1–27
doctrinal paradox, 70, 80–81
Douglas, Heather, 111, 122
Du Bois, W. E. B., 171, 204
Dummett, Michael, xxii, xxv, 62
Dutilh Novaes, Catarina, ix, xiii, xx, xxxii, xxxivn1, 63–64, 70–71, 74, 79, 81–82, 83n10, 87, 99, 110, 122, 138, 163, 195–96, 204–5

education, xiii, 23–24, 71, 89, 97, 101–2, 105, 126, 128, 176, 182, 199
eliminativism, xxxii, 85, 88, 99–102, 106, 189n11, 195, 197–98, 200–201
Ellison, Ralph, 171, 173, 204
England, xii, xxix, 75
epistemic hierarchy, 130, 133, 180, 182
epistemic injustice, 27nn20–21
epistemology, x, xii, xxxii, 51, 54, 63, 78, 82, 86, 111, 113, 116, 119–20, 128, 130–36, 138, 139n9, 140nn10–11, 154, 161n15, Ch. 7 *passim*, 163–189, 203
essence, 99–100, 102, 108n8, 130–31, 172, 182, 184, 187, 197, 199
ethics, xxix, xxxi–xxxii, 22, 24, 29–31, 33, 38, 40, 42, 44, 47–50, 55, 55n2, 56n6, 57n12, 63, 67, 85, 87–89, 92–99, 101–2, 104–7, 107n5, 108n7, 109–10, 165, 174, 186–87, 195, 204

Ethiopia, 76
eurocentrism, xvn2, 24, 55n2, 57n13, 62, 76–78, 139n1, 203–4
Europe, xxix, 24, 113, 123, 156, 203, 205n1, 206nn4–5
experience, xi, xiv, 3, 24, 44, 47, 49, 61, 64, 68, 77–82, 90, 101–2, 120, 123, 131, 154, 159, 168, 171, 177, 188n8, 201, 205n1
experimental philosophy, 67, 69, 83n6
externalism, 172, 181

falsificationism, 128–29
feminism, xii, xiv, 23, 27n17, 30–31, 50–51, 67, 102–3, 107n6, 125, 167, 187n2, 188n7, 194; in epistemology, 116–19, 122, 124, 129, 131–32, 138, 170, 172, 187n2, 196, 203; in metaphysics, 133, 172–74; in philosophy of science, 116–19, 122, 124, 129, 131, 138, 196, 203
Fitch, Frederic, 5–6, 8, 10, 12, 19
Fontaine, William, 112
Foot, Philippa, xxix, 27n19, 42, 44, 163, 165, 186
Frank, Philipp, xxix, 112, 114, 122–23, 126, 139nn3–4, 141
Frege, Gottlob, xxii, 2, 5, 25n5, 32, 34–35, 55n4, 56n5, 61, 63, 89, 135
Friedman, Michael, xxv, 111, 124

Gandhi, Mohandas, xxi, 30, 82n1
Garza, Alicia, 144–45, 150, 152, 160, 161n8
Gellner, Ernest, xx, xxxivn2
genocide, 156
Germany, 62
Glock, Hans-Johann, xx–xxi, xxiv, xxvi–xxviii, 14, 32, 38, 62, 87–89, 93, 127, 164–65, 167, 180
Godel, Kurt, xxii, xxix, 21, 32, 35
Gordon, Lewis, 62, 67, 82n3, 161nn6–7, 161n15, 204
Greece, xvn2, 56n5, 62, 74, 203

Grice, Paul, xxv, xxix, xxxii, Ch. 6 *passim*, 141–162, 196

Hacker, P. M. S., xxv–xxviii, xxxvn5
Hahn, Hans, 110–12, 114, 120, 122, 139n3, 141
Hardimon, Michael, 100, 103, 197–200
Hare, R. M., xxix, 15, 42
Harvard, xx, 126, 187n2
Haslanger, Sally, xi–xiii, xx–xxi, xxxii, xxxivn1, 26n13, 46–47, 50–54, 64, 70, 74, 82, 83n10, 99–100, 104–5, 122, 131, 133, 138, 161n15, 163, 165–66, 169–70, 172–74, 177, 180, 184, 187, 189n9, 195–98, 200–201, 204–5
hasty generalization, 49–50, 57n13, 71–72, 74, 80–81, 122, 176
Haudenosaunee, 24, 29, 57n16, 125, 202
Hegel, G. W. F., xxvi, 62–63
Hempel, Carl, 122
Henkin, Leon, 21, 35, 56n7
hermeneutics, 158
holism, 163, 165–70, 172–75, 177–80, 186–87, 196
Horkheimer, Max, xx, 93
Hume, David, 77–78; Hume's Guillotine, 42–44

Ibn al-Haytham, 55n2, 57n13, 206n4
Ibn Sina, 36, 55n2, 57n13
ideal, 78, 82, 117, 142, 174, 196
implicit definition, 166–67, 183–84
induction, 46, 48–50, 57nn13–14, 122, 139n3
internationalism, xxviii, 110–12, 127, 141
intersectionality, 47, 121–22, 157, 205
intuition, 66–67, 70–71, 83n9, 130–34, 139n8, 180, 182, 184
Islam, 36, 55n2, 55n5, 56n8, 57n13, 159, 203, 205
Italy, 76

judgment aggregation, xxxii, 61, 69, 80
justice, xi–xiii, xix–xxi, xxv, xxx, 1–2, 48, 56n6, 67, 81, 87–89, 92–93, 99, 102, 105, 110, 114, 117, 119, 157, 161n11, 163, 165, 187, 195–96, 202, 204

Kaepernick, Colin, 158
Kant, Immanuel, xxiii, xxvi, 23–24, 30–31, 55n2, 62–64, 89, 129, 131, 133–34, 180–81, 199
al-Khwarizmi, Muhammad ibn Musa, 55n5
al-Kindi, 56n5, 206n4
King Jr., Reverend Dr. Martin Luther, xxi, 30, 154
Kripke, Saul, xx, xxv–xxvi, xxix, xxxi–xxxii, xxxivn1, xxxvn3, Ch. 1 passim, 32, 37–44, 56n11, 130, 132, 134–35, 139n8, 163–64, 167, 179–82, 186, 205n1
Krishnamurthy, Meena, xiii, xxi, xxxvn4
Kukla, Rebecca, ix, xiii, xxx, 2, 4, 15–17, 23, 26n11, 26n13, 99, 195, 205

Lapointe, Sandra, xi–xii, xxii–xxiii, 55n4, 63
Left Vienna Circle, 110, 112–26, 131, 138, 139n3, 196
Leibniz, Gottfried, xxiii, 63, 114
Leiter, Brian, 14–15, 41
Lewin, Kurt, 101, 126
Lewontin, Richard, 100, 198, 200
LGBTQ+, xiv, 103, 153, 159, 102, 129, 196
linguistic turn, xxiii, xxvii
logic, xi, xiv, xix, xxii–xxv, xxix–xxxiv, 21–24, 25n2, 26n8, Ch. 2 passim, 29–57, 63–64, 67–70, 72, 74–76, 79–82, 86–89, 91–92, 94, 96, 98, 108n10, 111, 124, 127–28, 130, 139nn4–5, 142, 148, 150, 152–53, 159, 165–67, 178–83, 185–86, 187n2, 188n8, 194–97, 199–204; of conversation, xxxii, Ch. 6 passim, 141–162, 196; of domination, 50–51, 54; modal, xxix, xxxi–xxxii, 5, 21, 25n2, 26n8, 32, 34, 36–38, 40, 56n7, 56n11, 186; quantificational, 5, 21, 32–36, 167; sentential, 32–35, 90–92
logical atomism, xxvi–xxviii, xxxi, 85–90, 106, 110, 127, 141
logical constant, 90, 92, 166–67, 179
logical empiricism, xx, xxvi–xxxi, 75, 85, 100–101, Ch. 5 passim, 109–140, 141, 163, 166–67, 181–82, 187, 195
logical positivism. See logical empiricism
logicism, 33, 86
Lucas Brothers, 160n2
Lvov-Warsaw School, 35, 56n6, 109, 195–96, 205

MacIntyre, Alasdair, 15, 42
MacKinnon, Catharine, 51–52, 122
Malcolm X, xxi, 159
Marcus, Ruth Barcan, xxv, xxix, xxxi, Ch. 1 passim, 1–27, 31–32, 36, 38–47, 50, 55, 56n7, 56n11, 57n12, 163–64, 180, 186, 195
Marcuse, Herbert, xx, xxxivn2
Marxism, 40, 77, 102, 116, 132, 170, 173, 204
mathematics, xi, xxvi, xxviii, 21, 32–33, 36–37, 55n5, 56n7, 62, 86–87, 111, 122, 130, 143, 161n6, 176, 182–83, 185–86, 188n8, 195, 205
meta-philosophy, xxii, 13–14, 38–39, 107n14, 130, 163
metaphysics, xxv, xxvii, xxxii, 13, 26n11, 38, 54, 63, 78, Ch. 4 passim, 85–108, 109, 111, 113, 127, 164–65, 168, 173–75, 195, 197–99
method, xix–xx, xxiii–xxv, xxx, xxxii, xxxiv, 1, 7–8, 10, 12, 29, 32–33, 37–39, 48, 50–51, 56n5, 56n8, 57n13, 64, 67, 83n10, 86–87, 97, 105, 107n6, 117, 121, 127–29, 133–34, 143, 163, 166, 170, 171,

180, 182, 188n7, 193–94, 196–97, 202, 205
MeToo, 103, 156–57
Mexico, 73, 139n1
Mill, John Stuart, xiii
Mills, Charles, xiii, xx–xxi, xxxii, xxxivn1, 55n3, 61, 64, 72–74, 77–82, 99, 132–33, 138, 154–55, 161n7, 161n15, 163, 165, 169–74, 177, 180, 184, 187, 188n7, 189n9, 195–200, 204–5
Mo Di, 62, 204
modal argument, 5, 12, 41
Mohawk, John, 24, 29, 48, 50, 54, 57n16, 57n18, 202
molecular, 86, 90, 92, 107n2
Moore, G. E., xii, xxiii, xxvi–xxvii, xxix, xxxi–xxxii, xxxvn5, Ch. 3 *passim*, 61–83, 86–88, 93, 141, 184, 195, 203
moral dilemma, 45–47
moral solipsism, 98–99

Native Americans, 62, 145, 153, 155–57
naturalism, xxix, xxxi–xxxii, Ch. 7 *passim*, 163–189, 198
natural science, 87, 92, 100, 129, 168–69, 175, 197, 200
Nazism, xxix, 40, 102, 113, 123, 187n2, 205, 205n1
necessary a posteriori, 5, 7, 25n3, 25n5, 41, 130, 132, 134–35, 138, 180–82
necessity, 25n3, 83n5, 91, 130–31, 134–37, 167, 179–84, 188n5; of identity, 5–6, 8, 10, 12–13, 25n5, 41
Nelson, Lynn Hankinson, 165, 169–70, 187n2
Neurath, Otto, xxi, xxvii, xxix, 101, 108n13, 110–16, 120, 122–27, 139n3, 141, 175–76, 195
neutrality, xi, 52–53, 107n6, 115, 123–25, 131, 180, 184
new theory of reference, xxxi, 1–5, 7–12, 14, 19–21, 25n4
New Zealand, 40
Nigeria, 76

Noah, Trevor, 161n15
non-cognitivism, 42, 115, 123
non-ideal theory, 55n3, 78, 82, 174, 196, 201
nonsense, 88, 92–96, 99–100, 106; austere nonsense, 94–96, 106, 107n7; illuminating nonsense, 94–96, 106

objectification, 51–54
objectivity, 30, 33, 48, 51–55, 89, 107n6; assumed objectivity, 52–54, 122, 125, 129, 131, 138, 180, 184
obsessive compulsive disorder, 73–74, 184–87
oppression, xii–xiv, xx–xxv, xxx–xxxiii, 22, 26n11, 31, 46–47, 49–51, 54, 57n14, 64, 70–74, 77–78, 81, 92, 103–4, 110, 120, 133, 144–45, 152, 156–57, 161n7, 173, 203
ordinary language philosophy, xii, xx, xxv–xxix, xxxi–xxxii, xxxivn2, 82, 83n5, 110, 127, 141–42, 157, 163–64, 196
other minds, 77–78, 170
Oxford, xx, xxix, 40, 64, 164

paradox, 68–70, 80–82, 204
Park, Peter K. J., 23–24, 55n2, 62, 82n3, 203
Pateman, Carole, 104
Peacemaker, 24, 50, 57n18, 202
philosophy of language, xiv, xxiii, xxviii, xxx–xxxiv, 1, 14, 30, 50, 56n10, 82, 86, 89, 92, 94, 96, 98, 142, 150, 165, 194, 201–3
Plato, 30, 45, 62
pluralism (metaphysics), 61, 86, 195, 197
pluralism (politics), 121, 186
poetry, 62, 87, 108n9
political philosophy of science, xxxii, 109–10, 112, 114–16, 122–26, 138, 196
politics, xi, xiv, xxxii, 40, 51, 56n6, 85, 87, 89, 92–94, 97, 99, 103–4,

106, 109–10, 113, 115–16, 129, 169, 187n2
Popper, Karl, xxxii, 109, 111, 113, 126, 128–29, 138, 139n7
post-racial, 102–3, 108n12, 154
poverty, xvn1, 31, 40, 101, 103–5, 120, 128, 145, 170, 184
practicality, xi, xxi, xxx–xxxi, xxxiv, 21, 23, 30, 39, 52, 53, 61, 75, 78–80, 82, 83n10, 131, 141, 143–44, 158, 163
pragmatics, 124, 139n5, 161n10
pragmatism, xxix, 38, 40, 163–64, 186
prejudice, xxxii, 27n21, 31, 50, 61, 71, 73, 76, 101, 108n12, 126, 128, 158
Prior, A. N., xxv, xxix, xxxi, 31, 36–44, 47, 55, 56n7, 57n12, 164, 186
prison-industrial complex, 155, 162n16
proper names, 5–7, 10, 19, 25n5

Quine, W. V. O., xi, xiii, xx, xxii, xxiv, xxvi, xxviii, xxix, xxxii, 36, 55n4, 68, 135, Ch. 7 *passim*, 196, 205n1

racial contract, xiv, 104, 144, 154–55, 161n7, 174, 196
racism, xiii, xxxii, 23, 31, 55n2, 62, 72–73, 85, 102–5, 108n12, 132, 145–46, 153–54, 158–59, 161n15, 171, 184, 187, 187n2, 196, 198, 203
Ransby, Barbara, 152, 159
Rawls, John, xxi, xxv–xxvi, 44, 127–29, 133, 139nn6–7, 164, 174, 205n1
recursion, 33, 86
Reichenbach, Hans, 112, 139n1
revisionary, 64 , 74–75, 79–82, 83n10, 99, 122, 169, 184, 195–96, 201
Richardson, Sarah, xxxii, 110, 113–26, 129, 138, 139n3, 196, 203, 205
rigid designator, 5–6, 11, 41
Rosenberg, Noah, 100, 198, 200
Russell, Bertrand, xii, xxi, xxiii–xxviii, xxxi–xxxii, xxxvn5, 2, 19, 35, 61–64, 68–70, 74–75, 81–82, 85–89, 97, 106–7, 110–11, 122, 126–28, 141, 187n2, 195, 203–4, 206n3, 206n5
Russell, Dora, 89, 126
Russell, Gillian, 11, 25n3, 41, 134, 137–38, 166, 178–79, 181, 188n5
Ryle, Gilbert, 142, 164

Schroeder, Severin, 98, 180
Schwartz, Stephen, xxii, xxvi–xxvii, xxix, 14, 62, 66, 93, 109, 128, 139n7, 164–65
science, 101, 105, 111, 113, 119, 168, 204
scientific worldview, 101, 105, 111, 113, 119, 168, 204
semantics, xi, 2, 6, 32–38, 41, 56n11, 63, 111, 143, 164, 179, 181, 186
sense, xxii, xxiii, 90, 92–96
Serano, Julia, 103–4
set theory, 32–33
sexism, 4, 6, 19–23, 31, 73, 104–5, 117, 122, 124, 132, 146, 172, 184, 187
slavery, 72–73, 132, 156
Smith, Quentin, xxxi, 2–13, 19–23, 25nn3–4, 41, 56n10
Smullyan, Arthur, 5–6, 8, 10, 12, 19
SNCC, 159, 162n19
Soames, Scott, xi, xx–xxi, xxvi–xxviii, xxxi, xxxivn1, 1–14, 19, 22–23, 25n2, 26n6, 37, 39, 44, 56n11, 61–62, 66, 80, 88, 92–93, 109, 164–65, 201
social construction, 46, 100, 172, 187, 197–98, 200–201
socialism, 40, 89, 112, 115, 120, 125, 187n2
social science, 100, 116, 121, 129, 172, 174–75, 177, 188n8, 196–99
Somalia, 11
speech act theory, xxx, 15–19, 23, 26n11
SSHAP, xii, xxv
standpoint epistemology, xii, xiv, xxxiii, 77–79, 120, 139n9

Stebbing, Susan, xii, xxi, xxvii–xxix, xxxii, 27n19, 61, 64, 74–82, 87, 109, 111–13, 126–28, 138, 141, 195, 203
Steele, Claude, 165, 176–77
stereotype, 18, 20, 49, 51, 73, 103, 171
stereotype threat, xiv, 176–77
Strawson, P. F., 38, 64, 82, 93, 164
syntax, 32–36
synthetic a priori, 129–30, 134, 138, 180–82

Tarski, Alfred, xxii, 32, 35, 55n4
Tatum, Beverly Daniel, 102–3
theology, 55n2, 87, 92
Thomson, Judith Jarvis, xxix, 15, 42, 44, 165
tolerance, 57n12, 124
Tractatus Logico-Philosophicus, xxvi–xxviii, xxxii, 85, 88–90, 92–99, 106, 107n5, 166, 188n4
truth conditions, 37, 86, 90, 186

Uebel, Thomas, xxix, xxxii, 109–13, 115, 119, 124–26, 129–30, 138, 139n3
unity of science, xxviii, 110–11, 116, 123, 127
USA, xiii, xx, xxix, 40, 72–73, 123, 132, 145, 150, 156, 199, 205n1

veil of ignorance, 128
verificationism, xxxii, 128, 134, 168, 182
Vienna Circle, xii, xxvii–xxix, 110, 115, 120, 125–29, 166, 182, 196

Weber, Max, 116, 125
west, xxxiii, 24, 38, 50–51, 57n16, 62, 102, 108n12, 131, 170, 199, 203–4
West, Cornel, xvn1, xxiv, xxix, 204
white ignorance, xiv, xxxi, 55n2, 56n6, 71–74, 80–81, 108n12, 132–33, 144, 154–55, 161n15, 171
Wittgenstein, Ludwig, xi–xii, xx, xxiii–xxiv, xxviii, xxix, xxxi, xxxvn2, 2, 13, 26n7, 33, 35, 41, 68, 74, 82, Ch. 4 *passim*, 85–108, 127–28, 141–42, 164, 166, 188n4
Wollstonecraft, Mary, 23–24, 30, 133
Wuest, Amy, xxxii, 110–11, 118, 123, 126, 138, 139n4

Yap, Audrey, 110, 124, 129, 138, 195, 205

Zack, Naomi, 100, 195
Žižek, Slavoj, xx, xxxivn2

About the Author

Matt LaVine is assistant professor of interdisciplinary studies, coordinator of the exploratory program, and program analyst in the Division of Diversity, Equity, and Inclusion at SUNY Potsdam. He teaches courses on logic, environmental ethics, residential segregation, and global intellectual history. His previous publications have been on public philosophy and the history of analytic philosophy.

www.ingramcontent.com/pod-product-compliance
Lightning Source LLC
Chambersburg PA
CBHW050901300426
44111CB00010B/1332